AF894567

Machine Learning From Scratch

Intuition, Math and Code of ML Algorithms

Oleksandr Akimenko

Copyright © 2026 by Oleksandr Akimenko

All rights reserved. No part of this book may be reproduced in any form without permission from the author.

Contact: akm.oleksandr@gmail.com

Companion code: github.com/ml-from-scratch-book/code

ISBN: 978-1-0675197-0-4

Who Should Read This Book

This book is for two audiences: those with no machine learning (ML) experience and those seeking to deepen their understanding of core concepts. The only prerequisites are basic Python and high school math.

What Sets This Book Apart

This book is built around four core principles that guide how machine learning should be understood and applied: depth, simplicity, structure, and relevance.

Depth

The only way to truly understand how something works is to build it from scratch. Grasping how algorithms learn and make predictions at a fundamental level gives you the clarity to know when and how to apply them successfully in practice.

Simplicity

Machine learning has a reputation for being inaccessible. Many believe a STEM degree plus a master's or PhD is required to truly understand it – and gatekeeping within the community only reinforces that belief. This book exists to change that.

Understanding the basics of linear algebra, calculus, statistics, and computer science is necessary to fully grasp ML, but it doesn't have to be hard. The biggest obstacle isn't the math itself – it's that people give up before discovering its practical value. This book takes a pragmatic approach, presenting only the math needed to build real ML algorithms from scratch, letting these concepts sink in naturally through implementation.

Computer science here serves as a tool to formalize theory. Every concept is followed by a Python implementation – think of it as building a house once you have the blueprint, materials, and proportions.

Structure

There are many good individual tutorials about various ML concepts that exist online. However, building a proper foundation requires understanding how different concepts relate to each other. The connections between concepts are the key to clarity. This book builds up complexity incrementally with each ML section following the exact same logical structure.

Relevance

The concepts in this book are absolute essentials for both day-to-day ML work and acing ML theory interviews at any level. The industry recognizes these algorithms as the true foundation.

These four qualities together enable people with no formal technical background to fully understand and leverage core machine learning concepts to solve real problems.

This insight comes from an author who started learning machine learning with nothing more than high school math and basic Python – no formal university education at the time. Working through countless online lectures, courses, and tutorials from leading institutions, the process often felt fragmented and frustrating. That experience made one thing clear: this book needed to exist.

Years later – after completing relevant university courses, being mentored by industry veterans at top companies, and gaining hands-on experience at TD Bank, Kenvue (formerly Johnson & Johnson), and multiple startups – this book is in your hands.

Table of Contents

Setup

To get the most out of this book, it is strongly recommended that you implement the machine learning algorithms as you read. All examples in this book are designed to be run in Jupyter Notebooks. Unlike Python files, Jupyter Notebooks preserve code outputs alongside the code itself, which is useful for machine learning development.

There are multiple ways to set up your environment depending on your system and preferences. While this book assumes you are using Jupyter Notebooks, you are welcome to use any Python development environment you're comfortable with.

Running the Code without Local Installation

If you want to get started immediately without installing anything locally, you can use Google Colab throughout the entire book. Google Colab runs in the browser and works on any Mac or PC with Google Chrome installed. It is a simple and reliable way to run all the codes present in this book.

Here is the detailed instruction on how to get started:

1. Open Google Chrome and navigate to Google Drive (drive.google.com)
2. Create a new folder to store all the code for this book
3. Inside the folder: Right click, navigate to "More" and select "Google Colaboratory" – this creates a new Jupyter notebook
4. Start coding

Required Python Libraries

To run the examples in this book, several Python libraries are required. If you are using a local Python environment, these libraries need to be installed just once. Google Colab has most libraries pre-installed but those that are not must be downloaded inside each notebook that uses them.

Here's the list of all libraries that will be used throughout the book: NumPy, SciPy, Pandas, Scikit-learn, XGBoost, PyTorch, Optuna, OpenML.

If you already have a Python environment running locally, you can install all of them in the terminal using the following line:

```
pip install numpy scipy pandas scikit-learn xgboost torch optuna openml
```

If you choose to use Google Colab, most libraries are already pre-installed. However, whenever Optuna or OpenML are needed, you can install them with this line of code:

```
!pip install optuna openml
```

All substantial code examples are available in the GitHub repository at: **github.com/ml-from-scratch-book/code**

Fundamentals of ML

We will begin with some fundamental definitions you need to get comfortable with.

- Algorithm – a set of instructions that need to be followed in order.
- Artificial Intelligence (AI) – simulation of human intelligence in machines.
- Machine Learning (ML) – a subset of AI concerned with the development of algorithms that can learn from data and generalize to unseen data. Thus, ML algorithms can perform tasks without explicit instructions.

Most of the time when people talk about artificial intelligence, they refer to machine learning.

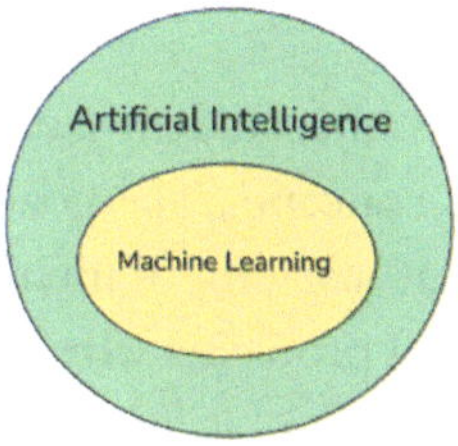

While there are multiple types of machine learning, supervised learning is the most practical. Most AI systems today run on supervised algorithms, and other approaches build heavily on its techniques. Therefore, all algorithms covered here focus on supervised machine learning, giving you skills that transfer to any ML subfield.

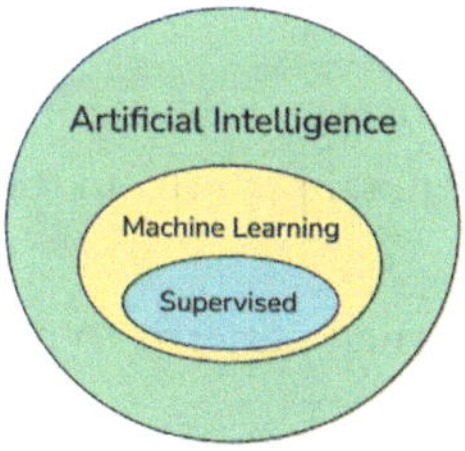

ML model – the result of training an ML algorithm on data.

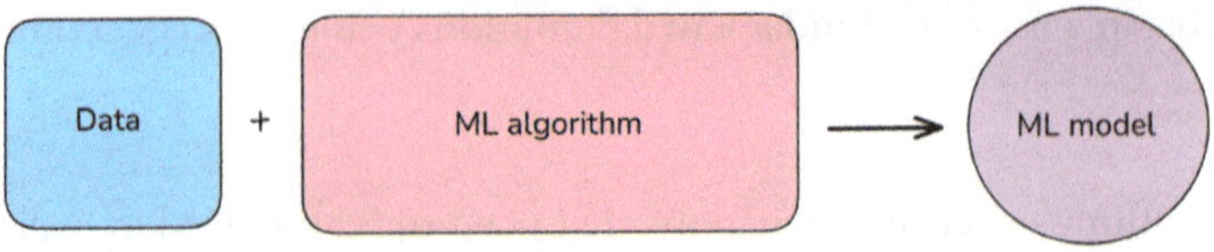

An ML model can be thought of as a student, who learns material from a book and then applies it in the real world. An ML professional who is developing that algorithm is a teacher.

Our Job as Teachers

As teachers, our goal is to create the ideal learning environment and provide the student with the right resources to master certain concepts. This comes down to selecting a relevant book that matches how that student learns best and giving them time to prepare.

In the end, the teacher tests the student on new problems that require understanding of the desired concepts. The goal of the test is to assess how well the student has learned information of interest. In other words, simulate how well they will solve desired problems when they leave the classroom and enter the real world.

Our goal is for the student to succeed in the real world. Hence, we train them until their performance on unseen problems – the test is sufficient.

Now, re-read this analogy by replacing the teacher with an ML professional (you), the student with an ML algorithm and the book with data.

Following this analogy, from our perspective ML algorithms have two modes:

1. Training – the learning process of the algorithm. In other words, the process of discovering general patterns in the data that apply to most problems of this kind.
2. Inference – leveraging learned patterns to make predictions on unseen data.

An important distinction that needs to be made is between seen and unseen data. Data is considered seen when it was part of the dataset the ML model was trained on – just like problems in the book a student used to prepare for the test. Conversely, data is considered unseen when the model wasn't trained on that data – new problems of similar kind the student faces on a test or when they enter the real-world.

As a professional we want the ML model to learn general patterns in the data. General patterns are those that are applicable to many problems of this kind – not just a single instance of it.

If a model succeeds in learning general patterns – it is said to have a right fit to the data. If not, there are two options for what could have happened:

1. Underfit – the model was unable to learn patterns because they are too complex, conversely the model is too simple
2. Overfit – the model memorized the data but didn't capture the general patterns

Both cases mean that the model will not be able to solve similar problems that were not previously seen.

Our goal as professionals is to balance the learning ability and memorization, so that our ML model learns only important patterns. Let's illustrate this with a continued student example.

Imagine these are the problems from the book our student was trained on:

1. John has 3 apples, Alisa has 7 apples and Dan has 2 apples. How many apples is there in total? The answer: 12
2. Anna has 4 apples, Robin has 7 apples and Li has 8 apples. How many apples is there in total? The answer: 19

Formally, a student learns in the following way:

1. Reads the problem description and solves the problem using their current knowledge
2. Compares their solution with the answer and tailors their approach if solution was incorrect

3. Repeats 1 and 2 for every problem in the book

Once the student was trained, we test them on a similar problem they haven't seen yet to observe how well they learned. For example, the following problem:

Gabe has 1 apple, Robin has 7 apples and Jane has 8 apples. How many apples is there in total? The answer: 16 but the student was not provided with the answer.

Let's explore three possibilities of what the student could have learned.

The Right Fit

The student learned the correct pattern. An example of the student's thinking: "I see the pattern! To find the total number of apples, you just need to add up the number of apples each person has. Let's apply it to the new problem. The total number of apples is 1 + 7 + 8 = 16."

In this case, the student identified the correct, general rule that works for both the training problems and the new, unseen problem. If we measure performance as "good" or "bad", we can conclude the following result:

- Seen data: good
- Unseen data: good

Underfit

The student learned an overly simple rule. An example of the student's thinking: "Maybe the answer is always just the number of apples the first person has? In the first problem, John had 3 (close-ish to 12?). In the second, Ana had 4 (close-ish to 19?). Let's apply this rule on the new problem. The first person is Gabe, who has 1 apple, so the total number of apples is 1."

In this case the student hasn't learned how to solve problems correctly (couldn't even match the answers in the book). Hence, no problems were solved, and the resulted performance is:

- Seen data: bad
- Unseen data: bad

Overfit

The student memorized unimportant details. An example of student's thinking: "Maybe certain names map to a particular number of apples in total. The first problem features name "Alisa" and the answer is 12. The second problem features name "Robin" and the answer is 19. Let's apply this rule on the new problem. I remember that second problem! It featured "Robin", and the answer was 19. This new problem also has "Robin" in it, so the answer must be 19 again!"

In this case, the student didn't learn the general concept. Instead, they fixated on a specific detail from the training data – "Robin" appeared in the problem with answer 19 and the student treated it as the rule. It works for that one example but fails to generalize.

- Seen data: good
- Unseen data: bad

Once a model is trained, we can figure out whether it has the right fit, underfits or overfits the data by looking at the performance on both seen and unseen data. To conclude:

- The right fit – seen: good, unseen: good. It is exactly what we want!
- Underfit – seen: bad, unseen: bad. The model is too simple, meaning it can't learn any pattern to produce a remotely correct answer even on seen data. Hence, we choose a more complex ML algorithm.
- Overfit – seen: good, unseen: bad. The model is too complex because it memorizes unimportant information. Hence, we choose a simpler ML algorithm.

Since there's no scenario when a model has bad performance on seen and good performance on unseen data – these three scenarios cover all possible cases.

Conclude: Our ultimate goal is to maximize performance of the model on unseen data as it mirrors model's performance in the real-world. By observing how the model performs on seen and unseen data – we can conclude whether it's the right fit, underfits or overfits the data to inform our further actions.

Let's now illustrate how problem in the example could be solved with an ML algorithm. Unlike a student, an ML algorithm needs a more structured representation of the information in order to learn. Hence, we convert problem from the example into a data table.

Training data looks as follows:

Name_1	Name_2	Name_3	Apples_1	Apples_2	Apples_3	Total
John	Alisa	Dan	3	7	2	12
Anna	Robin	Li	4	7	8	19

Structured data is usually represented by a table where every row corresponds to a separate observation and every column corresponds to a certain characteristic of every observation. In this case each problem corresponds to a row. Just like for a student, we need to explicitly indicate what ML model needs to learn. In this case it's the answer to a problem – column with the name "Total".

In every problem, the description and the answer must be treated separately. Hence, we give each of them a name and notation that applies to all ML problems.

- Features – a general name for a structured problem description in ML, denoted by X
- Target – a general name for an answer column, denoted by y

By following this convention, we can represent training data as follows:

Features – X:

Name_1	Name_2	Name_3	Apples_1	Apples_2	Apples_3
John	Alisa	Dan	3	7	2
Anna	Robin	Li	4	7	8

Target – y :

Total
12
19

Once data is ready, it's time to train an ML model. The goal is for the model to be capable of solving this kind of problems independently. The general idea behind the learning process of an ML model is to learn a rule (or set of rules) that maps features X to the target y. Thus, we conclude that during the training process model receives both X and y as inputs. Then it proceeds to learn general rule(s) of how to predict y based on X. In other words, infer answers based on problem descriptions.

Once the model was trained, we test it on unseen problems of similar kind. Thus, we prepare a new problem description of a similar kind in the same structured way.

Features – X:

Name_1	Name_2	Name_3	Apples_1	Apples_2	Apples_3
Gabe	Robin	Jane	1	7	8

The ML model takes features as input and predicts the target based on the patterns it learned during training. Recall, this process is also referred to as inference.

Once the prediction is made, we compare it with the true answer to measure how accurate the prediction is – just like testing a student. In case performance on unseen data is good – the fit is just right, and our model is ready to independently solve problems of this kind in the real-world.

If performance is not good, we can check whether the model underfits or overfits the data by assessing performance on seen data. This informs us of whether we should increase or decrease complexity of the model or select a new one.

In the real world we usually get a single dataset. Therefore, to train and test an ML model we need to split the data in two subsets. Seen data is also called training data because that's what we train our ML model on. Unseen data is also called test data because it is used to assess model performance to understand how well it will perform in the real world.

The proportion of the split depends on size of the dataset and the problem but usually we allocate 80% of rows for training and 20% for testing.

Let's formalize end to end ML project stages that we loosely defined so far:

Data Preparation

First, we have data in a table format, then we split it into features and targets, X and y respectively. Then we split it further for training and testing. As a result, our initial dataset is split into four subsets, two for training: *X_train*, *y_train* and two for testing: *X_test*, *y_test*:

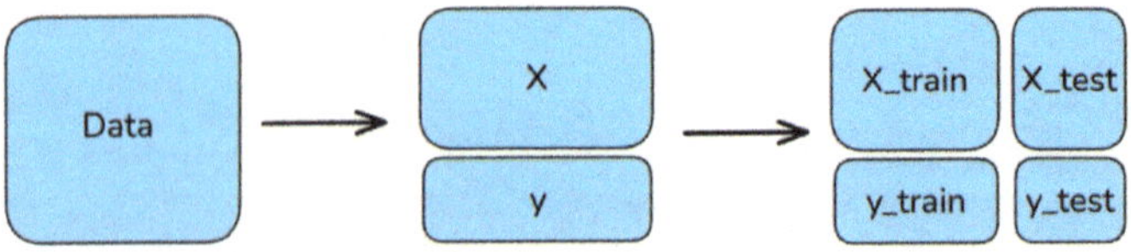

Training

During training, we pass *X_train*, *y_train* pairs as input into the ML algorithm to get a trained ML model.

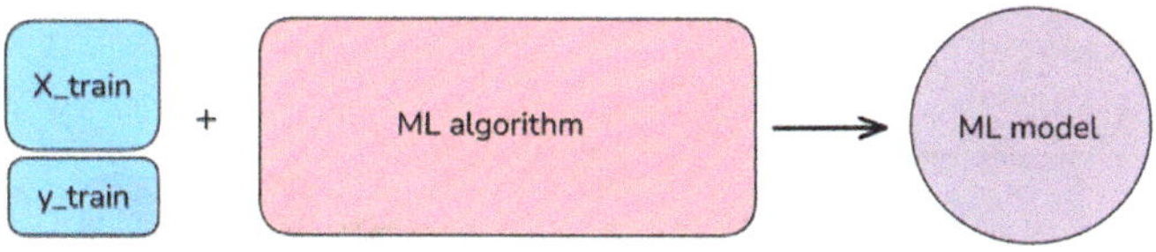

Testing

During testing, the model performs inference on *X_test* to make predictions.

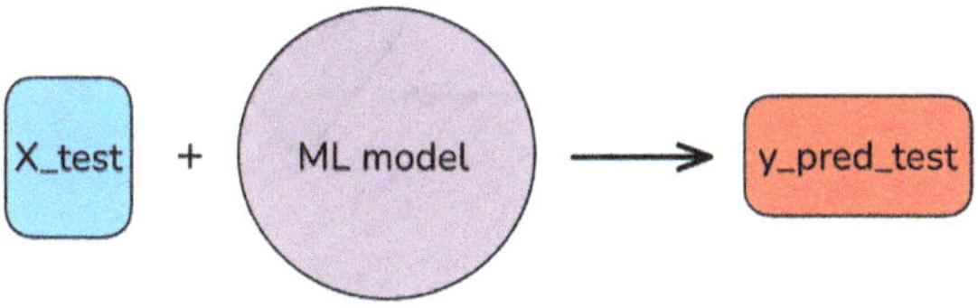

Then we compare *y_pred_test* with *y_test* to see how accurate the model's predictions are. This gives us insight into how well the model can deal with problems it hasn't seen during training.

The performance is measured by some metric that tells us how far *y_pred_test* is from *y_test*.

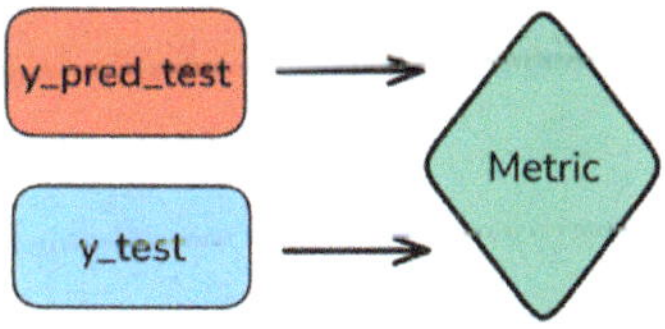

Based on the performance of the model on unseen data we decide whether the current model is good enough for our application. If we are satisfied – we proceed to use this model to solve our real-world problems. Note that using a model is equivalent to making the model perform inference on the new data of interest.

Otherwise, we measure the model's performance on seen data and decide whether our model underfits or overfits.

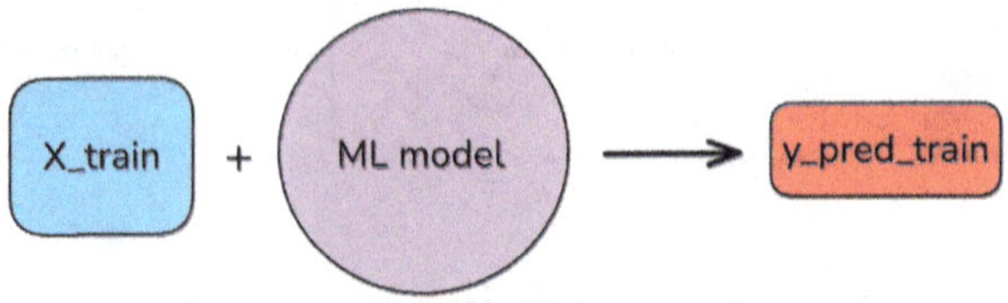

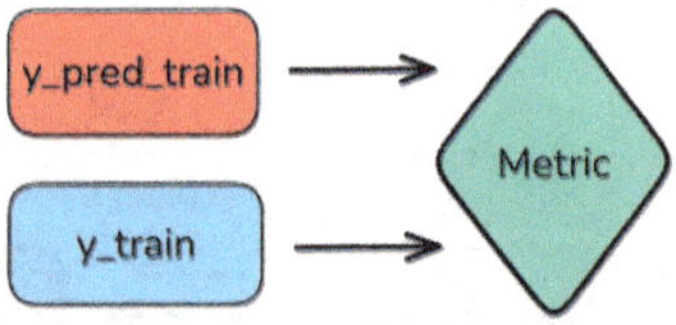

This tells us whether the model is too simple or too complex. With this insight, we gain more intuition about the nature of this problem, which helps us decide whether to adjust the model's complexity or try a different algorithm.

Congratulations on learning core ML definitions and the fundamental ML project structure. In this module we conceptually went from having a dataset to training and testing an ML model.

Introduction to Data

In the previous section we explored the core principles of ML by going over a very simple problem. It has done a perfect job playing along with the student analogy and showcasing general concepts in ML. However, it is too simple of a problem – in the real-world we would not bother using ML to solve an addition problem. In fact, if a problem can be solved sufficiently well with a deterministic method, there's no need to use ML. In this chapter we will get some feel to what real-world data looks like and how to deal with it.

How are problems and data in the real world different from the student example?

- Bigger and messier datasets. We could never train a good model on just two observations. In the real world it is common for datasets to consist of thousands or millions of observations. Additionally, in the student example we had complete and correct problem descriptions, which is not necessarily the case in the real world.
- More complex problems. In the student example we knew the perfect way to map features to targets – addition. In reality, we should only bother with ML if we don't know it. The goal of an ML model is to learn an equation or set of rules that allow it to predict target based on features.

An example of a real-world ML problem:

Predict the median house value in various California districts based on a range of features, which include demographic data and housing characteristics. Our goal is to train a model capable of accurately predicting median house value in a neighborhood.

Below is a snapshot of this dataset:

	median_income	housing_median_age	total_rooms	...	latitude	longitude	median_house_value
0	8.3252	41	880.0	...	37.88	-122.23	452600.0
1	8.3014	-99	NaN	...	37.86	-122.22	358500.0
2	7.2574	52	1467.0	...	37.85	-122.24	352100.0
3	0.0000	52	1274.0	...	37.85	-122.25	341300.0
4	3.8462	52	1627.0	...	37.85	-122.25	342200.0
...	...	...	...	...	...	...	...
20635	NaN	25	1665.0	...	39.48	-121.09	78100.0
20636	NaN	18	697.0	...	39.49	-121.21	77100.0
20637	NaN	17	2254.0	...	39.43	-121.22	92300.0
20638	NaN	18	1860.0	...	39.43	-121.32	84700.0
20639	NaN	16	2785.0	...	39.37	-121.24	89400.0

20640 rows × 9 columns

Let's explore the columns one by one. Note that the screenshot shows a subset of the data for illustration – you will work with the complete datasets in upcoming chapters.

Features:

- median_income – median income in the district (in tens of thousands of dollars)
- housing_median_age – median age of houses in the district
- total_rooms – the total number of rooms in the district
- total_bedrooms – the total number of bedrooms in the district
- population – the total population in the district
- households – the total number of households in the district
- latitude – latitude of the district (location data)
- longitude – longitude of the district (location data)

The target:

- median_house_value – median house value (price in dollars)

Let's see how differences between the student example and real-world problems manifest in this case.

As you can observe, this dataset contains 20,640 rows and 9 columns. Additionally, it has quality issues typical of real-world data: some values are missing (NaN), while others are impossible – such as the median income of $0 at cell (3,0) or the house age of -99 at cell (1,1). These errors arise from various sources: manual data entry mistakes, bugs in data collection systems, sensor malfunctions, etc.

The most important difference is that it would be difficult for a human to manually define an equation or a fixed set of rules to accurately relate features to the target variable. Therefore, we need ML to solve this problem.

Now that we identified points of difference – can we just split this data, train and test the model as outlined in the previous chapter?

Theoretically yes, but that would be like giving a student a textbook full of typos and missing pages.

In the previous section, it was mentioned that it's the teacher's job to provide the student with learning materials that best suit them. In other words, learning materials that make the student learn in the most effective way and thus maximize their performance on a fair test. After all, a student can learn as well as the learning materials teach them.

Additionally, different students learn best with different teaching approaches. Therefore, a teacher needs to truly know how the student thinks in order to provide them with the best suited learning materials.

This all makes sense, but how does it translate to machine learning?

As ML professionals, we're typically given raw data. Data preparation and algorithm selection are our responsibility. As you have already seen, raw datasets can contain errors and missing data. Training a model on that data is equivalent to teaching a student with problem descriptions that have missing information and errors. This leads both an ML model and a student to learn these mistakes, which we want to avoid. Therefore, always remember – we have complete freedom to transform the data however we want.

Different ML algorithms are like different students – they benefit from different learning approaches. When we understand how an algorithm learns (which you will discover in this book), we can prepare data that leverages its full potential. This maximizes the model's performance on unseen data, which reflects its real-world effectiveness.

How do we make the dataset ready for an ML algorithm?

Data preprocessing can be seen as a two-step process: Data Cleaning and Feature Engineering. Before diving in, there's one rule that governs both steps – every preprocessing operation falls into one of two types:

- Row-independent – the operation only looks at a single row to compute a value. These are safe to apply at any time, so we apply them on the whole dataset before the split. These tend to be column-wise operations.
- Row-dependent — the operation looks across multiple rows to compute a value. Consider why it must be applied after the split: if we use all data to compute a value, the test set is no longer truly unseen – its information has already quietly shaped our training set. This means our model's performance on the test set no longer reflects how it would perform in the real world because we wouldn't have access to unseen data there.

You will see an example of each operation type as we dive into the two steps of data preprocessing.

Data Cleaning

In this step, we handle missing values and errors by either deleting rows and columns or finding reasonable estimates.

If a row or column has many missing values, the simplest solution is to remove it. For example, we will remove 2nd row and 1st column of our dataset to get:

	housing_median_age	total_rooms	total_bedrooms	...	latitude	longitude	median_house_value
0	41	880.0	129.0	...	37.88	-122.23	452600.0
2	52	1467.0	190.0	...	37.85	-122.24	352100.0
3	52	1274.0	235.0	...	37.85	-122.25	341300.0
4	52	1627.0	280.0	...	37.85	-122.25	342200.0
5	52	919.0	213.0	...	37.85	-122.25	269700.0
...	...	...	...	...	...	...	...
20635	25	1665.0	374.0	...	39.48	-121.09	78100.0
20636	18	697.0	150.0	...	39.49	-121.21	77100.0
20637	17	2254.0	485.0	...	39.43	-121.22	92300.0
20638	18	1860.0	409.0	...	39.43	-121.32	84700.0
20639	16	2785.0	616.0	...	39.37	-121.24	89400.0

20639 rows × 8 columns

However, when a column is crucial and the dataset isn't large enough to freely delete rows, we need to estimate the missing values. Let's say we had kept "median_income" – what would be a reasonable estimate for its missing values?

A common approach is to fill the gap with an aggregated value – such as the mean "median_income" across all districts. We can also be more targeted: if location strongly influences income, we might use the mean income of the 10 nearest districts instead. This approach is called imputation of missing values.

Since it's a row-dependent operation, we will apply it after the split. For a simple imputation our plan is to compute mean "median_income" across all districts using training data. Then fill missing values in training and test data with the derived estimate.

Once our cleaning strategies are defined, we proceed to the next step.

Feature Engineering

This process involves transforming features to make patterns more obvious to the ML algorithm, just like simplifying problem descriptions for a student. The goal is to provide helpful hints without revealing the answer. Ask yourself: what indicators would make predicting house value easier?

A useful indicator could be ratio of the population to the total number of bedrooms. It reveals whether houses typically operate at full capacity or how "crowded" they are, which could be a strong indicator of a home's value.

We will call this new feature "used_capacity" and it is derived by dividing "population" by "total_bedrooms". The updated dataset looks as follows:

	housing_median_age	total_rooms	total_bedrooms	...	longitude	median_house_value	used_capacity
0	41	880.0	129.0	...	-122.23	452600.0	2.496124
2	52	1467.0	190.0	...	-122.24	352100.0	2.610526
3	52	1274.0	235.0	...	-122.25	341300.0	2.374468
4	52	1627.0	280.0	...	-122.25	342200.0	2.017857
5	52	919.0	213.0	...	-122.25	269700.0	1.938967
...	...	...	...	...	...	...	...
20635	25	1665.0	374.0	...	-121.09	78100.0	2.259358
20636	18	697.0	150.0	...	-121.21	77100.0	2.373333
20637	17	2254.0	485.0	...	-121.22	92300.0	2.076289
20638	18	1860.0	409.0	...	-121.32	84700.0	1.811736
20639	16	2785.0	616.0	...	-121.24	89400.0	2.251623

20639 rows × 9 columns

Since this operation is row-independent, we can apply it right away.

By creating features like this, we help the ML algorithm discover patterns that might otherwise remain hidden. We will develop much stronger intuition for feature engineering as we explore different ML algorithms. But you should remember that this step is more art than science. The better you understand how ML algorithms learn – the better your instincts will be for cleaning and engineering features that maximize performance.

Now that we have a general idea about data preprocessing, let's add this step to our ML project flow defined in the previous chapter:

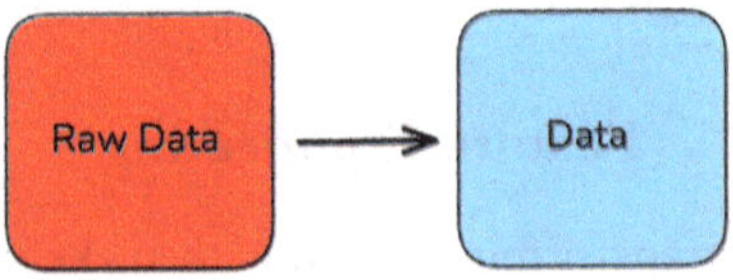

In this context, "Raw Data" is the initial dataset, while "Data" represents a state where all row-independent cleaning and feature engineering operations have already been applied. Any row-dependent operations – like calculating mean across rows to fill missing values are planned at this stage but not yet executed.

As the final data preparation step, the data is split – aggregations are then computed with just training data and used to transform both training and test sets.

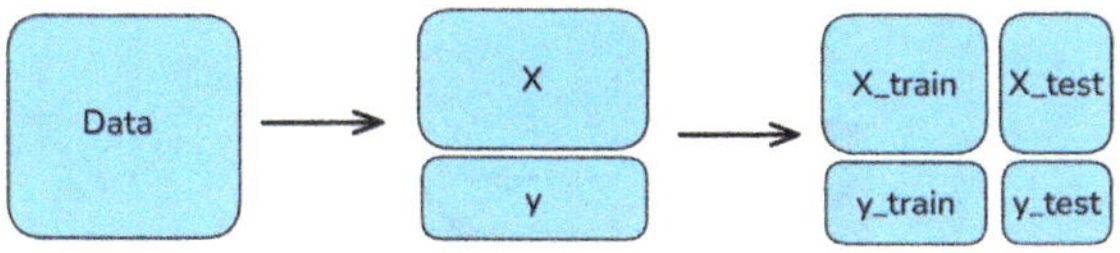

> Note: Though not shown in the diagram, this is the moment those planned row-dependent operations are executed – keep that in mind as you read forward.

With this new addition let's recap our finalized ML project flow at this stage:

Data Preparation

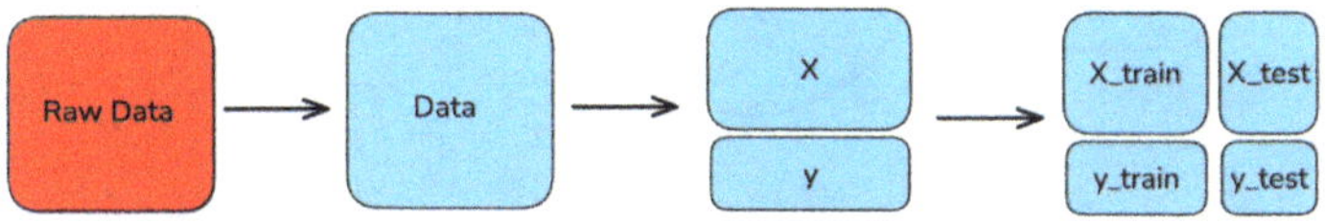

Training

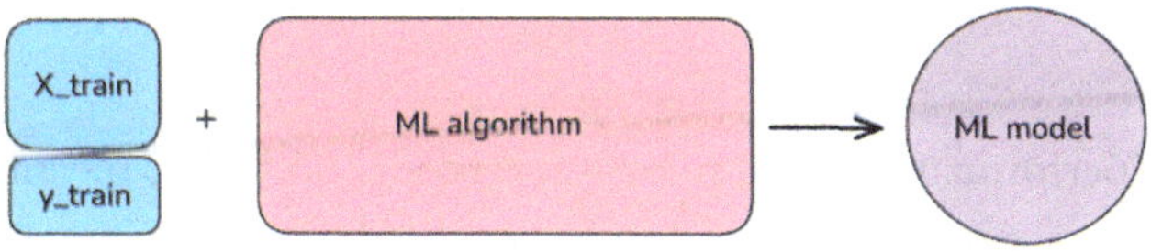

Testing

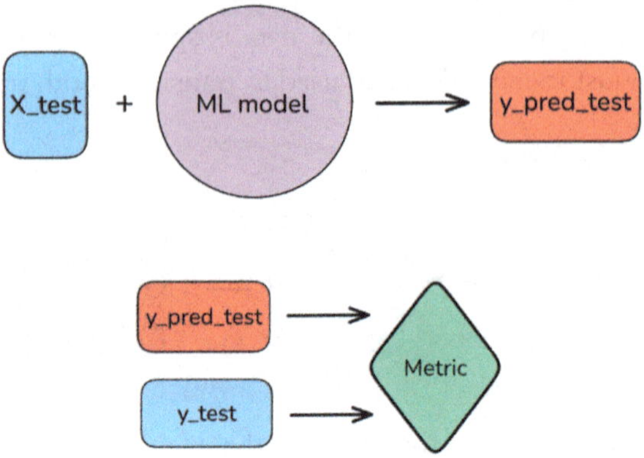

If we are satisfied with the performance – great, our model development is done! Otherwise, we check if the model underfits or overfits.

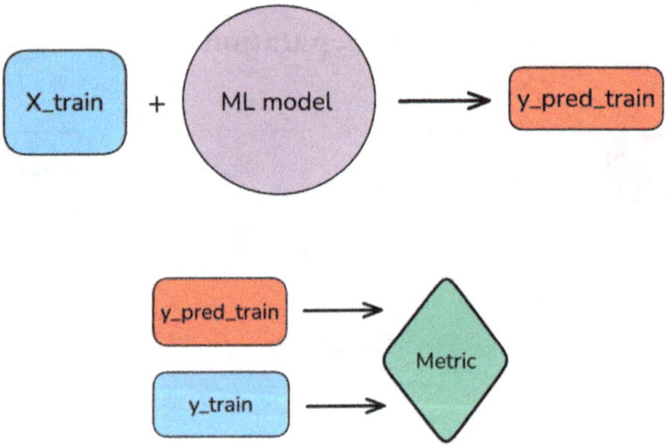

If training performance is still poor – the model underfits, meaning it's too simple to capture the underlying patterns in the data. If training performance is good or significantly better than test performance – the model overfits, meaning it's too complex and has memorized noise and irrelevant details instead of learning generalizable patterns.

Understanding how our ML algorithm learns from the preprocessed data allows us to reconsider both data preprocessing and algorithm selection. Perhaps our features need re-engineering to match the algorithm's learning style, or perhaps we need a different algorithm that better suits our current feature representation. These choices are interconnected – changing one often means reconsidering the other. Throughout this book you will learn how various algorithms learn and thus gain intuition on how to optimally leverage this information.

The Math You Actually Need for ML

Disclaimer: This chapter covers the practical math needed to build ML algorithms from scratch. While not as rigorous as a university math course, the information presented is accurate and sufficient for our purposes.

Manipulating Data (Linear Algebra Essentials)

This module will teach you all necessary data representations and operations to successfully navigate through theory and implementation of ML algorithms. Note that this module is not about strict mathematical concepts but rather practical application of linear algebra in programming. For convenience, we will revise all necessary concepts by employing NumPy – Python library for efficient computations. Let's begin by importing the necessary library:

```
import numpy as np
```

Importing "numpy as np", allows us to refer to the library by using just two letters instead of the full name – it's a standard convention for this library.

Generally, there are three primary ways to represent numeric data:

- Scalar – a single number. For example:

$$3$$

- Vector – a collection of numbers in one-dimensional list-like format. For example:

$$[1, 2, 3]$$

  The same information can be represented as:

$$\begin{bmatrix} 1 \\ 2 \\ 3 \end{bmatrix}$$

- Matrix – a collection of numbers in two-dimensional table-like format. For example:

$$\begin{bmatrix} 1 & 2 & 3 \\ 4 & 5 & 6 \end{bmatrix}$$

The most appropriate representation depends on the context. For instance, if we want to represent the total number of people on Earth, a scalar makes sense. If we need the population of each country individually, we naturally need a vector. Now suppose we want to store both the population and average height for each country – a scalar won't work, and a vector becomes inconvenient. This problem naturally suggests a matrix, where each row corresponds to a country and each column corresponds to a different aspect of data – population, height, etc.

Each data structure supports specific operations. Just as we can add, subtract, multiply, and divide scalars (except division by zero), vectors and matrices have their own operations with corresponding rules.

To learn what operations you can perform on each one of these structures is to learn all linear algebra you need to understand everything about ML algorithms covered in this book.

In Python we can define a scalar, vector and a matrix in the following way:

```
scalar = 1

vector = np.array([1, 2, 3])

matrix = np.array([[1, 2, 3], [4, 5, 6]])
```

Next, we will perform some operations so note down the vector and the matrix to follow along.

Operations between vectors and scalars work intuitively – the scalar operation is applied to each element of the vector individually.

```
print(vector * 3)

[3 6 9]

print(vector - 3)

[-2 -1  0]

print(vector + 3)

[4 5 6]

print(vector / 3)

[0.33333333 0.66666667 1.        ]

print(np.power(vector, 3))

[ 1  8 27]
```

This approach is equivalent to iterating over a Python list and performing operations on each element individually. Though NumPy is much more efficient because it performs computations in parallel

Standard operations between two vectors of the same size work element-wise – each operation occurs between elements at corresponding positions.

```
print(vector * vector)

[1 4 9]

print(vector - vector)

[0 0 0]

print(vector + vector)

[2 4 6]

print(vector / vector)

[1. 1. 1.]

print(np.power(vector, vector))

[ 1  4 27]
```

There are two more useful operations we can perform with vectors in NumPy. The first one is comparing each element in a vector to a scalar or each element in another vector.

```
print(vector > 3)

[False False False]

another_vector = np.array([4, 5, 6])

print(vector < another_vector)

[ True  True  True]
```

The second operation is sum of all elements in a vector.

```
print(np.sum(vector))

6
```

Now we get to matrices. All the standard operations between scalars and matrices work as expected – simply perform the operation elementwise.

```
print(matrix * 3)

[[ 3  6  9]
 [12 15 18]]

print(matrix - 3)

[[-2 -1  0]
 [ 1  2  3]]

print(matrix + 3)

[[4 5 6]
 [7 8 9]]

print(matrix / 3)

[[0.33333333 0.66666667 1.        ]
 [1.33333333 1.66666667 2.        ]]

print(np.power(matrix, 3))

[[  1   8  27]
 [ 64 125 216]]
```

Matrix multiplication is defined only when the number of columns in the first matrix matches the number of rows in the second matrix. The order of the operands matters. Conceptually, we can say that matrix multiplication is only defined when the first matrix is of $a \times b$ shape and the second is of $b \times c$ shape. We can always find out shape of the resulting matrix based on shapes of two operands:

$$a \times b \cdot b \times c = a \times c$$

In other words, the resulting matrix has the same number of rows as the first matrix, and the same number of columns as the second matrix.

For example, consider two matrices: $\begin{bmatrix} 1 & 2 \\ 3 & 4 \end{bmatrix}$ and $\begin{bmatrix} 5 & 6 \\ 7 & 8 \end{bmatrix}$. Both matrices are of 2×2 shape. Since the number of columns in the first matrix equals the number of rows in the second, the multiplication is valid. The resulting matrix will also have shape 2×2.

To compute the product of these two matrices, each entry of the resulting matrix is obtained as follows:

1. Take a row from the first matrix and a column from the second matrix
2. Multiply corresponding elements
3. Sum the products
4. Place the result in the corresponding position of the output matrix

This process is repeated for every row of the first matrix and every column of the second matrix. Elements of the resulting matrix are filled from left to right, top to bottom. To perform matrix multiplication, we follow the steps outlined above for all rows and columns of the matrices.

Here's the full process for two matrices above:

$\begin{bmatrix}1 & 2\\3 & 4\end{bmatrix}$ and $\begin{bmatrix}5 & 6\\7 & 8\end{bmatrix}$, then $\begin{bmatrix}1*5+2*7 & \\ & \end{bmatrix} = \begin{bmatrix}19 & \\ & \end{bmatrix}$

$\begin{bmatrix}1 & 2\\3 & 4\end{bmatrix}$ and $\begin{bmatrix}5 & 6\\7 & 8\end{bmatrix}$, then $\begin{bmatrix}19 & 1*6+2*8\\ & \end{bmatrix} = \begin{bmatrix}19 & 22\\ & \end{bmatrix}$

$\begin{bmatrix}1 & 2\\3 & 4\end{bmatrix}$ and $\begin{bmatrix}5 & 6\\7 & 8\end{bmatrix}$, then $\begin{bmatrix}19 & 22\\3*5+4*7 & \end{bmatrix} = \begin{bmatrix}19 & 22\\43 & \end{bmatrix}$

$\begin{bmatrix}1 & 2\\3 & 4\end{bmatrix}$ and $\begin{bmatrix}5 & 6\\7 & 8\end{bmatrix}$, then $\begin{bmatrix}19 & 22\\43 & 3*6+4*8\end{bmatrix} = \begin{bmatrix}19 & 22\\43 & 50\end{bmatrix}$

The result looks as follows:

$$\begin{bmatrix}1 & 2\\3 & 4\end{bmatrix} \cdot \begin{bmatrix}5 & 6\\7 & 8\end{bmatrix} = \begin{bmatrix}1*5+2*7 & 1*6+2*8\\3*5+4*7 & 3*6+4*8\end{bmatrix} = \begin{bmatrix}19 & 22\\43 & 50\end{bmatrix}$$

Recall, shape of operands helps you check validity of the operation and get to know shape of the resulting matrix.

Examples of valid matrix multiplications:

$$1 \times 5 \cdot 5 \times 10 = 1 \times 10$$

$$3 \times 3 \cdot 3 \times 5 = 3 \times 5$$

$$1 \times 10 \cdot 10 \times 1 = 1 \times 1$$

Examples of invalid matrix multiplications:

$$2 \times 2 \cdot 3 \times 2$$

$$10 \times 2 \cdot 10 \times 2$$

$$2 \times 2 \cdot 10 \times 2$$

Matrix multiplication between two vectors (arranged as row vector and column vector) produces a scalar, commonly called the dot product.

For example:

$$[1,2,3] \cdot \begin{bmatrix} 4 \\ 5 \\ 6 \end{bmatrix} = 1 * 4 + 2 * 5 + 3 * 6 = 32$$

Now let's explore matrix multiplication in Python. First, we will define matrices used in the example and verify our calculation.

```
A = np.array([[1, 2], [3, 4]])
B = np.array([[5, 6], [7, 8]])

print(np.dot(A, B))

[[19 22]
 [43 50]]
```

Let's do the same with vectors used in the example.

```
a = np.array([1, 2, 3])
b = np.array([4, 5, 6])

print(np.dot(a, b))

32
```

An alternative notation to perform matrix multiplication is as follows.

```
print(A @ B)

[[19 22]
 [43 50]]

print(a @ b)

32
```

NumPy treats one-dimensional arrays flexibly during matrix multiplication, automatically inferring whether to treat them as row or column vectors based on context to make the operation valid.

Since a vector is theoretically a special case of a matrix, we can also perform matrix multiplication between a vector and a matrix. For such operation to be valid in NumPy, either row or column form of the vector must be suitable.

For instance, let's explore $\begin{bmatrix} 1 & 2 & 3 \\ 4 & 5 & 6 \end{bmatrix}$ of shape 2×3 and $[1, 2]$ that can either by written in 1×2 or 2×1 format. How can we make this work? Well, the only arrangement that works shape-wise is:

$$1 \times 2 \cdot 2 \times 3 = 1 \times 3$$

Therefore:

$$[1, 2] \cdot \begin{bmatrix} 1 & 2 & 3 \\ 4 & 5 & 6 \end{bmatrix} = [1 * 1 + 2 * 4, \quad 1 * 2 + 2 * 5, \quad 1 * 3 + 2 * 6]$$

$$= [9, 12, 15]$$

We can verify this in code below.

```
C = np.array([[1, 2, 3], [4, 5, 6]])
c = np.array([1, 2])

print (c @ C)

[ 9 12 15]
```

Sometimes, it's useful to change the shape of a matrix in order to enable matrix multiplication. This transformation is called transpose, and it converts columns of the matrix into rows and vise-versa. The transpose operation is denoted by the superscript T:

$$\begin{bmatrix} 1 & 2 & 3 \\ 4 & 5 & 6 \end{bmatrix}^T = \begin{bmatrix} 1 & 4 \\ 2 & 5 \\ 3 & 6 \end{bmatrix}$$

This matrix went from 2×3 to 3×2 shape. Transpose swaps rows and columns and thus it also swaps the numbers in the shape of a matrix.

Generally, if we apply transpose on a n by m matrix it becomes m by n. Let's now perform the transpose operation in Python.

```
print(C.T)

[[1 4]
 [2 5]
 [3 6]]
```

This concludes linear algebra and NumPy content required to fully understand core ML algorithms.

Understanding Data (Statistical Foundations)

Statistics is useful to answer questions about data – let's explore its application through a practical example.

Grades for a university exam have just been released and we want to understand:

1. How well did the class of 30 students learn the material?
2. Did the professor do a good job teaching this class?
3. What grade should a future student in this class expect?

Intuitively, we want to see how well students performed on average, so we compute average exam score in this class, which turns out to be around 61. What can we conclude? On average, students tend to pass the class, which seems positive. But can we determine how good of a job the teacher did solely based on the average score? Not really. Let's see why.

We can visualize two classes of students with the same mean exam score of 61. We will use a histogram of counts – it shows all observed exam scores on x-axis and their frequencies on y-axis:

Class A

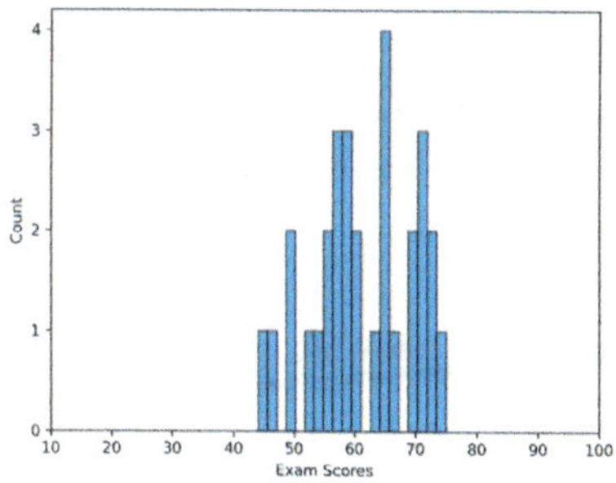

Class B

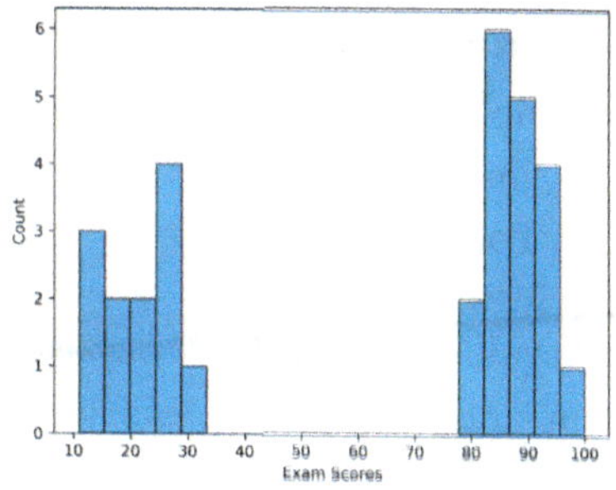

In Class A, most students scored in the middle range (55-75). This suggests the class was challenging, but students were generally able to grasp the material.

In Class B, students either failed (scoring below 40) or excelled (scoring above 75), with almost no one scoring near the average. Since this is a university-level course, we would expect students to have the necessary background and motivation to achieve at least moderate success. The absence of middle-range scores suggests potential problems with how the course was taught or assessed. Perhaps the material had a steep learning curve, or the assessment didn't align well with instruction.

Overall, despite same average score Class A's results appear more balanced and credible, suggesting better teaching effectiveness.

Measuring Spread of the Data

Our goal is to assess how student performance varies from one student to another. We use visualization to see this pattern, but we can compute a single number that captures the same information. This number is called variance, and it measures the dispersion of data, in other words, how much our observations differ from the mean value on average.

- Small variance indicates that most values are around the mean
- Large variance indicates the dataset contains values far from the mean – extreme values

Before diving deeper, let's establish some terminology:

- Population – all observation that exist of a specific type. Examples: All humans on Earth, all active students at the University of Toronto.
- Sample – one or more observation drawn from the population. Examples: 5000 random people, 400 random students from University of Toronto.

The key difference is that a population includes all possible observations of a certain kind, while a sample includes only some.

In practice, we usually want to infer information about a population using a sample because collecting data on the entire population is rarely feasible. For example, not all people who visit a restaurant (the population) leave a review – only some do (the sample) but we still draw conclusions based on rating calculated from that sample.

What makes a sample reliable? Think about restaurant ratings. We're more likely to trust a restaurant with 3,000 reviews and a 4.6-star rating than one with 30 reviews and a 4.7-star rating. Why? The larger sample size gives us more confidence that the rating reflects the true quality. The same principle applies across statistics – we need a sufficiently large sample to reliably represent the population.

Notation:

- n – sample size (30 students in our class).
- x_i – the i-th observation in our sample, where $i \leq n$ (represents score of a student with index i).
- $\bar{x}$ – sample mean or average, this is a sum of all observations in a sample divided by the sample size (e.g. mean score on the final exam). Formula to compute sample mean is as follows:

$$\bar{x} = \frac{\sum_{i=1}^{n} x_i}{n}$$

With the terminology in place, we can measure spread in the data with a single number. Intuitively, spread is how much observations tend to deviate from the mean. It is exactly what we will measure – average squared difference of all observations from the mean. However, there's one caveat – instead of dividing sum of squared differences by the sample size, we divide it by the sample size minus one:

$$Variance = \frac{\sum_{i=1}^{n}(x_i - \bar{x})^2}{n - 1}$$

Fundamentally, this change doesn't impact the intuition – it's just a formality that makes estimation of the population variance based on a sample more precise.

We want to measure how far every observation is from mean on average why square the differences?

If we simply averaged the raw differences $(x_i - \bar{x})$, positive and negative deviations would cancel out, giving us zero regardless of how spread out the data actually is.

For example: Suppose our sample has 2 observations and sample mean is 5, consider two datasets satisfying this condition:

- Dataset 1: {10, 0}
- Dataset 2: {5, 5}

These two datasets are very different – the first one has a large spread and the second one has absolutely no spread.

Without squaring, we get the following variances:

- Dataset 1:

$$\frac{(10-5)+(0-5)}{2-1} = \frac{5-5}{1} = \frac{0}{1} = 0$$

- Dataset 2:

$$\frac{(5-5)+(5-5)}{2-1} = \frac{0+0}{1} = 0$$

Both give zero, suggesting they have the same spread, but they clearly don't.

Once we square the differences – use variance formula, we get:

- Dataset 1:

$$\frac{(10-5)^2+(0-5)^2}{2-1} = \frac{25+25}{1} = \frac{50}{1} = 50$$

- Dataset 2:

$$\frac{(5-5)^2+(5-5)^2}{1}=\frac{0+0}{1}=0$$

Now we correctly identify that dataset 1 has a much larger spread.

As you can observe from the example above, variance gets large pretty fast. A more interpretable metric is standard deviation (SD), which is simply the square root of variance:

$$SD = \sqrt{Variance} = \sqrt{\frac{\sum_{i=1}^{n}(x_i-\bar{x})^2}{n-1}}$$

Back to our exam score example, after computing standard deviation using formula above, we get the following summary for each class:

- Class A: $\overline{x} = 61$ and $SD = 8$
- Class B: $\overline{x} = 61$ and $SD = 34$

These numbers tell a clear story: Class A has most students centered near the mean (low spread), while Class B has students scattered widely across the score range (high spread).

By knowing just two numbers – sample mean and standard deviation, we get a solid understanding of what the dataset looks like. These summary numbers are called statistics – single values computed from sample data that help us understand some characteristic of that data.

Probability

For a student entering Class A next term with the same professor, what grade should they expect to receive?

Obviously, this heavily depends on the individual student, but if we want to estimate a grade for a random student from the same university, we need to understand the likelihood of receiving each possible grade. One way to do this is to examine data from the previous term.

Let's plot the data for Class A:

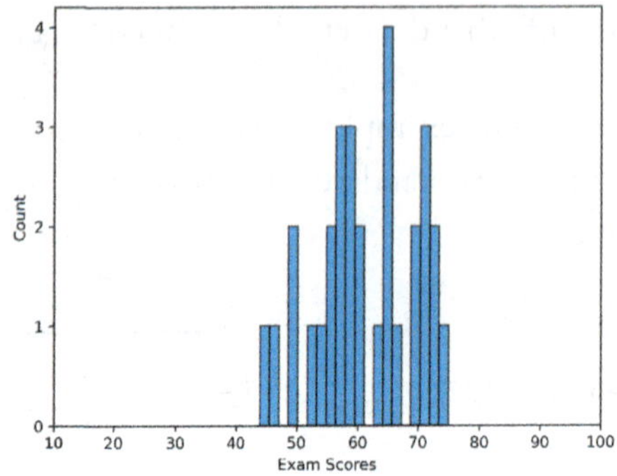

We can see how many students received each grade. To convert this into probabilities, we simply divide each count by the total number of students (30). Probability of receiving a certain grade is essentially just a proportion of times this grade was received in our sample.

$$Probability\ of\ a\ grade = \frac{\#\ of\ times\ the\ grade\ was\ received}{Total\ \#\ of\ grades}$$

Let's plot the result:

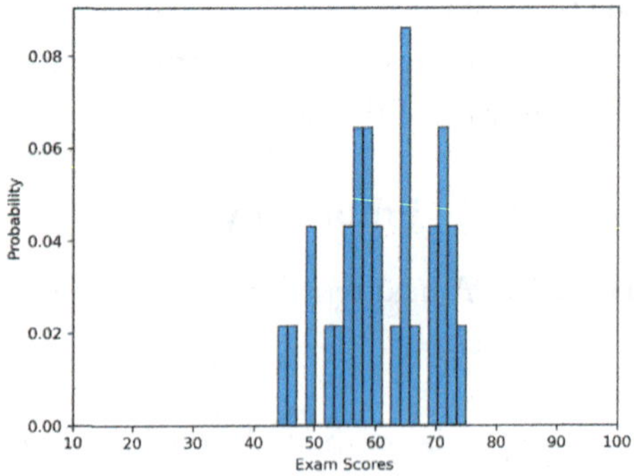

Notice that the shape hasn't changed – only y-axis scale. Instead of counts, we now have proportions (or probabilities).

From this plot, we can see that a random student from that university has about 8% chance of scoring 65 and 4% chance of scoring 50. This way we can infer probability of receiving any score. Additionally, we can compute probability of receiving a score more or less than a certain value – by summing up probabilities of all scores above or below it respectively.

An important caveat: This analysis relies on a crucial assumption that our sample of 30 students is representative of all students who will take this class with this professor. In other words, we're assuming that future students will be similar to past students in terms of preparation, motivation, and ability.

How confident can we be in this assumption? As we discussed earlier, sample size is the key factor. A sample of 30 students is modest, meaning it gives us some insight, but we should be cautious about over-interpreting these exact probabilities. Ideally, we'd want to collect data from multiple previous terms (perhaps 3-5 terms, giving us 90-150 students) to get more stable probability estimates.

What this means in practice: While we shouldn't treat these probabilities as exact predictions, they do provide useful ballpark estimates. A future student of Class A can reasonably expect that:

- Scores in the 60-70 range are fairly common (higher probabilities)
- Extreme scores (below 40 or above 85) are relatively rare (lower probabilities)

The overall distribution gives a sense of what's typical versus unusual in this class. Think of it like a restaurant with 30 reviews versus 300 reviews – both provide information, but you'd be more confident in conclusions drawn from the larger sample.

Distribution

A set of values with corresponding probabilities is called a probability distribution. Why is this useful?

While a histogram of counts is specific to our sample of 30 students, a probability distribution is more general. It's not tied to a specific measurement type or sample size. Instead, it represents the underlying pattern of how values are distributed in the population.

This generality is powerful – a single type of probability distribution can represent many unrelated phenomena, such as:

- Height distribution among NBA players
- Age distribution of first-time homebuyers worldwide
- Lifespan distribution of clownfish

Since certain patterns appear repeatedly in nature, statisticians have identified and named several "famous" probability distributions. Each of those distributions has some useful properties that allow us to infer useful information from data that follows that distribution.

We'll explore the most important one – normal distribution (also called the Gaussian distribution or bell curve). The general shape of this distribution looks as follows:

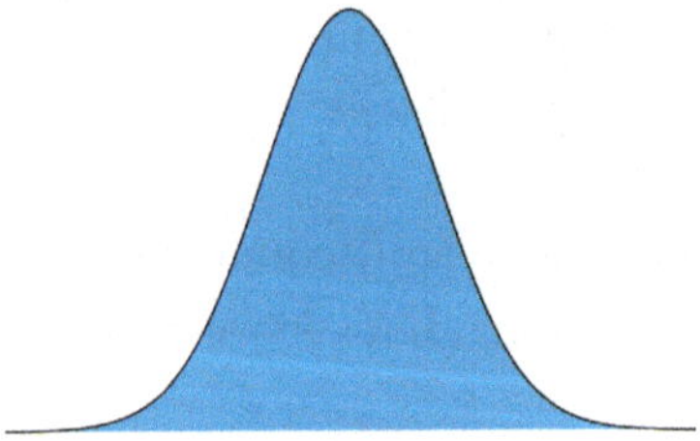

In practice, if we drew a large sample from a population that follows a normal distribution, it would look as follows:

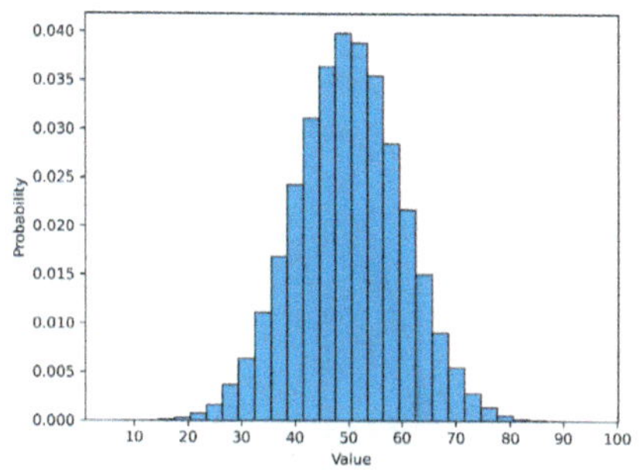

What are properties of this distribution?

1. Symmetry: The distribution is perfectly symmetric around its center. The mean, median, and mode are all equal.
2. The 50-50 split: The mean divides the data in half – 50% of values fall below the mean, and 50% fall above it (directly related to symmetry).
3. The Empirical Rule (68-95-99.7). By knowing mean (*M*) and standard deviation (*SD*), we can estimate percentage of data points that lie within certain intervals:

   - 68% of data points lie in the interval $[M - SD, M + SD]$
   - 95% of data points lie in the interval $[M - 2 * SD, M + 2 * SD]$
   - 99.7% of data points lie in the interval $[M - 3 * SD, M + 3 * SD]$

This pattern can be easily observed through a normal distribution with mean 0 and standard deviation of 1:

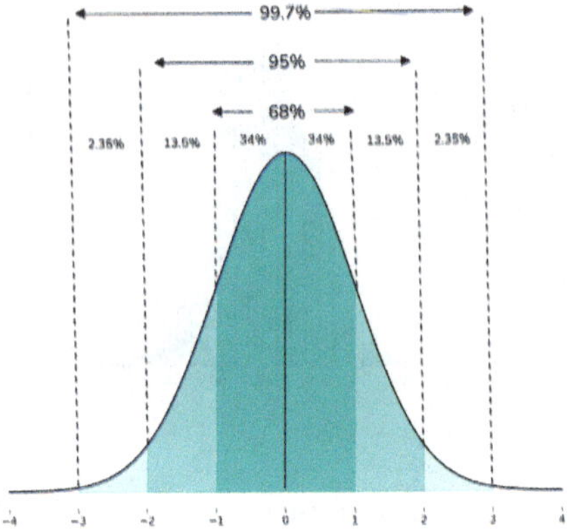

In fact, normal distribution is completely defined by just two numbers – its mean (*M*) and standard deviation (*SD*). These are called parameters of the distribution.

The type of a distribution and its parameters is all we need to generate data that follows the distribution. In fact, we can generate infinitely many of different normal distributions by varying values of mean and standard deviation.

In practice, we are not given a distribution, just raw data – it's our job to decide whether it follows a certain "famous" distribution or not. In order to safely assume a distribution, we need a large sample size.

To illustrate why sample size matters – let's sample from the same distribution and plot histogram after 20, 200, 2 thousand and 20 thousand samples.

$n = 20$

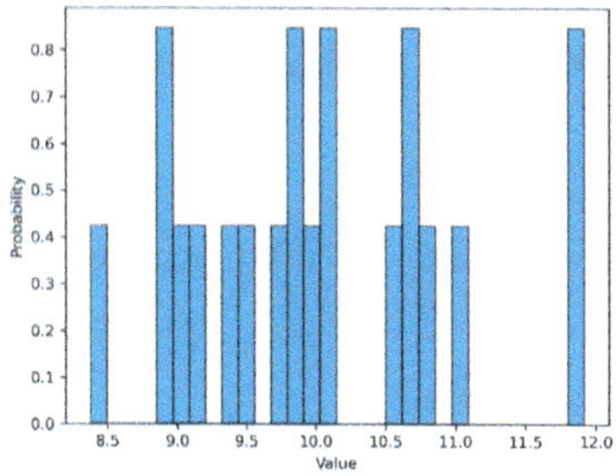

$n = 200$

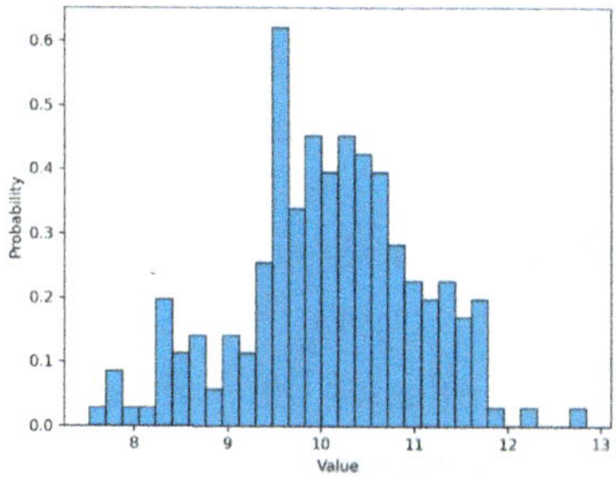

n=2,000

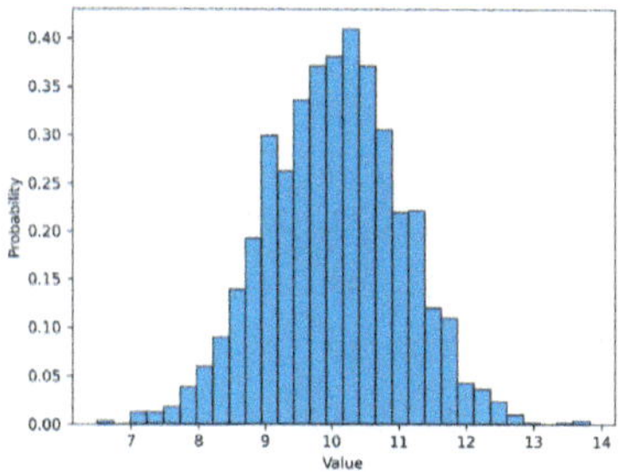

n=20,000

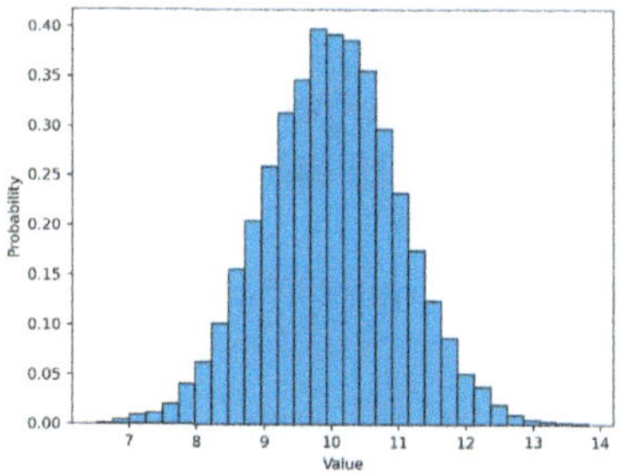

- $n = 20$: Doesn't look normal
- $n = 200$: Starting to show bell shape
- $n = 2{,}000$: Clear bell curve emerges
- $n = 20{,}000$: Smooth, nearly perfect bell curve

Conclude: Even data drawn from a perfectly normal population won't look normal with a small sample size. The underlying pattern only becomes clear as sample size increases. This is why we should be cautious about drawing strong conclusions from small datasets.

Now let's come back to the initial questions and answer them using the information we learned in this chapter.

For illustration purposes, we will answer these questions for Class A.

1. How well did the class of 30 students learn the material?
2. Did the professor do a good job teaching this class?
3. What grade should a future student in this class expect?

Since we can only infer information from the grades of these 30 students, we must make several strong assumptions:

- These 30 students represent the broader population of students who take this class
- The professor will teach similarly in future terms
- Course content and difficulty will remain stable
- No major external factors will change between terms

These are strong assumptions, which means we should not be overly confident in our conclusions. However, with these caveats in mind, it's reasonable to expect that future classes will perform similarly, making questions 1 and 3 essentially equivalent.

Before answering questions – let's take another look at the data of interest:

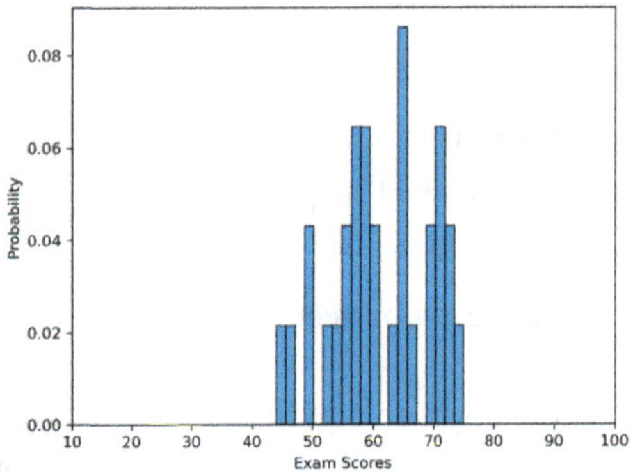

Question 1 and 3:

The typical score is around 61 (the mean), which indicates that on average students tend to pass this class.

Standard deviation is equal to 8. While the sample size of 30 is too small to reliably assume normality – by looking at the histogram, we can see that most data is centered around the mean.

Therefore, it is safe to say that most data points lie within one standard deviation from the mean, that is within this interval: $[61 - 8, 61 + 8] = [53, 69]$. This indicates that most people tend to achieve at least moderate success.

Note: If we were confident the data followed a normal distribution, we could use 68-95-99.7 rule and say that this interval contains approximately 68% of student scores. Without that formal assumption, but observing that the data clusters around the mean, we can still reasonably say "most students" fall in this range. In practice, we can loosely apply the intuition from the 68-95-99.7 rule even when we haven't formally verified normality, as long as we see similar clustering patterns.

Question 2:

In question 1 and 2, we determined that most scores lie within $[53, 69]$ interval. Paired with the fact that histogram shows a relatively even distribution without extreme values – the teacher has done a decent job teaching the class as most students achieved at least moderate success.

In this module you got a gist of how we can leverage statistics to answer interesting questions about data.

Learning From Data (Optimization)

In this module, you will learn about the backbone of a great number of ML algorithms. We will derive the desired approach intuitively by solving a very simple problem.

The Language of Machine Learning (Functions)

The concept of a function is used throughout ML, so let's make sure you're comfortable with it first.

A function can be casually defined as a black box that requires some input and always produces output. Crucially, for the same input, a function must always produce the same output.

Let's look at an example:

$$y = f(x) = x + 5$$

In this case, y value depends on x; therefore, it is referred to as dependent variable. On the other hand, x doesn't depend on anything and thus is referred to as independent variable.

A function consists of exactly one dependent (output) and one or more independent variables (inputs). Here are some examples of functions with multiple independent variables:

$$y = r(x_1, x_2) = x_1 + x_2$$

$$y = k(x_1, x_2, x_3) = 7x_3 * (x_1^2 - \frac{x_2}{2})$$

$$y = z(x_1, x_2, x_3, x_4, x_5) = \frac{9x_1}{e^{x_5^{11}}}$$

Get comfortable with the fact that a function can take many inputs, perform any kind of transformation and produce exactly one output.

Let's solve a simple problem where we want to make predictions about future based on historical data.

Our dataset:

	x	y
0	0.791320	1.551080
1	0.035284	0.030772
2	0.525270	1.020041
3	0.856293	1.812797
4	0.043562	0.065656
5	0.651788	1.546606
6	0.493195	1.122662
7	0.899229	1.750989
8	0.086825	0.266201
9	0.309275	0.692684
10	0.698256	1.419231
11	0.465975	0.970432
12	0.051959	-0.022401
13	0.574756	1.298906
14	0.157858	0.223998

Plotted:

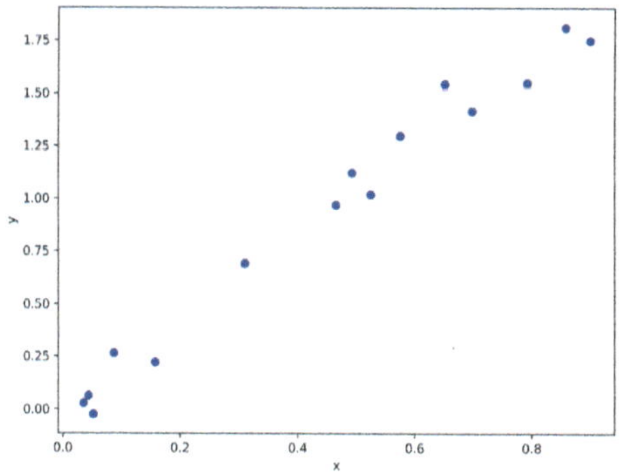

Before diving in, we need to understand the data by answering two critical questions:

1. What are we trying to predict?
2. What will we use to predict that?

In the real world, a clear answer to both questions is always the most important part of the problem statement.

For this dataset, we want to predict y based on x. Looking at the graph, we can see that x and y have a positive linear relationship – as x increases, y increases at roughly the same rate.

> Note: Predicting one value based on another means figuring out the pattern of their relationship. We can formalize this pattern using a function.

Based on our observation, a linear function seems like a good fit:

$$y = f(x) = \omega * x$$

Where:

- x – is a feature (input) from a single data point
- ω – is a scalar we need to find

This simple model can solve many different problems because the prediction pattern changes as ω changes. ω is a learnable parameter – it makes our ML algorithm generic. We'll soon discover why it's called "learnable."

Let's observe what kind of models we can potentially create with different values for ω:

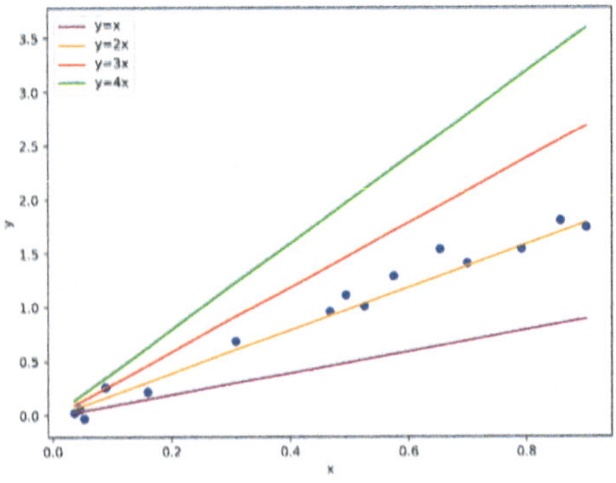

Any of these models could be used to predict y for any value of x. From the graph, we can see that $y = 2x$ fits the data best, so $\omega = 2$ appears optimal.

Our model is done!

Now let's use our model to make a prediction for a new data point. For example, when $x = 0.6$:

$$y = 2 * 0.6 = 1.2$$

Great, we just made our first prediction!

The Problem With "Eyeballing It"

The intuition is good, but this approach has major issues for real-world problems. In practice:

- We have thousands or millions of observations
- The relationships are more complex
- There are usually many features (not just one x) and as many parameters

Let's try the same approach with a slightly more complex dataset:

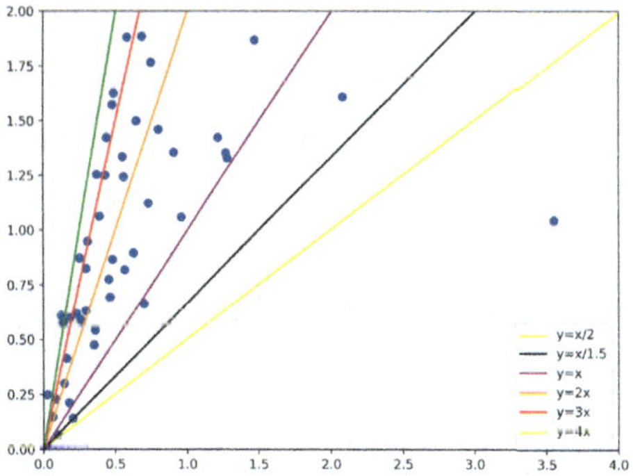

Now it's unclear which value of ω is best or if it's even among the ones we plotted. Keep in mind, we're still dealing with only one feature. Imagine trying this with:

- Thousands or millions of data points
- Multiple features (3+ features are impossible to visualize)
- More complex relationships

It would be simply impossible.

Conclusion: After choosing a general model structure, we need a quantitative approach to find the optimal parameter value ω.

First, we need to understand, what "optimal" means.

- Optimal value – the parameter value that achieves our objective.
- Our objective – create the most accurate model. In other words, one that predicts values as closely to actual values as possible and learns the general pattern rather than memorizes training data.

To optimize is to find the optimal solution to our objective. Hence, optimization in this case refers to the process of finding learnable parameter value that achieves the objective.

To create a model is to train it, if we want to excel at this task – we need to understand how ML algorithms learn. Now, let's come back to student analogy and understand how they actually learn.

Training a Student

Until a student learned the pattern, for every problem in the book:

1. Take the problem description
2. Solve the problem with current knowledge
3. Compare the solution to the correct answer
4. Adjust approach based on the feedback

Training an ML Model

Until a model learned the pattern, for every data point in the dataset:

1. Take its feature
2. Make a prediction
3. Compare to the target
4. Adjust the current approach based on the feedback

Now let's formalize steps 2, 3, and 4 to train our model.

Step 2 – Making a Prediction

Recall, our model has the following general form:

$$y = \omega * x$$

There are two parts to the prediction – actual data point (x) and learnable parameter (ω). Data is constant; therefore, the only way to change prediction is through the learnable parameter.

The goal of the training process for this ML algorithm is to learn (find) value of this parameter that results into the most accurate predictions. But what happens when it makes its first prediction? It makes a guess. Hence, at the beginning of training we just assign a random value to ω.

Step 3 – Comparing to the Target

Every time the model makes a prediction, it needs feedback to learn. We formalize this using a loss function that computes how far the prediction is from the truth. The smaller the loss – the better the prediction.

Depending on a problem, we may prefer to use different loss functions – the one used in this sub-module is the most common loss for predicting a continuous target.

Loss function – error for a single observation, denoted by l:

$$l(y_{pred_i}, y_{actual_i}) = \left(y_{pred_i} - y_{actual_i}\right)^2$$

In words: Loss function in this case is squared difference between the predicted and actual target value for any single data point.

The loss function gives feedback about a single prediction. But if we want the model to receive feedback on multiple observations, we need to compute the average loss across a batch of data.

Cost function – average loss across all observations, denoted by *J*:

$$J(y_{pred}, y_{actual}) = \frac{1}{n} * \sum_{i=1}^{n} l(y_{pred_i}, y_{actual_i})$$

Equivalently:

$$J(y_{pred}, y_{actual}) = \frac{1}{n} * \sum_{i=1}^{n} (y_{pred_i} - y_{actual_i})^2$$

Cost function is like a student solving n problems without looking at solutions, then receiving an average score for all n problems. This particular cost function measures mean squared error (MSE). Different cost functions can be thought of as different grading system.

Step 4 – Learning From Feedback

That's where the quantitative part begins – actual learning from the feedback.

First, recall our prediction equation:

$$y_{pred} = \omega * x$$

Let's rewrite the cost function by substituting in our prediction equation:

$$J(\omega * x, y_{actual}) = \frac{1}{n} * \sum_{i=1}^{n} (\omega * x_i - y_{actual_i})^2$$

Notice, all values are given except ω. Therefore, the cost function depends only on ω. Recall, it's our objective to minimize the cost function – equivalently, make the most accurate prediction. Thus, we need to find ω that makes J as small as possible.

Let's code up the cost function defined earlier.

```
def cost(omega, x, y_actual):

    n = len(x)

    return (1 / n) * sum((omega * x - y_actual) ** 2)
```

Now, we can check how the cost function changes with different values of ω.

```
import numpy as np

omega_values = np.linspace(0, 4, 100)

cost_values = [cost(omega, x, y) for omega in omega_values]
```

Code above generates 100 omega values in the range from 0 to 4 and then computes cost function value for each one of them. Note that this is just an illustration to show the concept – you don't need to implement this yourself.

Let's plot the cost function value for different values of omega:

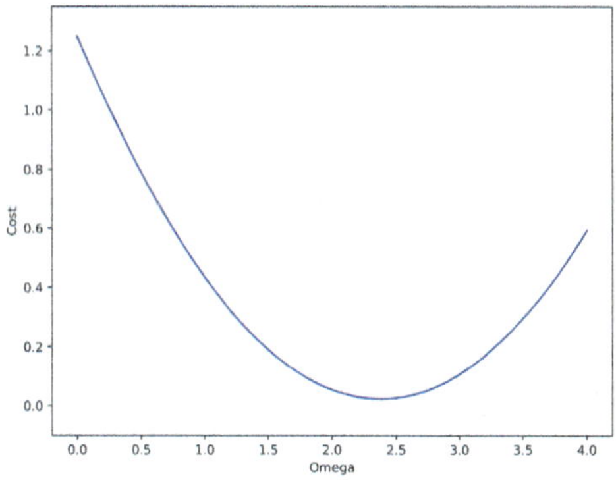

This plot shows how value of the cost J changes as learnable parameter ω changes. It allows us to visually identify the optimal value for ω – the one that makes cost the smallest, which is somewhere between 2 and 3. We could find the minimum value in "cost_values" and track the corresponding ω in "omega_values".

This approach works for this simple problem, but it doesn't scale – in the real world, we have many learnable parameters that affect J. Since it's not even possible to produce this plot for two or more learnable parameters, we conclude this approach is not general enough. Similarly, "cost_values" array becomes too large and expensive to construct very fast.

We need a better approach that works for any number of learnable parameters.

Begin Learning

Our ML model begins by making a guess for the first prediction. In other words, we initialize value for the learnable parameter ω to be a random value, say 0.5. Let's represent the current omega with a purple circle and produce the plot:

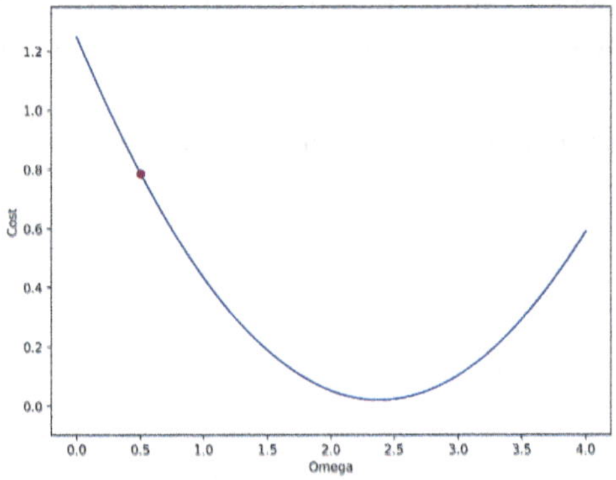

Note: In practice, we can't visualize this graph – at this point all information we have is about the location of the purple dot. In other words, all the model knows is that the cost function value is 0.8 when omega equals to 0.5.

Here's where it becomes fun!

Think of the learnable parameter as a person trying to walk down a hill, where the hill is the cost function. The purple dot is the person, and blue curve is the hill:

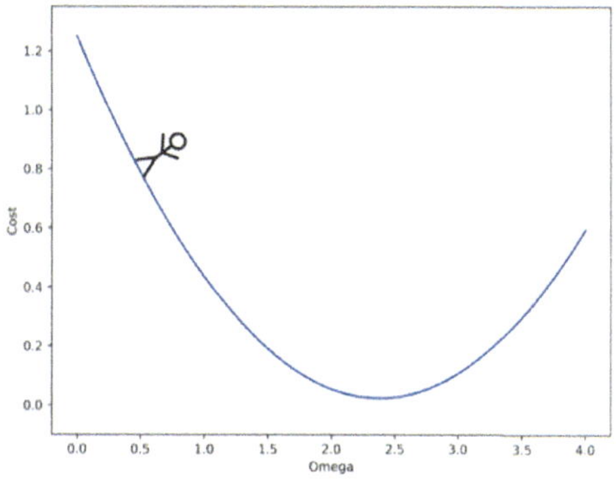

This person going down the hill is equivalent to us finding omega (ω) that minimizes the cost (maximizes accuracy) of the model.

While a person can feel the ground (giving them information about direction and steepness), we don't have that information by default.

That's where calculus comes into play, giving our person the information they need – which direction to step and how far. In other words, whether to increase or decrease omega and by how much.

But how do we get that information?

The good news: Every smooth function is locally linear, meaning if we zoom in close enough at any point, it looks like a straight line.

For instance, if we zoom in close enough at $\omega = 0.5$, the surface looks flat – just like a straight line. Extending that line reveals:

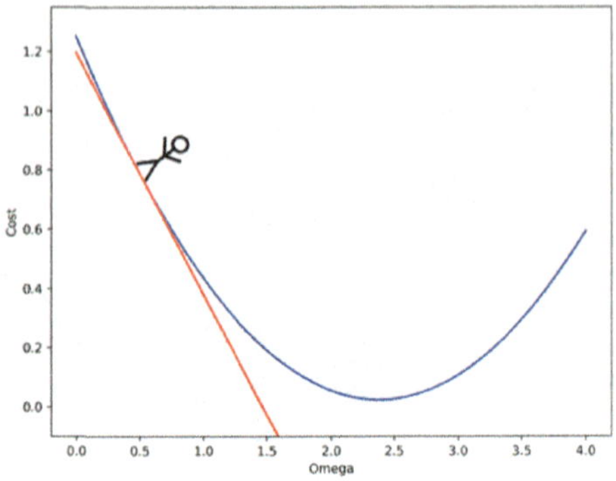

This means we can define a straight line at any point along the cost function. Intuitively, the slope of this line tells our person how steep the surface is and which way it tilts – which is exactly what we need.

Eventually, the goal is to go down the hill – in other words reach flat surface:

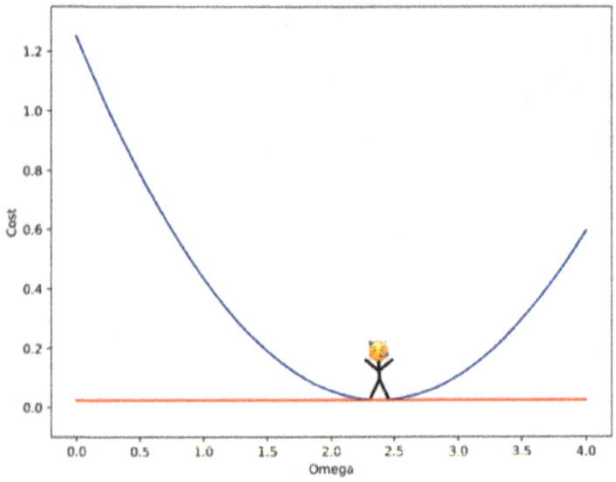

At this point, the slope of the straight line beneath our person is equal to 0.

To recap: A straight line (tangent) can be defined at any point on the cost function. The slope of that line guides us toward the flat surface where our objective is achieved.

Conclude the learning process:

1. Initialize omega to be random
2. Until we reach flat surface (slope equal to 0):
    - Compute slope of the straight line at the current point
    - Use it to inform whether we need to increase or decrease omega and by how much

The key is computing slope of the tangent line at every point and using it to inform how to change omega to minimize the cost. Now, let's observe how this movement downhill is manifested in math.

To find the slope of a line, we need two points. Recall that the slope between points (x_1, y_1) and (x_2, y_2) is:

$$\frac{y_2 - y_1}{x_2 - x_1}$$

Since y is a function of x, we can rewrite equation as:

$$\frac{f(x_2) - f(x_1)}{x_2 - x_1}$$

To find the slope at a specific point, we need two points that are infinitely close to each other. Let's say the distance between them is h, a tiny number approaching 0. Then we use the formula above to find the slope of straight line between two infinitely close points.

Two infinitely close points with distance h between them are: $(x, f(x))$ and $(x + h, f(x + h))$. Thus, the slope of a line defined by these two points is:

$$\frac{f(x + h) - f(x)}{(x + h) - x} = \frac{f(x + h) - f(x)}{h}$$

We can denote that h is infinitely close to 0 using limit notation:

$$\lim_{h \to 0} \frac{f(x+h) - f(x)}{h}$$

Conclude: The equation above allows us to compute the slope of a straight (tangent) line at any point x to any smooth function f. The slope of the tangent line tells us how a tiny change in x affects f – using this information we can keep changing x to decrease f until slope becomes close to 0.

In our case, we want to figure out how to change ω to make J as small as possible. J is at its minimum value when bottom of the hill is reached, which is indicated by slope of the tangent line being close to 0 (flat surface).

Using the slope formula, we can find how change in ω affects J:

$$\lim_{h \to 0} \frac{J(\omega+h) - J(\omega)}{h}$$

This quantity is also called derivative of J with respect to ω – those terms are equivalent. Hence, above equation can also be denoted as:

$$\frac{dJ}{d\omega} = \lim_{h \to 0} \frac{J(\omega+h) - J(\omega)}{h}$$

This gives our person information about the surface they're standing on. They use it to decide which way to step and how far.

Starting from their current ω, they keep taking steps guided by the slope until it reaches 0 – the bottom of the hill!

The Learning Algorithm

Let's formalize what we just learned purely in ML context:

1. Select random omega
2. Compute slope of the tangent line, that is $\frac{dJ}{d\omega}$
3. Until slope of the tangent line is around 0, that is $\frac{dJ}{d\omega} \approx 0$:
   - Update omega using slope, that is $\omega = \omega - \frac{dJ}{d\omega}$
   - Compute slope of tangent line at newly updated omega, that is $\frac{dJ}{d\omega}$
   - Repeat (3)

Eventually, slope becomes 0, which indicates minimum of the cost was reached and we learned optimal value for omega – model has been trained!

Now that we know how the algorithm works, let's compute slope of the tangent line of our cost function:

$$\frac{dJ}{d\omega} = \lim_{h \to 0} \frac{J(\omega) - J(\omega + h)}{h} =$$

$$\lim_{h \to 0} \frac{\sum_{i=1}^{n} \left[\left(\omega * x_i - y_{actual_i}\right)^2 - \left((\omega + h) * x_i - y_{actual_i}\right)^2 \right]}{h * n}$$

It may look scary, but we just used definition of the cost function. You are encouraged to revisit definition of J to make sure you fully understand the expression above.

Let's simplify the expression above, it's not necessary to go through this process as it's nothing but tedious math. If we expand the squared terms and perform some algebra, we get the following form:

$$\frac{dJ}{d\omega} = \frac{2}{n} * \sum_{i=1}^{n} x_i * \left(\omega * x_i - y_{actual_i}\right)$$

In code, this is done as follows.

```
def cost_derivative(omega, x, y_actual):

    n = len(x)

    return (2 / n) * sum(x * (omega * x - y_actual))
```

Now we can implement the full algorithm.

```
import random

omega = random.uniform(0, 4)
slope = cost_derivative(omega, x, y)

while abs(slope) > 0.0001:
    omega = omega - slope
    slope = cost_derivative(omega, x, y)

print(omega)

2.083087164799504
```

Note: Each line of code (aside from import and print) represents a step we defined earlier in our learning algorithm. To recap, we initialize omega, compute the slope, then keep updating omega using the slope until it gets close to 0. Finally, we reach our objective and print the optimal value for omega.

Let's illustrate what is happening after each iteration of this learning algorithm using our cost-omega graph.

The starting point (random omega):

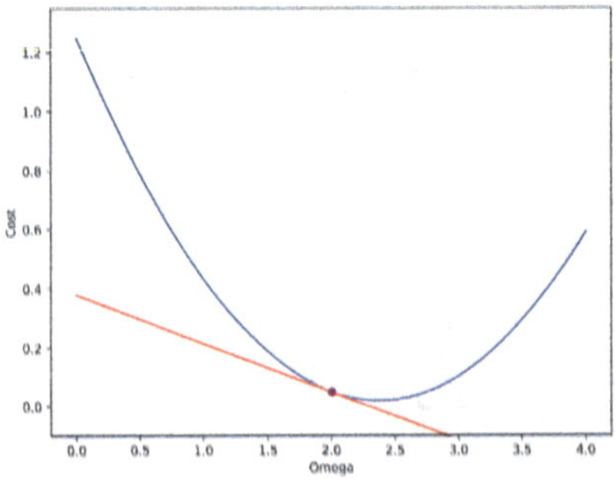

After each iteration:

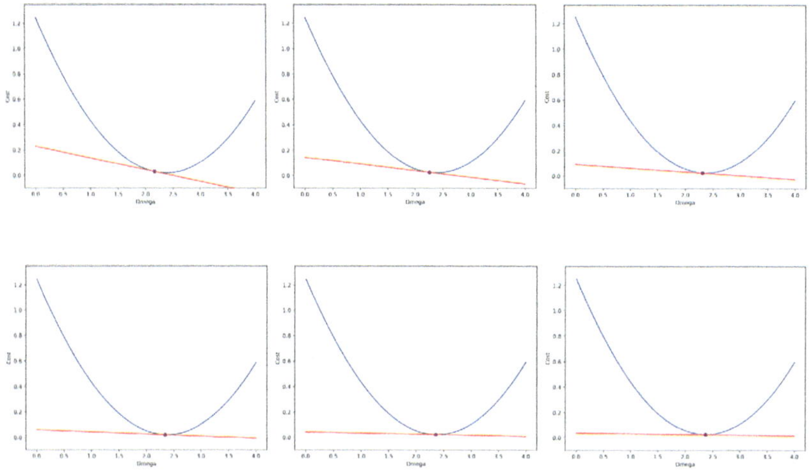

This illustrates how after each iteration we get closer and closer to the bottom of the hill until we reach it. The slope of the red line is what guides our next move at every iteration until eventually it becomes 0.

You now understand how the most important training algorithm in ML works! This core idea powers countless algorithms, including large language models (LLMs).

There are two more modifications that we need to consider making this algorithm more robust. In the original explanation, we keep training the algorithm until slope approaches 0. While it's the ideal state we want to reach – in practice training algorithms on a lot of data becomes computationally expensive. In order to finish training within a reasonable time and computational constraint – algorithms are trained for a set number of iterations. Simply put, instead of a while loop, we use for loop to restrict training expanses. The number of iterations needs to be large enough for the algorithm to converge, that is for the slope to become relatively small.

We know that information from the slope (derivative) provides learnable parameter with direction and magnitude of its next step. What if we were to introduce a variable to control size of each step?

This allows us to control how fast the person gets down the hill, which directly relates to the number of steps they need to make to reach the bottom (number of iterations). This new variable provides us with more flexibility, allowing to make training faster and more efficient. The variable can be thought of as step size and is formally defined as learning rate denoted by alpha (α).

In essence, we scale derivative by alpha to control step size on each iteration:

$$\omega = \omega - \alpha * \frac{dJ}{d\omega}$$

Let's update the learning algorithm with these two changes.

```
num_iterations = 100
alpha = 0.1

omega = random.randint(0, 4)
slope = cost_derivative(omega, x, y)

for _ in range(num_iterations):

    omega = omega - alpha * slope
    slope = cost_derivative(omega, x, y)

print(omega)

2.077084848143789
```

We replaced while loop with a for loop and introduced alpha to control step size on each iteration – as the result we get an identical result to the previous version of this algorithm. What's important is that this version scales with complexity of the real-world problems.

The number of iterations and step size are values that interfere with how an ML algorithm works and are set by ML professionals, such quantities are referred to as hyperparameters.

The next logical question is: How to select appropriate values for the hyperparameters?

While there's no ultimate answer to this question as it depends on the problem, size and complexity of the dataset – we will explore how professionals approach this.

The Number of Iterations

The number of iterations is equivalent to the number of times learnable parameter gets updated. There's no point updating ω when the model stops making substantial progress, that is when the slope becomes very small (nearly flat surface).

Good starting points in the real world are 1,000 or 5,000 iterations, depending on dataset size and complexity.

How to know if it's right? Monitor the cost as training progresses:

- Too small: Algorithm stops before the model hits diminishing returns
- Too big: Algorithm runs long after progress stops
- Just right: Algorithm stops when cost stops changing significantly.

If the number is too small, the ML model will underperform as parameters never become optimal. If it's too large, performance usually won't decline – we are just wasting time and resources by performing unnecessary computations. You will get more understanding of this as we move forward.

Learning Rate

Step size is crucial for robust learning process and what is too big and too small is best shown visually.

Good starting points in the real world are 0.01, 0.001 or 0.0001, depending on the size and complexity of the dataset. We will use our learning algorithm with number of iterations set to 1000. To illustrate learning process under different step sizes, we will plot cost-omega graph at the beginning and after each 10 iterations of learning.

$\alpha = 0.001$ – too small:

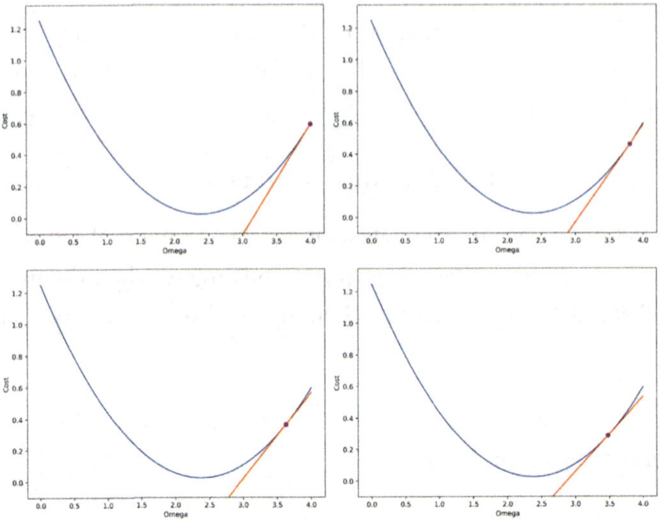

$\alpha = 5$ – too big:

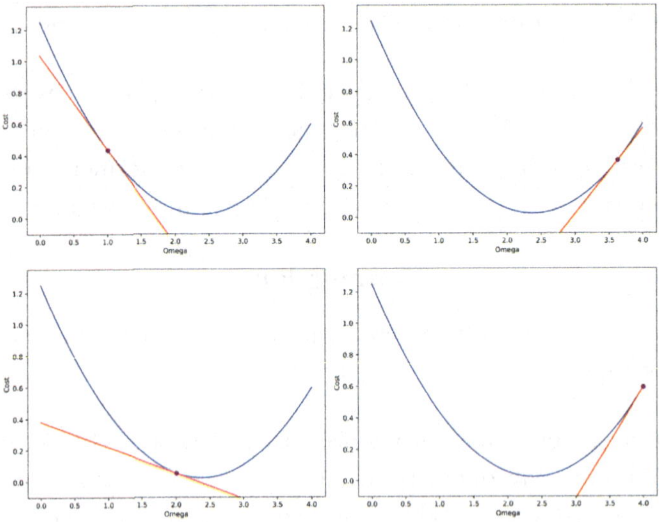

$\alpha = 0.01$ – just right:

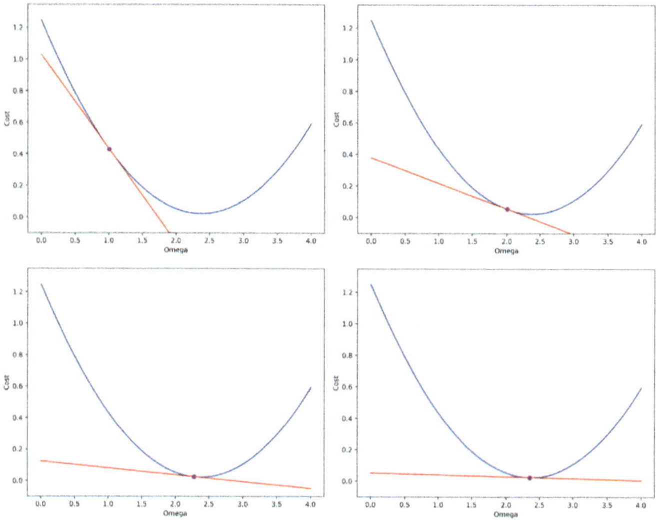

How do you know whether it's too big, too small or just right without the visual? Think about what the visuals tell us. Learning rate is too small when value of the cost function doesn't change much starting from the very beginning. Alpha is too big when value of the cost function sometimes becomes substantially bigger as the model is being trained (opposite of what we want), meaning value of the cost is erratic. In both cases we never achieve optimal learnable parameter value. The value is just right when model makes substantial incremental progress towards the minimal value of the cost function.

To recap: The number of iterations and learning rate account for the number of steps and step size of the learnable parameter towards minimal value of the cost function. They are also referred to as hyperparameters of a model.

Multiple Learnable Parameters

So far, we have explored how to train a linear model with a single learnable parameter. Let's expand to multiple learnable parameters. The core ideas remain the same.

The new dataset with multiple features:

	x1	x2	y
0	0.374540	0.642032	2.805723
1	0.950714	0.084140	2.155949
2	0.731994	0.161629	2.017069
3	0.598658	0.898554	3.861953
4	0.156019	0.606429	2.163741
...	...	...	...
195	0.349210	0.930757	3.407596
196	0.725956	0.858413	4.054195
197	0.897110	0.428994	3.076179
198	0.887086	0.750871	4.002891
199	0.779876	0.754543	3.732623

200 rows × 3 columns

Plotted:

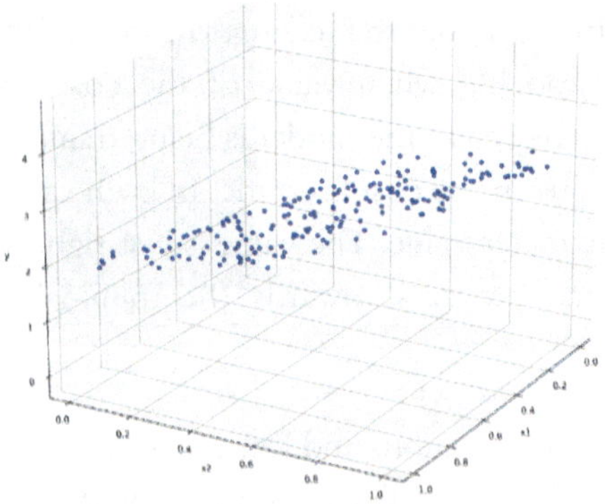

We'll still use a linear model, but now we predict y based on two features: x_1 and x_2. Each feature provides different information and has different influence on the target. Therefore, each feature gets its own "weight" – its own learnable parameter that represents its influence on the target.

Our new prediction equation becomes:

$$y = \omega_1 * x_1 + \omega_2 * x_2$$

Let's update the algorithm with these changes:

1. Select multiple random omegas
2. For a set number of iterations:

   - Compute slope of the tangent line for each omega
   - Update each omega using corresponding slope, scaled by learning rate

Our cost function remains the same, it still measures average squared difference between predicted and actual value:

$$J = \frac{1}{n} * \sum_{i=1}^{n} \left(y_{pred_i} - y_{actual_i}\right)^2$$

Since our y_{pred} has changed, it now involves two learnable parameters – *J* becomes dependent on two parameters, instead of just one:

$$J(\omega_1, \omega_2) = \frac{1}{n} * \sum_{i=1}^{n} \left(\omega_1 * x_{1_i} + \omega_2 * x_{2_i} - y_{actual_i}\right)^2$$

Because we have two parameters to tune, we need to calculate the slope (the derivative) for each one individually.

Think back to our hill analogy. Previously, our person was stuck on a single path and could only move forward or backward (increasing or decreasing a single ω value). But now, with two parameters, our person can move freely in any direction, not just forward or backward along a fixed path. The movement happens when we change parameter values for ω_1 and ω_2.

Here's what the cost surface looks like for two parameters:

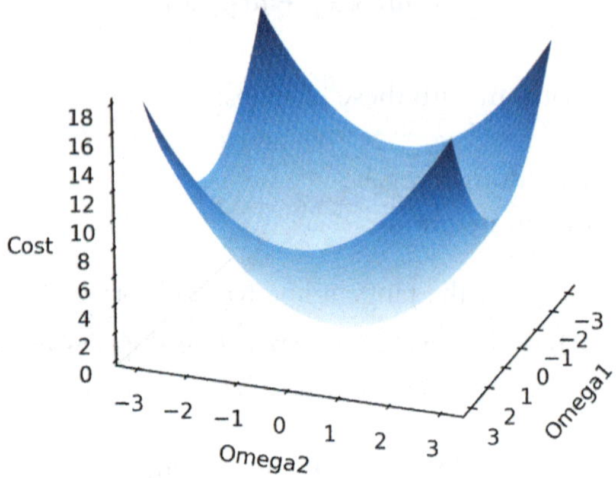

While we can only visualize the hill in 2D or 3D, the beauty of this math is that it works for any number of parameters. Even if you have 100 or 1 million features, the logic remains the same: we find the slope for each individual parameter and take a small step downhill to minimize our error.

To find the way down, we look at the slope of the tangent line for the first parameter:

$$\frac{dJ}{d\omega_1} = \lim_{h \to 0} \frac{J(\omega_1 + h, \omega_2) - J(\omega_1, \omega_2)}{h}$$

And for the second:

$$\frac{dJ}{d\omega_2} = \lim_{h \to 0} \frac{J(\omega_1, \omega_2 + h) - J(\omega_1, \omega_2)}{h}$$

> Note: In each case, the other parameter stays the same – we are isolating how a tiny change in just one specific parameter affects the total cost J.

Finally, our person uses the information from the slope across each axis to take an informed step in the right direction:

$$\omega_1 = \omega_1 - \alpha * \frac{dJ}{d\omega_1}$$

$$\omega_2 = \omega_2 - \alpha * \frac{dJ}{d\omega_2}$$

Congratulations! You just learned how to train a linear model with multiple learnable parameters!

Matrix Notation

Whenever we deal with multiple quantities of the same kind, it is useful to consider whether they can be represented in a more comprehensive structure. In this case we have multiple features (x_1, x_2), learnable parameters (ω_1, ω_2) and derivatives $(\frac{dJ}{d\omega_1}, \frac{dJ}{d\omega_2})$. Each feature is a vector, while each parameter and derivative is a scalar. Therefore, we can create a matrix of features:

$$X = \begin{bmatrix} x_1 & x_2 \\ \vdots & \vdots \end{bmatrix}$$

A vector of learnable parameters:

$$\omega = \begin{bmatrix} \omega_1 \\ \omega_2 \end{bmatrix}$$

And a vector of derivatives with respect to each parameter:

$$\frac{dJ}{d\omega} = \begin{bmatrix} \frac{dJ}{d\omega_1} \\ \frac{dJ}{d\omega_2} \end{bmatrix}$$

Vector $\frac{dJ}{d\omega}$ represents how change in every learnable parameter affects cost J. It can be thought of as ultimate information to guide the person down the hill at any point of their journey. This type of vector has a special name – the gradient, denoted by nabla symbol next to the cost:

$$\nabla J = \frac{dJ}{d\omega} = \begin{bmatrix} \frac{dJ}{d\omega_1} \\ \frac{dJ}{d\omega_2} \end{bmatrix}$$

With matrix notation, our learning rule becomes compact and scales to any number of parameters.

This equation can be used to make a prediction for datasets with arbitrary number of features:

$$y_{pred} = X \cdot \omega$$

On each iteration compute the gradient and update parameters:

$$\nabla J = \frac{2}{n} * X^T \cdot (y_{pred} - y_{actual})$$

$$\omega = \omega - \alpha * \nabla J$$

Note: If you're curious how this matrix form relates to the individual derivatives we derived earlier, you can verify that it is equivalent to computing each derivative separately and stacking the results into a vector. The matrix multiplication and transposition covered in the "Manipulating Data" chapter make this operation both efficient and general – this equation works whether you have 3 parameters or 3 million.

Finally, the concept of gradient is crucial in ML as it allows us to optimize parameters. In practice, the term gradient is loosely used to refer to any vector of derivatives of a single objective function.

Let's implement complete training algorithm and solve our problem.

```
def cost_gradient(omega, X, y_actual):

    n = len(X)

    return (2 / n) * X.T @ (X @ omega - y_actual)

num_params = X.shape[1]

num_iterations = 1000
alpha = 0.01

omega = np.array([random.randint(0, 4) for _ in
range(num_params)])

for _ in range(num_iterations):

    gradient = cost_gradient(omega, X, y)
    omega = omega - alpha * gradient

print(omega)

x1     1.920969
x2    3.072803
```

First, we defined a function to compute the gradient, then we identified the number of parameters (equal to the number of features) and finally trained the model using our learning algorithm.

At this point the model learned optimal values for ω and is ready to predict targets based on unseen features. In mathematical terms our model can be defined as follows:

$$y_{pred} = 1.92 * x_1 + 3.07 * x_2$$

Or in matrix form as:

$$y_{pred} = X \cdot \begin{bmatrix} 1.92 \\ 3.07 \end{bmatrix}$$

This training algorithm that we learned is called gradient descent because the gradient of the cost function guides the parameters to progressively descend toward the minimum cost. Gradient descent is an optimization technique, as it seeks the optimal values of learnable parameters.

This algorithm or its variations power everything from simple linear models to massive neural networks.

Congratulations! You've just learned how the most fundamental ML algorithms actually learn from data!

Data Preparation

So far, we've only worked with toy datasets – it's time for something more realistic! In this module, we will explore three different datasets that will be used throughout this book. We need three datasets because there are three common problem types in classical ML each represented by its own dataset.

The key question that determines problem type: What does our target variable look like?

Regression

Goal: Predict a continuous value – one that can potentially take on an infinite number of values.

Examples:

- What will a house sell for? ($250,000, $892,300, ...)
- How tall will a child grow to be? (178.5 cm, 192 cm, ...)
- How far will a customer travel to our store? (2.3 km, 8.1 km, ...)

All these problems have a very large number (theoretically infinite) of possible distinct values within a reasonable range.

Our dataset: California housing data. You're already familiar with it – we need to predict house value based on information about its neighborhood.

	median_income	housing_median_age	total_rooms	...	latitude	longitude	median_house_value
0	8.3252	41	880.0	...	37.88	-122.23	452600.0
1	8.3014	21	7099.0	...	37.86	-122.22	358500.0
2	7.2574	52	1467.0	...	37.85	-122.24	352100.0
3	5.6431	52	1274.0	...	37.85	-122.25	341300.0
4	3.8462	52	1627.0	...	37.85	-122.25	342200.0
...	...	...	...	...	...	...	...
20635	1.5603	25	1665.0	...	39.48	-121.09	78100.0
20636	2.5568	18	697.0	...	39.49	-121.21	77100.0
20637	1.7000	17	2254.0	...	39.43	-121.22	92300.0
20638	1.8672	18	1860.0	...	39.43	-121.32	84700.0
20639	2.3886	16	2785.0	...	39.37	-121.24	89400.0

20640 rows × 9 columns

As part of data preprocessing, we will scale our targets down by 100,000, as most ML algorithms benefit from smaller scales for continuous targets.

Note: In one of the previous chapters, we explored the dirty version of this dataset – this one is cleaned, ready to be used for training.

Binary Classification

Goal: Predict which of two possible classes an observation belongs to.

Examples:

- Will a customer cancel their subscription this week? (yes/no)
- Is an email spam? (yes/no)
- Is a particular person in this photo? (yes/no)

All these problems have only two potential answers: yes or no (often encoded as 0 or 1).

Our dataset: Medical data about breast cancer. The target takes value benign for patients without the condition and malignant for those with the condition. The goal is to predict whether a new patient has the condition based on various medical features.

	Clump_Thickness	Cell_Size_Uniformity	Cell_Shape_Uniformity	...	Normal_Nucleoli	Mitoses	Class
0	5.0	1.0	1.0	...	1.0	1.0	benign
1	5.0	4.0	4.0	...	2.0	1.0	benign
2	3.0	1.0	1.0	...	1.0	1.0	benign
3	6.0	8.0	8.0	...	7.0	1.0	benign
4	4.0	1.0	1.0	...	1.0	1.0	benign
...	...	...	...	...	...	...	...
694	3.0	1.0	1.0	...	1.0	1.0	benign
695	2.0	1.0	1.0	...	1.0	1.0	benign
696	5.0	10.0	10.0	...	10.0	2.0	malignant
697	4.0	8.0	6.0	...	6.0	1.0	malignant
698	4.0	8.0	8.0	...	4.0	1.0	malignant

699 rows × 10 columns

As part of data preprocessing, we will encode the target, meaning assign a number to each possible class. In this case, benign will be encoded as 0 and malignant as 1.

Multiclass Classification

Goal: Predict which of multiple classes (more than two) an observation belongs to.

Examples:

- What grade does a student belong to? (1st, 2nd, 3rd, 4th, 5th, ...)
- What subscription tier will a user buy? (Basic, Pro, Enterprise)
- What phone brand does a customer own? (Apple, Samsung, Google, Lenovo, ...)

All these problems have a limited number of distinct outcomes, greater than two (often encoded as 0, 1, 2, 3, ...).

Our dataset: Iris flower data with the goal of predicting the species of the iris. Values 0, 1, and 2 are all discrete, with each representing a different iris species (Setosa, Versicolor, and Virginica).

	sepallength	sepalwidth	petallength	petalwidth	class
0	5.1	3.5	1.4	0.2	Iris-setosa
1	4.9	3.0	1.4	0.2	Iris-setosa
2	4.7	3.2	1.3	0.2	Iris-setosa
3	4.6	3.1	1.5	0.2	Iris-setosa
4	5.0	3.6	1.4	0.2	Iris-setosa
...	...	...	...	...	...
145	6.7	3.0	5.2	2.3	Iris-virginica
146	6.3	2.5	5.0	1.9	Iris-virginica
147	6.5	3.0	5.2	2.0	Iris-virginica
148	6.2	3.4	5.4	2.3	Iris-virginica
149	5.9	3.0	5.1	1.8	Iris-virginica

150 rows x 5 columns

Similarly to binary classification, we will encode each possible class with a respective numeric value beginning with 0. Setosa, Versicolor, and Virginica will be encoded as 0, 1 and 2 respectively.

Technical Note

These datasets will be used to train and test models as we develop them throughout the book. To avoid repetitive work and focus on the ML part later, let's develop a script to load and preprocess all the data right now.

Since we aim to build a system once and then import it each time we need the data – we will first ensure that files in our system can talk to each other.

If you are using a local environment, make sure the file containing the code from this chapter is named "data_loader.py". Store this file in the same directory where you plan to save all the ML algorithms we will build later. This is the only place we need to use a Python file to enable "importing" its contents into our notebooks.

If you are using Colab, we need to go through a couple of steps:

Every new notebook you create for this book (including the one for this chapter) must begin with the following code cell. Replace "YOUR_FOLDER_NAME" with the folder you created to store your files for this book:

```
from google.colab import drive
drive.mount('/content/drive')

%cd "/content/drive/MyDrive/Colab Notebooks/YOUR_FOLDER_NAME"

!pip install openml
```

> Note: This connects the notebook to your Google Drive, navigates to your specific folder, and installs the OpenML library used to import raw data.

To create a Python file from our notebook, we will store the entire data preparation system within a single notebook cell. To save that cell's contents as a file, the very first line of that cell must be:

```
%%writefile data_loader.py
```

This command automatically writes all the code within the cell to a file named "data_loader.py" inside your book's folder. This allows us to easily import its contents into our future ML algorithm files.

Data Preparation System

Our goal is to make data loading and preparations as simple as possible, something like:

```
dataset = Dataset("regression")

X_train, X_test, y_train, y_test = dataset.load_split_data()
```

With this interface, we can load any dataset using two lines of code by simply specifying the problem type. Let's build it.

First, we import all necessary libraries.

```
import pandas as pd
import openml
from IPython.display import display
from sklearn.model_selection import train_test_split
from sklearn.preprocessing import StandardScaler, LabelEncoder
```

All the datasets are provided by OpenML, so no additional downloads are necessary. Each dataset we explored has a special id – the following function will take in dataset id, load it from server and return the data frame (df) along with column name for the target.

```
def load_openml_df(dataset_id):
    dataset = openml.datasets.get_dataset(dataset_id)

    X, y, _, _ = dataset.get_data(
        target=dataset.default_target_attribute
    )

    df = X.copy()
    df[dataset.default_target_attribute] = y

    return df, dataset.default_target_attribute
```

Let's create dataset class that will be used to load and split the data. It takes in the problem type and loads corresponding data using function we defined above. Then, depending on the problem type, it transforms the target column to meet appropriate standards.

- For regression problems, we scale targets by 100,000 to make training process smoother. Generally, ML algorithms benefit from targets on a reasonable scale. You can get good intuition by asking yourself: "What is a sufficiently small scale for this problem?". In case with house prices, we can represent house value in hundreds of thousands of dollars reasonably well.

- For classification problems the transformation is very straightforward – models can't predict text directly. Therefore, we represent each class with an integer, this process is also referred to as label encoding. In code below, you can observe how it can be nicely done with the help of Scikit-learn.

```
class Dataset:

    def __init__(self, problem_type):

        if problem_type == "regression":
            self.df, target_col = load_openml_df(537)

            self.df[target_col] = self.df[target_col] / 100000

        elif problem_type == "binary classification":
            self.df, target_col = load_openml_df(15)

            self.df[target_col] =
LabelEncoder().fit_transform(self.df[target_col])

        elif problem_type == "multiclass classification":
            self.df, target_col = load_openml_df(61)

            self.df[target_col] =
LabelEncoder().fit_transform(self.df[target_col])

        else:
            raise ValueError(
                "Choose between regression, binary classification,
or multiclass classification"
            )

        self.df.dropna(inplace=True)

        self.X = self.df.drop(columns=[target_col]).values
        self.y = self.df[target_col].values
```

The final touch of the initial method is to remove all rows with missing data for simplicity and define two instance variables that represent features and targets of the chosen dataset.

Next, we define a method to display the dataset in desired format – in case we ever want to take another look at it.

```
    def display(self):

        pd.set_option("display.max_columns", 6)

        display(self.df)
```

Finally, we split the data for training and testing using 80-20 split.

```
    def load_split_data(self):

        X_train, X_test, y_train, y_test =
train_test_split(self.X, self.y, test_size=0.2, shuffle=True,
random_state=1)

        return X_train, X_test, y_train, y_test
```

This is industry standard to split data for a typical ML problem. "train_test_split" function shuffles the data and randomly takes sample of rows of for test and leaves out the rest for training. "test_size" parameter specifies the proportion of rows used for test. Finally, "random_state" set to a particular value (1 in this case) ensures that the resulted split is same for everyone following this book.

Time-series problems involve a date column where the order of observations matters. Shuffling such data would leak future information into the training set, so instead we split chronologically – training on earlier dates and testing on the most recent ones.

If you need a refresher on why we separate features and targets or why we need to split the data into train and test subsets feel free to revisit "Fundamentals of ML" chapter.

Feature Scaling

In the "Learning from Data (Optimization)" chapter, we learned how to train a linear model on many features. Each feature is assigned a weight that gradient descent adjusts during training.

Ideally, we want learnable parameters to act as importance scores that we can interpret.

However, when features are on different scales, features with higher values dominate the smaller ones. For instance, let's use linear model to predict person's credit scores based on:

- Age – x_1 with range (18 – 120)
- Number of children – x_2 with range (0 – 12)
- Salary – $x_3$with range (20,000 – 500,000)

Each feature is assigned an importance score towards prediction of their credit score.

$$y_{pred} = \omega_1 * x_1 + \omega_2 * x_2 + \omega_3 * x_3$$

Let's explore how significant a 10-unit change should be for each feature.

- 10 years of age should make a lot of difference towards person's credit score
- 10 children significantly change person's profile, in combination with their salary it may indicate how responsible they are, which is very relevant to a credit score prediction
- 10 dollars in annual salary make no meaningful difference

Recall, gradient contains information of how change in each learnable parameter affects the cost. Since importance of a change is very different for the features – some gradients will be huge while others tiny. This mismatch makes training slow and unstable.

What's the solution? Bring features to the same scale.

One of the common ways to achieve this is to use standardization. This technique transforms every feature to have mean value of 0 and standard deviation equal to 1. Crucially, it doesn't change the shape of distribution of the feature, which is exactly what we want to preserve. In other words, relative variation within a feature is not affected – just its absolute value.

The technique is straightforward, say x denotes a single feature column, then standardized column becomes:

$$\frac{x - M}{SD}$$

We subtract every feature value by its mean and divide by standard deviation. Repeat this process for every feature within a dataset. As the result, each feature has mean 0 and standard deviation 1, which indicates they are on the same scale.

Gradient descent is not the only training algorithm that benefits from this transformation – you will learn about others as we move forward. Given its usefulness, let's add it to our data preparation system to perform the transformation in one line of code whenever we need it.

Let's define our function and use Scikit-learn to apply standardization.

```
def standardize(X_train, X_test):

    scaler = StandardScaler()

    scaler.fit(X_train)

    X_train = scaler.transform(X_train)
    X_test = scaler.transform(X_test)

    return X_train, X_test
```

Note: Since it's a row-dependent operation (mean and standard deviation are computed across rows) – we apply it after the split.

First, statistics are computed from the training data and then are applied to both train and test sets. This function takes in and transforms both training and testing feature matrices. It is crucial to standardize the whole dataset at once using mean and standard deviation calculated from the training data to prevent revealing test data to the algorithm.

This data preparation system allows us to obtain training-ready data in just a few lines of code, enabling us to focus on the ML part throughout this book!

Module Structure

When it comes to building a strong foundation, structure is the key. Therefore, all chapters covering ML algorithms follow the same structure outlined below.

Intuition

Each module begins with intuition about what ML algorithm is used for and how it makes predictions. Each algorithm is backed up by common sense of why it works – that's what we explore here.

Formalization

This part formalizes the intuition and turns conceptual understanding into practical explanation of each step using formal notation.

Implementation

In this part, we implement earlier formalized concepts in code, so that we can use the ML algorithm to solve real problems.

Test

The test part is responsible for testing our implementation. Here, we leverage an established library to train the same model we built from scratch and compare their performance. Apart from validation of our custom implementation, you get to learn how this same ML algorithm is trained and evaluated in practice.

Tips

In the last part you get guidelines on when to apply the algorithm in the real world, rooted in what we learned in this chapter. This module also explores additional practical information that will help you understand strengths and weaknesses of the algorithm.

Linear Regression

Intuition

Linear regression is a linear model that works in a very similar way to the one we already explored. It assigns a weight to each feature – a learnable parameter that measures the influence of the respective feature on the target, which can also be thought of as an importance score. These weights are then optimized with gradient descent. The ultimate goal is to capture linear relationship between features and a continuous target. This part is absolutely identical to the first ML algorithm you learned.

The only difference is that now we have a base parameter, which acts as a starting point of our line. Whenever all feature values equal to 0 – the model predicts this base value.

If you look more closely at the graphs that we have explored for linear models so far – the line always started at $y = 0$. However, for many problems the target never equals to 0. Think about house prices, annual salaries in Canada, or age of employees at a company – these values have natural minimum thresholds far above zero.

The following graph represents the difference between a linear model with and without the base parameter using the housing data:

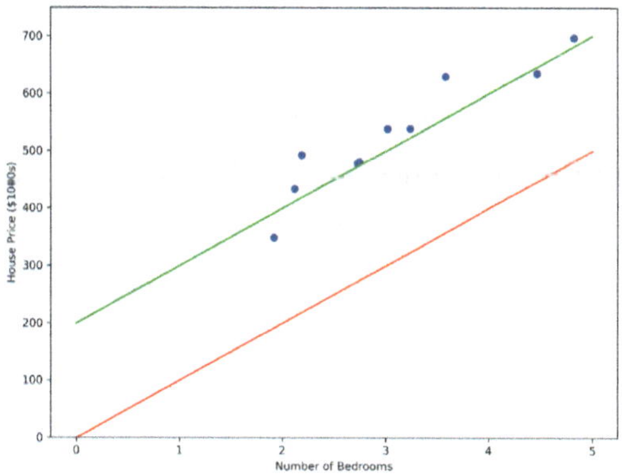

Each line represents a linear model with the same weights assigned to the feature. However, the model represented by the green line has a base value of 200, while the red one has no base term.

The green line is linear regression, and the red one represents the linear model we learned in the "Learning from Data (Optimization)" chapter. As you can observe, it's a small but crucial difference that makes the model adaptable to different scales of the target.

> Note: The base number is also a learnable parameter – the model learns it through gradient descent the same way it learns every other parameter.

Formalization

Recall formula for the linear model from the optimization chapter:

$$y_{pred} = X \cdot \omega$$

Now we add base b, which is also called bias or intercept because it represents value at which the line intercepts y-axis. As the result we get the equation of linear regression:

$$y_{pred} = X \cdot \omega + b$$

Bias is a single number that allows the fitted line to shift up or down, making the model more flexible and able to handle targets of any scale.

Imagine the number of features in our dataset is m, then linear regression has $m + 1$ learnable parameters. Since the cost J is a function of the prediction – it depends on $m + 1$ learnable parameters. Recall, the gradient of J is a vector of derivatives of J with respect to each parameter it depends on.

Equation of the cost function:

$$J(\omega, b) = J(\omega_1, \omega_2, \dots, \omega_m, b) = \frac{1}{n} * \sum_{i=1}^{n} \left(y_{pred_i} - y_{actual_i}\right)^2$$

The gradient of the cost becomes:

$$\nabla J = \left[\frac{dJ}{d\omega}, \frac{dJ}{db}\right] = \left[\frac{dJ}{d\omega_1}, \frac{dJ}{d\omega_2}, \dots, \frac{dJ}{d\omega_m}, \frac{dJ}{db}\right]$$

We just wrote the definition of a gradient – each element of the vector answers "How does change in value of this learnable parameter affects the cost?". This way the gradient acts as the ultimate guide for linear regression on each iteration of the learning process – gradient descent.

Here's what happens if we expand each term:

$$\frac{dJ}{d\omega_1} = \lim_{h \to 0} \frac{J(\omega_1 + h, \dots, \omega_m, b) - J(\omega_1, \dots, \omega_m, b)}{h}$$

$$\frac{dJ}{d\omega_2} = \lim_{h \to 0} \frac{J(\omega_1, \omega_2 + h, \dots, \omega_m, b) - J(\omega_1, \dots, \omega_m, b)}{h}$$

$$\vdots$$

$$\frac{dJ}{d\omega_m} = \lim_{h \to 0} \frac{J(\omega_1, \dots, \omega_m + h, b) - J(\omega_1, \dots, \omega_m, b)}{h}$$

$$\frac{dJ}{db} = \lim_{h \to 0} \frac{J(\omega_1, \dots, \omega_m, b + h) - J(\omega_1, \dots, \omega_m, b)}{h}$$

Note: We measure how a tiny change (h) in each parameter individually affects value of the cost – this is all there is to the gradient!

Once we represent weights in a vector form and simplify the equation we get:

$$\frac{dJ}{d\omega} = \frac{2}{n} * X^T \cdot (y_{pred} - y_{actual})$$

$$\frac{dJ}{db} = \frac{2}{n} * \sum_{i=1}^{n} (y_{pred_i} - y_{actual_i})$$

Let's now formally define training process of linear regression:

1. Initialize learnable parameters ω and b with random values
2. For a set number of iterations:

   - Compute the gradient of the cost function:

$$\nabla J = \left[\frac{dJ}{d\omega}, \frac{dJ}{db}\right]$$

   - Update learnable parameters (ω and b) using gradient:

$$\omega = \omega - \alpha * \frac{dJ}{d\omega}$$
$$b = b - \alpha * \frac{dJ}{db}$$

This way, linear regression learns the optimal parameters and is therefore ready to make predictions on unseen data!

Implementation

We will use NumPy for data manipulation, so let's import it.

```
import numpy as np
```

Begin by defining class for the linear regression that takes hyperparameters as input – learning rate (α) and the number of iterations. Recall, hyperparameters are quantities that influence learning process of the algorithm that are manually defined by us – ML professionals.

```python
class CustomLinearRegression():

    def __init__(self, learning_rate=0.001, num_iterations=10000):

        self.learning_rate = learning_rate
        self.num_iterations = num_iterations
```

Each hyperparameter is initialized with a reasonable default value to serve as a baseline for training.

Next, we will define method to train the model. Traditionally, such method is called "fit" because training can be thought of as fitting data to the model. Since linear regression uses gradient descent for optimization, that's what we'll implement here.

```python
    def fit(self, X, y):

        n, m = X.shape

        self.weights = np.random.randn(m)
        self.bias = np.random.randn()

        for _ in range(self.num_iterations):

            y_pred = self.predict(X)

            dw = (2 / n) * np.dot(X.T, (y_pred - y))
            db = (2 / n) * np.sum(y_pred - y)

            self.weights -= self.learning_rate * dw
            self.bias -= self.learning_rate * db
```

This method:

1. Takes training features and targets as input
2. Extracts the total number of observations (n) and features (m)
3. Initializes learnable parameters with random values
4. For a set number of iterations:

    - Makes a prediction using current parameters (see "predict" below)
    - Computes the gradient using our derived formula
    - Updates parameters

Finally, we define method that implements the prediction equation of linear regression.

```
    def predict(self, X):

        return np.dot(X, self.weights) + self.bias
```

Once the model is trained, this method will be used for inference.

Test

In this section we will make sure our custom linear regression performs as expected by training and comparing its performance to the linear regression model offered by Scikit-learn.

Begin by importing our data preparation system to load and split dataset for training and testing.

```
from data_loader import Dataset, standardize
```

We also want to import linear regression offered by Scikit-learn to train and test it alongside our custom implementation.

```
from sklearn.linear_model import LinearRegression
```

The final dependency is the metric we will use to evaluate both models. In this case it is our cost function – mean squared error (MSE).

```
from sklearn.metrics import mean_squared_error
```

Let's use our data preparation system to load, split and then standardize data.

```
dataset = Dataset("regression")
X_train, X_test, y_train, y_test = dataset.load_split_data()
X_train, X_test = standardize(X_train, X_test)
```

Recall, "regression" parameter indicates we are working with California housing dataset. Since linear regression can only be used to solve regression problems – it is the one we want to use. Additionally, the features are standardized to ensure smooth training performance.

Let's define, train and test our custom linear regression model.

```
custom_model = CustomLinearRegression()
custom_model.fit(X_train, y_train)
y_pred_custom = custom_model.predict(X_test)

print(f"Custom Linear Regression MSE:
{mean_squared_error(y_pred_custom, y_test):.3f}")

Custom Linear Regression MSE: 0.513
```

Note: The model is trained on the training data and makes prediction on the test features, then we compare prediction with actual test targets.

What does MSE of 0.513 mean?

MSE represents the average squared difference between predicted and actual values. However, this number is meaningless without context – we need to consider the scale of our target variable.

Let's examine our dataset to understand the target's scale.

```
dataset.display()
```

	median_income	housing_median_age	total_rooms	...	latitude	longitude	median_house_value
0	8.3252	41	880.0	...	37.88	-122.23	4.526
1	8.3014	21	7099.0	...	37.86	-122.22	3.585
2	7.2574	52	1467.0	...	37.85	-122.24	3.521
3	5.6431	52	1274.0	...	37.85	-122.25	3.413
4	3.8462	52	1627.0	...	37.85	-122.25	3.422
...	...	...	...	...	...	...	...
20635	1.5603	25	1665.0	...	39.48	-121.09	0.781
20636	2.5568	18	697.0	...	39.49	-121.21	0.771
20637	1.7000	17	2254.0	...	39.43	-121.22	0.923
20638	1.8672	18	1860.0	...	39.43	-121.32	0.847
20639	2.3886	16	2785.0	...	39.37	-121.24	0.894

20640 rows × 9 columns

The target represents house values in hundreds of thousands of dollars. This means our model's average squared error translates to approximately 0.513 × 100,000 = $51,300 per house. Now we can properly assess our model's performance because we've connected the metric to its real-world meaning.

Let's train and test the same model using Scikit-learn.

```
sklearn_model = LinearRegression()
sklearn_model.fit(X_train, y_train)
y_pred_sklearn = sklearn_model.predict(X_test)

print(f"Scikit-learn Linear Regression MSE:
{mean_squared_error(y_pred_sklearn, y_test):.3f}")

Scikit-learn Linear Regression MSE: 0.487
```

Notice that Scikit-learn's interface mirrors our custom implementation. The difference in performance is negligible, indicating our implementation is correct. You are encouraged to experiment with "learning_rate" and "num_iterations" hyperparameters by passing different values during initialization of "CustomLinearRegression" object.

Tips

When should you use it? By definition, linear regression captures linear relationships between variables. Therefore, it works best for data where the target and feature values change proportionally – meaning when one variable goes up, the other increases or decreases at a constant rate.

How do you know if there's a linear relationship? Theoretically, you can plot each feature against the target to look for linear patterns or perform statistical tests, but this is rarely done in practice. In applied ML, experimentation is cheap. Therefore, for any regression problem, the first step most professionals take is to train a simple linear regression model to establish a performance benchmark.

Can we still use linear regression with non-linear data? Most of the time, features and targets do not have a perfect linear relationship, but they might be related in other ways. We can often apply transformations (such as logarithmic or square-root functions) to the features or the target to "linearize" the relationship, allowing the model to capture it effectively.

What if multiple features have strong linear relationship? How does the model decide how to distribute the weights between them? Simple answer is – it can't. This issue is known as multicollinearity and leads to unstable weights that can swing wildly with small data changes.

This compromises the model's interpretability, making it impossible to isolate the individual effect of specific features. To address this, we typically diagnose the issue using the Variance Inflation Factor (VIF). VIF measures how well a feature can be predicted using all other features. VIF of 10 indicates the feature is linearly related to others and should likely be removed or merged. If interpretability and stability matter to your project, checking for multicollinearity is highly recommended.

Why is interpretability crucial for decision making? When developing a model that guides important decisions, it is crucial to know how the model makes predictions. With linear regression, we can clearly see the magnitude and direction of how each feature impacts the outcome – making it a highly interpretable ML algorithm.

This section introduced key strategies for applying linear regression effectively in practice. You now have the foundation to explore any of these techniques in greater depth.

Conclude: Linear regression is simple, fast, and interpretable. This makes it the perfect starting point for any regression problem and an excellent baseline to try and beat with more complex models.

Logistic Regression

Intuition

Logistic regression is the most fundamental ML algorithm for binary classification tasks. The core difference from linear regression is that instead of predicting a continuous target, we want to predict a category – essentially answering "yes" or "no". As we explored in the "Data Preparation for ML Algorithms" chapter, "yes" is encoded as 1 and "no" as 0.

Naturally, a model cannot know the true class with certainty – there's always some uncertainty, just as in real-world situations where no answer is guaranteed from a rational standpoint. Therefore, instead of directly predicting 0 or 1, logistic regression predicts a probability: a number between 0 and 1 that represents how certain the model is in class 1.

Since there are only two possible outcomes and exactly one must be true, knowing the probability of one class tells us everything about the other. If we're 80% certain an observation belongs to class 1, we're automatically 20% certain it belongs to class 0. The two probabilities must always sum to 1.

A probability like 0.95 means high certainty that the true class is 1, while 0.1 means low certainty in class 1 – or equivalently, high certainty (0.9) in class 0.

Why can't we just use linear regression to predict probability?

There are two fundamental problems:

- Range problem. Probability ranges from 0 to 1, while linear regression can produce literally any output. Negative values or values greater than 1 have no meaning as probabilities.
- Constant rate of change. Most classification problems have a steep tipping point, meaning a small change in the feature value makes a big difference in the outcome. Linear regression increases at the same rate throughout all values of a particular feature, making it impossible to capture that subtlety.

The following plot illustrates how using linear regression for binary classification task would look like:

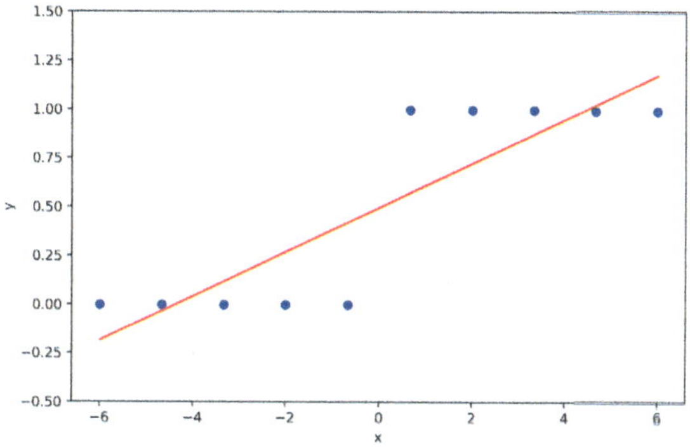

Notice that all observations have a y value of either 0 or 1, corresponding to the class they belong to. The linear fit extends beyond the valid probability range and fails to capture the natural "tipping point" around x at 0.

The solution addresses both issues simultaneously. We ensure the model's output lies within the range from 0 to 1, and the prediction takes on an "S" shape that accounts for the tipping point inherent to binary classification problems. This is achieved by transforming the linear model with a sigmoid function that guarantees both properties.

The resulting model looks as follows:

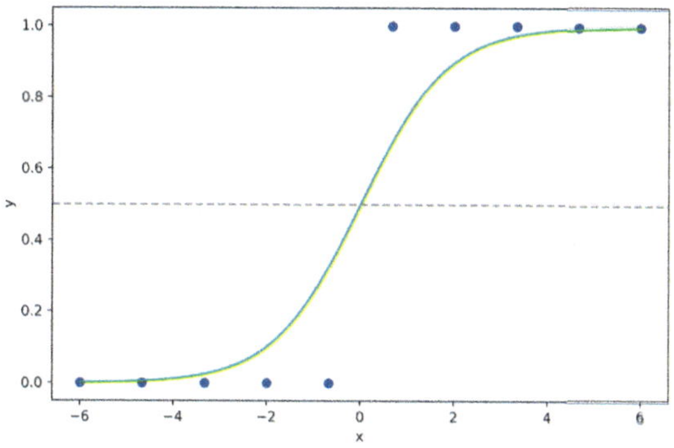

Now the predictions smoothly transition from 0 to 1, staying within valid probability bounds. The steep middle section captures the tipping point, while the flat regions near 0 and 1 reflect high certainty.

Given we mastered linear regression, it's best to get last bit of intuition about logistic regression by answering two questions:

What stays the same?

Logistic regression has the same parameters as linear regression (weights and bias) that are trained in the same way using gradient descent.

What is different?

- The transformation. We apply sigmoid function to the linear model, squeezing outputs into the 0 to 1 range.
- The objective. Instead of minimizing squared error, we use a different loss function designed for probabilities – one that rewards confident correct predictions and heavily penalizes confident wrong ones.

Conclude: While gradient descent, parameter updates, the optimization loop remain fundamentally the same, we simply change the shape of our predictions and how we measure success.

Formalization

Logistic regression can be thought of as generalization of a linear model for a binary classification task. It estimates probability (p) of an observation belonging to class 1, then the probability is interpreted to make the final prediction. A common practice is to classify an observation as class 1 when $p > 0.5$ and as class 0 otherwise.

Linear model we explored so far can only be used to predict a continuous target. How do we modify the approach to predict probabilities – values between 0 and 1?

First, let's recall the prediction equation for linear regression:

$$y = X \cdot \omega + b$$

Output of this equation y has a range of $(-\infty, +\infty)$, in other words its boundless. Our desired range is $[0,1]$, representing probability of an observation belonging to class 1.

We mainly think of uncertainty in two ways – probabilities and odds. Both are equally valid ways to quantify likelihood of a binary outcome. When we say "odds are 3 to 1 that this horse will win the race", this translates to saying "this horse's chance of winning is 3 times higher than losing".

We can represent winning as class 1 and losing as class 0, by convention we can denote probability of an observation belonging to class 1 as p. Since it's a binary outcome – horse either wins or loses – probabilities of both events need to sum up to 1. Thus, probability of class 0 (horse losing) can be denoted as $1 - p$. Verify that probabilities of all possible outcomes (winning and losing) sum up to 1: $p + (1 - p) = 1$.

Let's leverage this notation to quantify odds through example: "this horse's chance of winning is 3 times higher than losing", this translates to:

$$\frac{p}{1-p} = 3$$

Notice: Unlike probability, odds are not bound by 1 – there's no upper bound. We previously said that odds and probabilities are equivalent, let's verify. By knowing odds are 3 to 1 and quantifying them as a ratio of class 1 over class 0 probability, we can solve the equation for p:

$$\frac{p}{1-p} = 3$$

$$3 * (1 - p) = p$$

$$3 - 3 * p = p$$

$$4 * p = 3$$

$$p = \frac{3}{4} = 0.75$$

We just derived that odds 3 to 1 translate to probability of 0.75. Conclude, we can equally represent uncertainty as odds or probabilities. Why does it matter?

Odds lie within $[0, +\infty)$, while probabilities lie within $[0,1]$. Odds got us much closer to matching range of the linear model, which is $(-\infty, +\infty)$.

We now need to find a transformation that can remove the lower bound – this can be done with a function that can translate small positive inputs into negative ones. A function that can shift the scale, without breaking core intuition behind odds – "the bigger the value of odds – the higher the probability of an outcome".

Such function happens to be a natural logarithm of a number:

$$f(x) = log_e(x) = ln(x)$$

It shifts the scale, making odds of 1 the new "0" because $f(1) = 0$ and all inputs below 1 become negative.

If we apply natural logarithm to odds, we get:

$$ln\left(\frac{p}{1-p}\right)$$

This quantity is also called log-odds or logits for short. Log-odds lie within $(-\infty, +\infty)$ – just like output of a linear model. Therefore, we can use linear model to predict log-odds and then translate them to probabilities – desired output format.

Let's denote output of linear model as out:

$$out = X \cdot \omega + b$$

Since we can use linear model to estimate logits, we can say:

$$out = ln\left(\frac{p}{1-p}\right)$$

Now, let's solve this for p:

Apply exponent to both sides – natural logarithm will cancel out.

$$e^{out} = \frac{p}{1-p}$$

$$e^{out} * (1-p) = p$$

$$e^{out} - e^{out} * p = p$$

$$e^{out} = e^{out} * p + p$$

$$p * (e^{out} + 1) = e^{out}$$

$$p = \frac{e^{out}}{e^{out} + 1}$$

Divide both numerator and denominator of the left-hand side by e^{out}.

$$p = \frac{1}{1 + \frac{1}{e^{out}}}$$

$$p = \frac{1}{1 + e^{-out}}$$

This way we can estimate probability of class 1 by transforming output of a linear model. The final equation for logistic regression becomes:

$$y_{pred} = p = \frac{1}{1 + e^{-(X \cdot \omega + b)}}$$

We can also think of the final equation as output of a linear model transformed by a sigmoid function. Sigmoid function is:

$$s(x) = \frac{1}{1 + e^{-x}}$$

Then, passing output of linear model as its input we get the same equation:

$$y_{pred} = s(X \cdot \omega + b) = \frac{1}{1 + e^{-(X \cdot \omega + b)}}$$

To conclude, the logical flow is:

1. We want to leverage linear model to predict probabilities.
2. Linear model output lies within $(-\infty, +\infty)$, while probability lies within $[0,1]$ – any number outside of this range is meaningless.
3. Translate probability to odds without losing meaning, now range becomes $(0, +\infty)$.
4. Transform odds with natural logarithm without losing meaning, now range becomes $(-\infty, +\infty)$ – same as output of linear model.
5. This allows us to estimate log-odds using linear model. This means that all we learned in the linear regression chapter applies here – conceptually we just use that model to predict a transformed target (log-odds).
6. Since odds and probabilities are equivalent, we solve this equation to translate prediction of the linear model (log-odds) into probability – our desired output.

This way, we derive the final equation that lets us predict the probability of an observation belonging to class 1.

Sigmoid function is known to transform input into "S" shaped curve, such that our final prediction curve becomes:

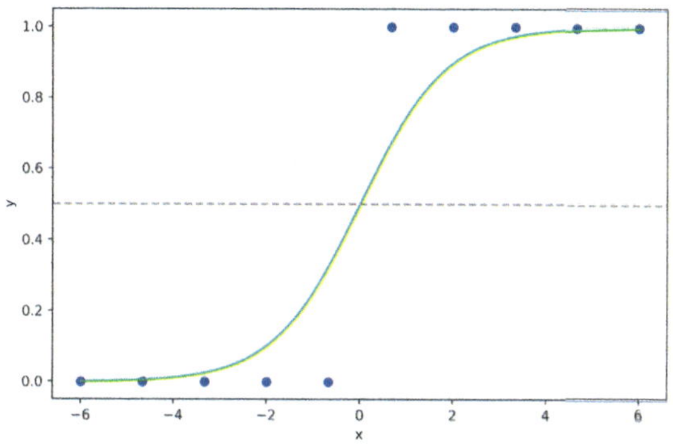

As usual, blue circles are observations (with y being 0 or 1) and the green line representing predicted probability for any value of x. The intersection of the grey dotted line and the curve marks the "tipping point" – the usual 0.5 threshold used to interpret the predicted probability.

Similarly to a linear model, we use gradient descent to train the model but now our objective is different.

Since output of our model is a probability, we no longer want to minimize squared difference between prediction and actual value. Instead, we want to use a more suitable way to tell the model what's bad and what's good during training. Let's think about what behaviour we want to encourage:

We want the model to be confidently correct – the more certain it is about the right answer, the better. Conversely, we should heavily penalize high confidence in wrong answers, and we want to avoid indecisiveness (probabilities around 0.5).

Let's plot two functions that may be of use given our request:

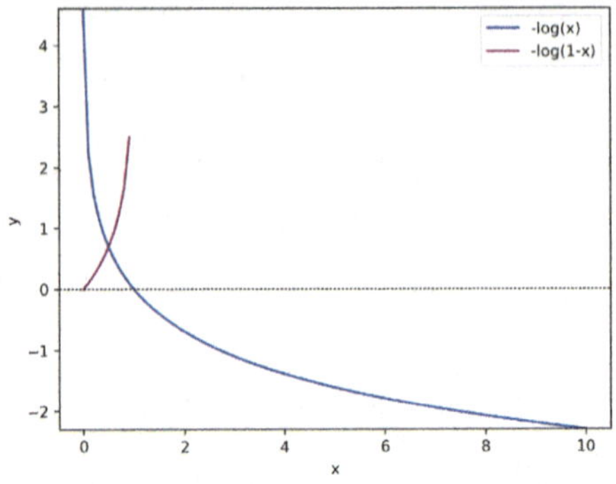

Consider this as our loss function. Since probabilities lie within $[0, 1]$, we will zoom in to that range on the x-axis:

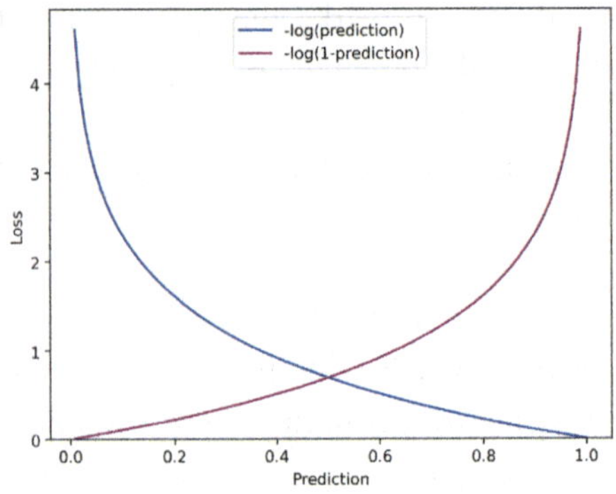

Predicted probability is on x-axis and loss is on y-axis. We can observe two curves with opposite behaviour:

- The purple curve has a very small loss when probability is small and explodes as probability becomes big. This is exactly the behaviour we want when the actual target is 0 – greatly appreciate small probability of class 1 and strongly penalize high probability of class 1.
- The blue curve is the opposite – it strongly penalizes small probability and greatly appreciates big probability, which is exactly what we want when actual target class is 1.

This is why our loss function is $-log\,(1-x)$ when the actual target is 0 and $-log\,(x)$ when the actual target is 1 makes sense.

We can unite this conditional loss function into a single equation with a simple trick that changes the loss function based on the actual target:

$$-\left[y_{actual_i} * log\left(y_{pred_i}\right) + \left(1 - y_{actual_i}\right) * log\left(1 - y_{pred_i}\right)\right]$$

Verify that the scary looking function above is actually quite simple – either blue or red part of the equation becomes 0 depending on value of the target.

- If $y_{actual_i} = 0$, equation becomes: $-log\left(1 - y_{pred_i}\right)$
- If $y_{actual_i} = 1$, equation becomes: $-log\left(y_{pred_i}\right)$

This loss function is called log-loss.

The cost function is average loss, which becomes:

$$J(\omega, b) =$$

$$-\frac{1}{n} * \sum_{i=1}^{n} y_{actual_i} * log\left(y_{pred_i}\right) + \left(1 - y_{actual_i}\right) * log\left(1 - y_{pred_i}\right)$$

Note: If we were to come back to the hill metaphor – the right choice of the cost function manifests in a smooth hill with a single absolute bottom. This ensures that learnable parameters are guaranteed to become optimal. On the other hand, if we were to use the wrong cost function (e.g. MSE for logistic regression) – the hill would be bumpy. This would result into multiple flat surfaces, making training unstable and potentially resulting into non-optimal learnable parameters.

As before, the cost function is only dependent on learnable parameters ω and b. Logistic regression employs gradient descent for training, so let's compute and simplify gradient of the cost above:

$$\nabla J = \left[\frac{dJ}{d\omega}, \frac{dJ}{db}\right]$$

Where

$$\frac{dJ}{d\omega} = \frac{1}{n} * X^T \cdot (y_{pred} - y_{actual})$$

$$\frac{dJ}{db} = \frac{1}{n} * \sum_{i=1}^{n} (y_{pred_i} - y_{actual_i})$$

The gradient is very similar to the one we computed for linear regression, but it comes from a different cost function. Note that while gradient looks similar, the prediction is different from the linear regression:

$$y_{pred} = \frac{1}{1 + e^{-(X \cdot \omega + b)}}$$

Essentially, logistic regression is a general linear model tailored to binary classification tasks. Implementation wise, the only differences from linear regression are the prediction equation and a small change in the gradient of the cost.

Implementation

Begin by importing NumPy and initializing class for logistic regression.

```
import numpy as np

class CustomLogisticRegression():

    def __init__(self, learning_rate=0.001, num_iterations=10000):

        self.learning_rate = learning_rate
        self.num_iterations = num_iterations
```

Define training method, same in structure as for linear regression.

```
    def fit(self, X, y):

        n, m = X.shape

        self.weights = np.random.randn(m)
        self.bias = np.random.randn()

        for _ in range(self.num_iterations):

            y_pred = self.predict(X, predict_class=False)

            dw = (1 / n) * np.dot(X.T, (y_pred - y))
            db = (1 / n) * np.sum(y_pred - y)

            self.weights -= self.learning_rate * dw
            self.bias -= self.learning_rate * db
```

Next, we define method for inference – this is where it gets very different. Recall, logistic regression predicts probability of an observation belonging to class 1 – we then need to interpret it to make the final prediction. A common rule is to treat probability of 0.5 or higher as class 1 and class 0 otherwise. Therefore, our predict method will have two modes, one that outputs probability (raw output) and the other predicted class (final prediction).

```
    def predict(self, X, predict_class=True):

        linear_model = np.dot(X, self.weights) + self.bias

        y_pred = 1 / (1 + np.exp(-linear_model))

        if predict_class:
            y_pred = np.array([1 if i >= 0.5 else 0 for i in
y_pred])

        return y_pred
```

Output of the linear model is transformed by sigmoid function to get the probability and is then optionally converted to the final prediction.

Test

We will evaluate performance of logistic regression using accuracy metric – it is a ratio of correct predictions over all predictions. Other than that, the data loading and preprocessing stays the same as for linear regression, we just use a different dataset.

```
from data_loader import Dataset, standardize
from sklearn.linear_model import LogisticRegression
from sklearn.metrics import accuracy_score

dataset = Dataset("binary classification")
X_train, X_test, y_train, y_test = dataset.load_split_data()
X_train, X_test = standardize(X_train, X_test)
```

Next, we train and test both custom and Scikit-learn implementation.

```
custom_model = CustomLogisticRegression()
custom_model.fit(X_train, y_train)
y_pred_custom = custom_model.predict(X_test)

print(f"Custom Logistic Regression Accuracy:
{accuracy_score(y_pred_custom, y_test):.3f}")

model_sklearn = LogisticRegression()
model_sklearn.fit(X_train, y_train)
y_pred_sklearn = model_sklearn.predict(X_test)

print(f"Scikit-learn Logistic Regression Accuracy:
{accuracy_score(y_pred_sklearn, y_test):.3f}")

Custom Logistic Regression Accuracy: 0.964
Scikit-learn Logistic Regression Accuracy: 0.985
```

Accuracy of around 96-99% indicates both models fit our data well, as before tiny difference in performance is tied to the choice of hyperparameters. This performance proves our implementation to be correct!

Tips

Logistic regression can be thought of as linear regression for binary classification tasks. Just like linear regression models linear relationships between features and continuous target, logistic regression models linear relationships between features and log-odds.

Just like with linear regression, many professionals start with logistic regression as their first attempt at any classification problem. It serves as an excellent baseline model due to its simplicity, speed, and interpretability. You can easily understand how it makes predictions – the coefficients represent how much each feature increases or decreases log-odds, which directly translates to how they affect probability of the positive class (1).

Logistic regression suffers from the same multicollinearity issues as linear regression. When multiple features have strong linear relationship, the model cannot properly distribute importance between them, leading to unstable coefficients that swing wildly with small data changes. Use the same VIF diagnostic approach – as a rule of thumb, remove or merge features with VIF scores above 10 to maintain model stability and interpretability.

Think of logistic regression as the classification equivalent of linear regression – simple, interpretable, and an excellent starting point for any binary classification problem.

Regularization

Intuition

Regularization is not a model – it's a technique that can be applied to many models to prevent them from overfitting the data. It's like tidying up clutter to reveal the underlying pattern. By doing so, the model becomes more general and performs better on unseen data – not merely memorizing examples "word for word," but focusing on the recurring pattern. It's especially useful when a dataset has outliers or a lot of noise – a situation when small fluctuations in the inputs can cause large swings in the target.

Regularization achieves the goal by adding a penalty term to the cost function. This encourages smaller weights, reducing the influence of noisy or less important features, making the model more stable.

No Regularization Regularization

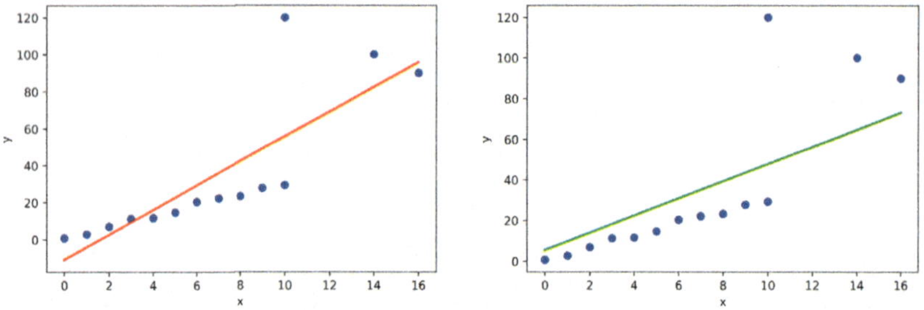

As can be seen from the graphs above, regularization encourages the model to prioritize simplicity and don't pay as much attention to outliers.

Formalization

There are multiple regularization techniques, each one offering a different penalty added to the cost function of the original model. The penalty is regulated a hyperparameter called regularization strength – often denoted by lambda (λ). Regularization strength refers to the degree to which we want to penalize weights, equivalently simplify the model.

L1 Regularization

L1 regularization adds a penalty proportional to the absolute values of weights:

$$L1 = \lambda * \sum_{i=j}^{m} |\omega_j|$$

This encourages weights to shrink, often driving many to exactly zero, effectively removing unimportant features.

L2 Regularization

L2 regularization uses a penalty based on the square of weights:

$$L2 = \frac{\lambda}{2} * \sum_{i=j}^{m} \omega_j^2$$

This penalizes large weights more heavily, causing all weights to shrink smoothly, but typically not to zero. Unlike L1, which promotes sparsity, L2 distributes penalty evenly. This benefits models trained on datasets with features that have strong linear relationship.

Elastic Net

Elastic Net blends the strengths of L1 and L2 regularization, combining both penalties:

$$Elastic\ net = \lambda_1 * \sum_{i=j}^{m} |\omega_j| + \frac{\lambda_2}{2} * \sum_{i=j}^{m} \omega_j^2$$

This regularization technique has two regularization parameters: one controlling the strength of the L1 penalty and another controlling the strength of the L2 penalty.

Regularization Applied to an ML Algorithm

These techniques are very general – they are used to tackle overfitting with a variety of ML algorithms. We will explore them in application to the algorithms we already know inside out – linear and logistic regression.

Let's use variable reg as a placeholder for any of the three regularization techniques we explored.

Then applying a regularization to linear regression is equivalent to adding respective regularization term to the cost:

$$J(\omega, b) = \frac{1}{n} * \sum_{i=1}^{n} \left(y_{pred_i} - y_{actual_i}\right)^2 + reg$$

Similarly for logistic regression:

$$J(\omega, b) =$$

$$\frac{1}{n} * \sum_{i=1}^{n} y_{actual_i} * log\left(y_{pred_i}\right) + \left(1 - y_{actual_i}\right) * log\left(1 - y_{pred_i}\right) + reg$$

Now, depending on the regularization technique we would simply replace reg with an appropriate term – $L1$, $L2$ or $Elastic\ Net$.

Everything we changed was the hill itself (cost) – not the way we get information about the surface (compute gradient) or the goal of reaching the bottom by making steps (progressively minimizing cost).

As we changed the hill – information about its surface that we get on each iteration also changed. We still compute gradient but now of the updated cost functions we defined above. Let's now define updated gradient of the cost. We will use reg' as a placeholder for differentiated regularization term of any of the three techniques.

Gradient notation stays the same:

$$\nabla J = \left[\frac{dJ}{d\omega}, \frac{dJ}{db}\right]$$

Using updated cost to compute gradient for linear regression we get:

$$\frac{dJ}{d\omega} = \frac{2}{n} * X^T \cdot \left(y_{pred} - y_{actual}\right) + reg'$$

$$\frac{dJ}{db} = \frac{2}{n} * \sum_{i=1}^{n} (y_{pred_i} - y_{actual_i})$$

Gradient of the updated cost of logistic regression:

$$\frac{dJ}{d\omega} = \frac{1}{n} * X^T \cdot \left(y_{pred} - y_{actual}\right) + reg'$$

$$\frac{dJ}{db} = \frac{1}{n} * \sum_{i=1}^{n} (y_{pred_i} - y_{actual_i})$$

All that happens is reg' term is added to the derivative of the cost with respect to weights – that's the only change for both algorithms. Depending on the chosen regularization technique reg' will have a different value.

L1 regularization:

$$reg' = \lambda * sign(\omega)$$

Where $sign(\omega)$ represents -1 if weight is negative and 1 if it's positive.

L2 regularization:

$$reg' = \lambda * \omega$$

Elastic net:

$$reg' = \lambda_1 * sign(\omega) + \lambda_2 * \omega$$

Conclude: Regularization is a technique that prevents overfitting by adding a penalty term to the model's cost function. This modifies the training objective (and consequently the gradient), ensuring that the model assigns less weight or even zero weight to unimportant features.

The strength of this penalty is controlled by a hyperparameter, typically denoted as λ. For L1 and L2 regularization, λ determines how strictly the model is constrained. Elastic net combines both techniques and therefore requires hyperparameters to manage the balance between them. Ultimately, higher regularization strength promotes model simplicity, while setting λ to 0 reverts the model to its original, unregularized state.

Implementation

First, we define a function that depending on the regularization strength parameters, returns reg' to be used in the computation of the gradient.

```
import numpy as np

def get_reg(reg_l1, reg_l2, weights):

    reg = 0

    if reg_l1 and reg_l2:
        reg = reg_l1 * np.sign(weights) + reg_l2 * weights

    elif reg_l1:
        reg = reg_l1 * np.sign(weights)

    elif reg_l2:
        reg = reg_l2 * weights

    return reg
```

The function works as follows:

- If both "reg_l1" and "reg_l2" are non-zero – apply elastic net
- If only "reg_l1" is not 0 – apply L1 regularization

- If only “reg_l2” is not 0 – apply L2 regularization

Next, we define linear regression with regularization. Conceptually, the only change is that now differentiated regularization term is added to $\frac{dJ}{d\omega}$. To make linear regression class generalizable for any regularization technique – it takes both L1 and L2 regularization strengths as input and creates instance variables for them.

```
class CustomLinearRegression():

    def __init__(self, reg_l1=None, reg_l2=None,
learning_rate=0.001, num_iterations=10000):

        self.learning_rate = learning_rate
        self.num_iterations = num_iterations

        self.reg_l1 = reg_l1
        self.reg_l2 = reg_l2

    def fit(self, X, y):

        n, m = X.shape

        self.weights = np.random.randn(m)
        self.bias = np.random.randn()

        for _ in range(self.num_iterations):

            y_pred = self.predict(X)

            reg = get_reg(self.reg_l1, self.reg_l2, self.weights)

            dw = (2 / n) * np.dot(X.T, (y_pred - y)) + reg
            db = (2 / n) * np.sum(y_pred - y)

            self.weights -= self.learning_rate * dw
            self.bias -= self.learning_rate * db

    def predict(self, X):

        return np.dot(X, self.weights) + self.bias
```

Regularization term is re-computed using updated weights and used to compute gradient on each iteration of the algorithm.

Note: When we apply regularization to linear regression, the resulting ML algorithm gets a special name – lasso regression for L1 and ridge regression for L2.

The exact same changes are made to implement regularized logistic regression.

```
class CustomLogisticRegression():

    def __init__(self, reg_l1=None,
reg_l2=None,learning_rate=0.001, num_iterations=10000):

        self.learning_rate = learning_rate
        self.num_iterations = num_iterations

        self.reg_l1 = reg_l1
        self.reg_l2 = reg_l2

    def fit(self, X, y):

        n, m = X.shape

        self.weights = np.random.randn(m)
        self.bias = np.random.randn()

        for _ in range(self.num_iterations):

            y_pred = self.predict(X, predict_class=False)

            reg = get_reg(self.reg_l1, self.reg_l2, self.weights)

            dw = (1 / n) * np.dot(X.T, (y_pred - y)) + reg
            db = (1 / n) * np.sum(y_pred - y)

            self.weights -= self.learning_rate * dw
            self.bias -= self.learning_rate * db

    def predict(self, X, predict_class=True):

        linear_model = np.dot(X, self.weights) + self.bias

        y_pred = 1 / (1 + np.exp(-linear_model))

        if predict_class:
            y_pred = np.array([1 if i >= 0.5 else 0 for i in
y_pred])

        return y_pred
```

Test

As usual, we import established models, metrics and data – this time for two different problem types.

```
from data_loader import Dataset, standardize
from sklearn.linear_model import Lasso, Ridge, ElasticNet,
LogisticRegression
from sklearn.metrics import mean_squared_error, accuracy_score

dataset_r = Dataset("regression")
X_train_r, X_test_r, y_train_r, y_test_r =
dataset_r.load_split_data()
X_train_r, X_test_r = standardize(X_train_r, X_test_r)

dataset_b = Dataset("binary classification")
X_train_b, X_test_b, y_train_b, y_test_b =
dataset_b.load_split_data()
X_train_b, X_test_b = standardize(X_train_b, X_test_b)
```

Begin by testing our algorithms – linear and logistic regressions with each regularization term applied individually. The only change is that now we specify regularization type and strength.

Linear regression:

```
custom_model = CustomLinearRegression(reg_l1=0.1)
custom_model.fit(X_train_r, y_train_r)
y_pred_custom = custom_model.predict(X_test_r)
print(f"Custom Linear Regression L1 (Lasso) MSE:
{mean_squared_error(y_test_r, y_pred_custom):.3f}")

custom_model = CustomLinearRegression(reg_l2=0.1)
custom_model.fit(X_train_r, y_train_r)
y_pred_custom =  custom_model.predict(X_test_r)
print(f"Custom Linear Regression L2 (Ridge) MSE:
{mean_squared_error(y_test_r, y_pred_custom):.3f}")

custom_model = CustomLinearRegression(reg_l1=0.05, reg_l2=0.05)
custom_model.fit(X_train_r, y_train_r)
y_pred_custom = custom_model.predict(X_test_r)
print(f"Custom Linear Regression Elastic Net MSE:
{mean_squared_error(y_test_r, y_pred_custom):.3f}")

Custom Linear Regression L1 (Lasso) MSE: 0.559
Custom Linear Regression L2 (Ridge) MSE: 0.504
Custom Linear Regression Elastic Net MSE: 0.534
```

Logistic regression:

```
custom_model = CustomLogisticRegression(reg_l1=0.1)
custom_model.fit(X_train_b, y_train_b)
y_pred_custom = custom_model.predict(X_test_b)
print(f"Custom Logistic Regression L1 Accuracy:
{accuracy_score(y_test_b, y_pred_custom):.3f}")

custom_model = CustomLogisticRegression(reg_l2=0.1)
custom_model.fit(X_train_b, y_train_b)
y_pred_custom = custom_model.predict(X_test_b)
print(f"Custom Logistic Regression L2 Accuracy:
{accuracy_score(y_test_b, y_pred_custom):.3f}")

custom_model = CustomLogisticRegression(reg_l1=0.05, reg_l2=0.05)
custom_model.fit(X_train_b, y_train_b)
y_pred_custom = custom_model.predict(X_test_b)
print(f"Custom Logistic Regression Elastic Net Accuracy:
{accuracy_score(y_test_b, y_pred_custom):.3f}")

Custom Logistic Regression L1 Accuracy: 0.934
Custom Logistic Regression L2 Accuracy: 1.000
Custom Logistic Regression Elastic Net Accuracy: 0.964
```

Our custom implementation uses a slightly different interface than Scikit-learn. In Scikit-learn, "Ridge", "Lasso", and "ElasticNet" are separate classes, which removes ambiguity in how hyperparameters are applied.

For "Lasso" and "Ridge", Scikit-learn uses a single parameter, alpha, to define the regularization strength.

```
sklearn_model = Lasso(alpha=0.1)
sklearn_model.fit(X_train_r, y_train_r)
y_pred_sklearn = sklearn_model.predict(X_test_r)
print(f"Scikit-learn Lasso MSE: {mean_squared_error(y_test_r,
y_pred_sklearn):.3f}")

sklearn_model = Ridge(alpha=0.1)
sklearn_model.fit(X_train_r, y_train_r)
y_pred_sklearn = sklearn_model.predict(X_test_r)
print(f"Scikit-learn Ridge MSE: {mean_squared_error(y_test_r,
y_pred_sklearn):.3f}")
```

When it comes to "ElasticNet", alpha represents the total regularization penalty, which is then partitioned between L1 and L2 terms. This partitioning is controlled by the "l1_ratio" parameter, which specifies the proportion of alpha assigned to the L1 ("Lasso") penalty.

```
sklearn_model = ElasticNet(alpha=0.1, l1_ratio=0.5)
sklearn_model.fit(X_train_r, y_train_r)
y_pred_sklearn = sklearn_model.predict(X_test_r)
print(f"Scikit-learn ElasticNet MSE: {mean_squared_error(y_test_r,
y_pred_sklearn):.3f}")

Scikit-learn Lasso MSE: 0.664
Scikit-learn Ridge MSE: 0.487
Scikit-learn ElasticNet MSE: 0.611
```

Scikit-learn's "LogisticRegression" class supports L1, L2, and elastic net penalties through a single penalty parameter. Unlike linear models, which use alpha to represent regularization strength directly, logistic regression uses an inverse parameter "C", defined as $C = \frac{1}{\lambda}$ – so a smaller "C" means stronger regularization.

```
sklearn_model = LogisticRegression(penalty="l1", C=1/0.1,
solver="saga")
sklearn_model.fit(X_train_b, y_train_b)
y_pred_sklearn = sklearn_model.predict(X_test_b)
print(f"Scikit-learn Logistic Regression L1 Accuracy:
{accuracy_score(y_test_b, y_pred_sklearn):.3f}")

sklearn_model = LogisticRegression(penalty="l2", C=1/0.1,
solver="lbfgs")
sklearn_model.fit(X_train_b, y_train_b)
y_pred_sklearn = sklearn_model.predict(X_test_b)
print(f"Scikit-learn Logistic Regression L2 Accuracy:
{accuracy_score(y_test_b, y_pred_sklearn):.3f}")

sklearn_model = LogisticRegression(penalty="elasticnet", C=1/0.1,
l1_ratio=0.5, solver="saga")
sklearn_model.fit(X_train_b, y_train_b)
y_pred_sklearn = sklearn_model.predict(X_test_b)
print(f"Scikit-learn Logistic Regression Elastic Net Accuracy:
{accuracy_score(y_test_b, y_pred_sklearn):.3f}")

Scikit-learn Logistic Regression L1 Accuracy: 0.985
Scikit-learn Logistic Regression L2 Accuracy: 0.985
Scikit-learn Logistic Regression Elastic Net Accuracy: 0.985
```

For logistic regression in Scikit-learn, different penalties require specific solvers to optimize the cost function. While the default "lbfgs" is designed for L2 regularization, it is incompatible with L1 or Elastic Net. For these penalties, you must use the "saga" solver, which is capable of handling the non-smooth gradients associated with L1 terms.

As with previous algorithms, any slight differences in performance stem from technical subtleties in how Scikit-learn performs computations under the hood, rather than any conceptual discrepancy. You might have noticed that applying regularization didn't boost performance in our case, but it doesn't mean it never does. The datasets we use are still small and have clearly defined patterns, which is not always the case in the real world. Therefore, when it comes to noisy real-world data – these techniques come in handy.

Tips

These techniques should be applied whenever there's a slightest suspicion that a model overfits the data. Another good clue to use regularization would be a big number of linearly dependent or unimportant features. As for the regularization strength hyperparameter – one should start experimenting with values in 0 to 1 range and tweak the value such that model has the right fit. See "Fundamentals of ML" to recall on how to spot overfit.

K-Nearest Neighbors

Intuition

What if we don't want to train a model at all – what's the simplest way to make predictions using our dataset?

Say we have a dataset with features and targets. Let's skip the whole ML algorithm selection, training, and testing process. We receive a new set of features and need to predict its target.

The most logical solution:

1. Find observations with the most similar feature values to the one we want to predict
2. Look at their targets
3. Choose the most common target among them – that's our best bet

It's that simple – we predict based on what the most similar observations have as their target.

The algorithm's name is intuitive: neighbors are those located close to one another. Specifically, the algorithm considers k closest (or nearest) observations to the new data point as its neighbors, where k can be any number we choose, such as 5, 10, or 50. The prediction is simply the most common target among these k nearest observations.

Just like people, data points can be located in space – each one has a position. Let's visualize a multiclass dataset:

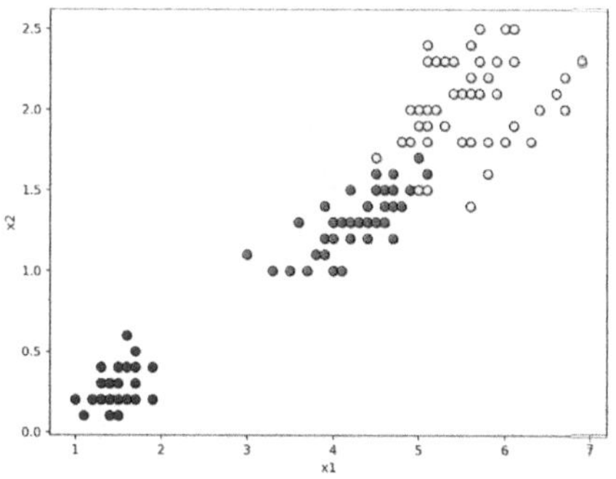

Unlike previous plots, both x and y axes represent feature values, while color indicates the target class. Notice that observations belonging to the same class tend to cluster together – they're neighbors.

Now say we receive a new data point with an unknown target, marked in cyan:

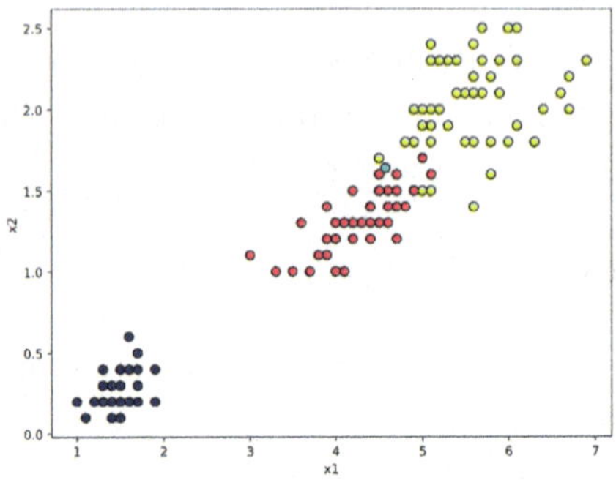

We haven't done any computations yet – just plotted the data. The algorithm simply finds the closest points and selects the most common target among them. We just need to specify how many neighbors to consider. Let's choose $k = 3$:

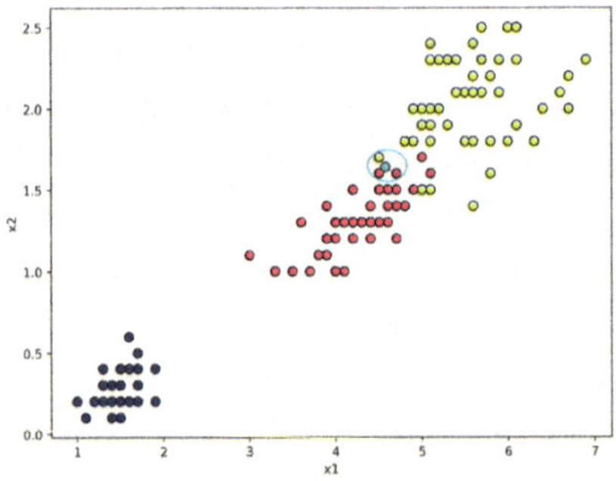

The 3 closest points are two purple and one yellow – so we predict purple (the majority). That's it! We can repeat the same process for any number of neighbors by specifying value of k – the only hyperparameter.

Formalization

To select the k closest data points, we measure the distance between the new point and all points in our dataset, then choose the k with the smallest distances. Let's see how to measure distance between two points.

The most straightforward solution is to measure the length of a straight line connecting them. Say we have two data points – blue at ($x_1 = 2, x_2 = 3$) and red at ($x_1 = 5, x_2 = 7$).

Let's connect them with a straight line:

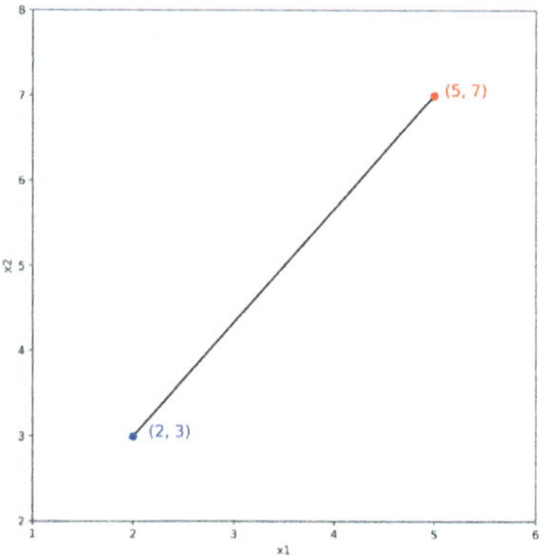

Treating these as points in space, let's call the blue point p and the red one q. The straight-line distance is called Euclidean distance, computed as:

$$d(p,q) = \sqrt{(2-5)^2 + (3-7)^2} = 5$$

The straight-line distance between these points is 5.

For the general case with m features, the formula is:

$$d(p,q) = \sqrt{\sum_{j=1}^{m} (p_j - q_j)^2}$$

Let's think about what happens if two features are on different scales.

Consider two houses:

- House A – 3,000 sq ft, 2 bedrooms
- House B – 3,100 sq ft, 5 bedrooms

$$d = \sqrt{(3{,}000 - 3{,}100)^2 + (3 - 5)^2} = \sqrt{10{,}000 + 9} \approx 100$$

The square footage difference (100) contributes 10,000 to the distance, while the bedroom difference (3) contributes only 9. The algorithm will treat these houses as nearly identical neighbors, completely ignoring that one has 3 more bedrooms.

From this example we can see that features on larger scales dominate features on smaller scales. What we actually want to measure is the relative difference for each feature – this way we can meaningfully compare a square footage difference with a bedroom difference. The solution is to bring all features to the same scale through standardization!

Once we standardize the dataset, all features contribute equally based on their relative differences, not their original scales.

Now let's formalize the complete algorithm for predicting a new observation's target:

1. Compute Euclidean distance between the new observation and each observation in the training dataset
2. Select the k observations with the smallest distances (the k neighbors)
3. Predict the most common target class among these neighbors

This is the algorithm for classification problems. For regression, instead of taking the most common class, we simply average the targets of the k nearest neighbors.

Implementation

First, let's define function to compute distance between two points.

```
import numpy as np

def euclidean_distance(p, q):

    return np.sqrt(np.sum((p - q) ** 2))
```

Next, define initial method and a purely formal "fit" method to mirror Scikit-learn's interface. These two methods essentially create instance variables for features, targets and hyperparameter *k*.

```
class CustomKNN():

    def __init__(self, k=5):

        self.k = k

    def fit(self, X, y):

        self.X_train = X
        self.y_train = y
```

We learned that inference is done by measuring distance between each observation in the dataset and the new one, selecting k closest data points and predicting their most common target. Unlike with previous algorithms, we can't perform any matrix operations here, so we will make prediction for one observation at a time. Therefore, we will first define main method that iterates over each observation and applies helper method to make one prediction at a time.

```
    def predict(self, X):

        y_pred = [self._predict(x) for x in X]

        return np.array(y_pred)
```

```
    def _predict(self, x):

        distances = [euclidean_distance(x, x_train) for x_train in
self.X_train]

        neighbors_idx = np.argsort(distances)[: self.k]

        y_neighbors = [self.y_train[i] for i in neighbors_idx]

        y_pred_i = self._get_label(y_neighbors)

        return y_pred_i
```

In the helper method we:

- Compute distances to the new point
- Select indices of *k* closest data points from our dataset
- Select their targets
- Use a method to get the final prediction (see "_get_label" below)

Remember, our prediction is the most common class for classification (either binary or multiclass) and the mean value of the k targets for regression problems. This method simply determines the problem type based on the training targets – less than 20 unique target values indicate classification and regression otherwise. Then, it applies appropriate logic to make the prediction depending on the problem type.

```
    def _get_label(self, y):

        if len(set(self.y_train)) <= 20:
            return max(y, key=y.count)
        else:
            return np.mean(y)
```

> Note: This is not a universal method to the determine problem type but it's good enough to illustrate the concept in full.

Test

Let's import dependencies, load and standardize all datasets.

```
from data_loader import Dataset, standardize
from sklearn.neighbors import KNeighborsClassifier,
KNeighborsRegressor
from sklearn.metrics import accuracy_score, mean_squared_error

dataset_m = Dataset("multiclass classification")
X_train_m, X_test_m, y_train_m, y_test_m =
dataset_m.load_split_data()
X_train_m, X_test_m = standardize(X_train_m, X_test_m)

dataset_b = Dataset("binary classification")
X_train_b, X_test_b, y_train_b, y_test_b =
dataset_b.load_split_data()
X_train_b, X_test_b = standardize(X_train_b, X_test_b)

dataset_r = Dataset("regression")
X_train_r, X_test_r, y_train_r, y_test_r =
dataset_r.load_split_data()
X_train_r, X_test_r = standardize(X_train_r, X_test_r)
```

Now, train a custom model for each problem type.

```
custom_model_m = CustomKNN()
custom_model_m.fit(X_train_m, y_train_m)
y_pred_custom_m = custom_model_m.predict(X_test_m)
print(f"Custom Multiclass Classification Accuracy:
{accuracy_score(y_test_m, y_pred_custom_m):.3f}")

custom_model_b = CustomKNN()
custom_model_b.fit(X_train_b, y_train_b)
y_pred_custom_b = custom_model_b.predict(X_test_b)
print(f"Custom Binary Classification Accuracy:
{accuracy_score(y_test_b, y_pred_custom_b):.3f}")

custom_model_r = CustomKNN()
custom_model_r.fit(X_train_r, y_train_r)
y_pred_custom_r = custom_model_r.predict(X_test_r)
print(f"Custom Regression MSE: {mean_squared_error(y_test_r,
y_pred_custom_r):.3f}")

Custom Multiclass Classification Accuracy: 0.967
Custom Binary Classification Accuracy: 0.993
Custom Regression MSE: 0.380
```

Note: Since this algorithm checks distance from the new point to each data point in the dataset one by one – it takes a long time to execute. For instance, the regression dataset we are using has more than 20k rows and with our implementation it takes 5-10 minutes to execute the code above.

Scikit-learn offers two separate KNN classes for classification and regression problems.

```
sklearn_model_m = KNeighborsClassifier()
sklearn_model_m.fit(X_train_m, y_train_m)
y_pred_sklearn_m = sklearn_model_m.predict(X_test_m)
print(f"Scikit-learn Multiclass Classification Accuracy:
{accuracy_score(y_test_m, y_pred_sklearn_m):.3f}")

sklearn_model_b = KNeighborsClassifier()
sklearn_model_b.fit(X_train_b, y_train_b)
y_pred_sklearn_b = sklearn_model_b.predict(X_test_b)
print(f"Scikit-learn Binary Classification Accuracy:
{accuracy_score(y_test_b, y_pred_sklearn_b):.3f}")
sklearn_model_r = KNeighborsRegressor()
sklearn_model_r.fit(X_train_r, y_train_r)
y_pred_sklearn_r = sklearn_model_r.predict(X_test_r)
print(f"Scikit-learn Regression MSE: {mean_squared_error(y_test_r,
y_pred_sklearn_r):.3f}")

Scikit-learn Multiclass Classification Accuracy: 0.967
Scikit-learn Binary Classification Accuracy: 0.993
Scikit-learn Regression MSE: 0.380
```

The reason this code executes within seconds is that Scikit-learn uses an optimized approach to significantly reduce computation time, even with large datasets. Instead of directly measuring distance from the new point to every point in the dataset, it first organizes the data into a spatial structure (like a tree) and then only searches within relevant regions to find the k nearest neighbors.

Note: Both custom and Scikit-learn implementations have identical performance, as expected. For our dataset, k-NN with $k = 5$ considerably outperforms linear regression.

Standardization makes a huge difference here – without it, the regression dataset would yield an MSE of 1.2 instead of 0.38, a significant degradation in performance. This instance shows how much standardization can help model performance when different scales interfere with how the ML algorithm captures relationships.

You're encouraged to experiment with different k values and observe how they affect performance.

Tips

k-NN usually works best for classification problems with a small number of features. The reason is that this algorithm treats all features equally and with a larger number of features there's a higher chance to have unimportant features that skew the results.

As for the k parameter – it is very dependent on the size of a dataset and the underlying pattern. The larger the dataset – the higher k should be and vise-versa.

Let's get some more intuition on how different values of k change the model. Color of the area represents what a new observation would be classified as if it happened to be in the respective area.

$k = 5$

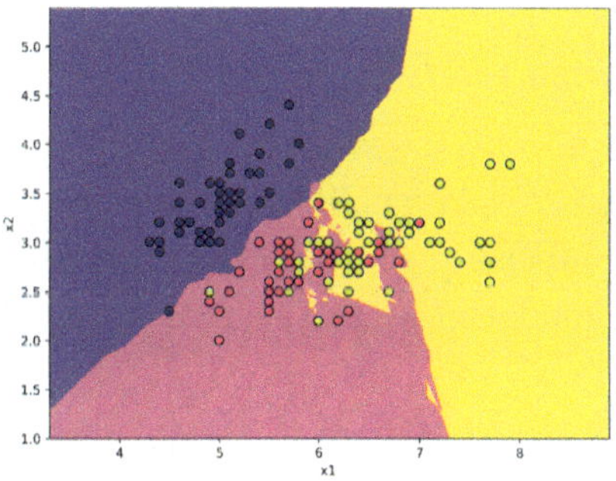

$k = 50$

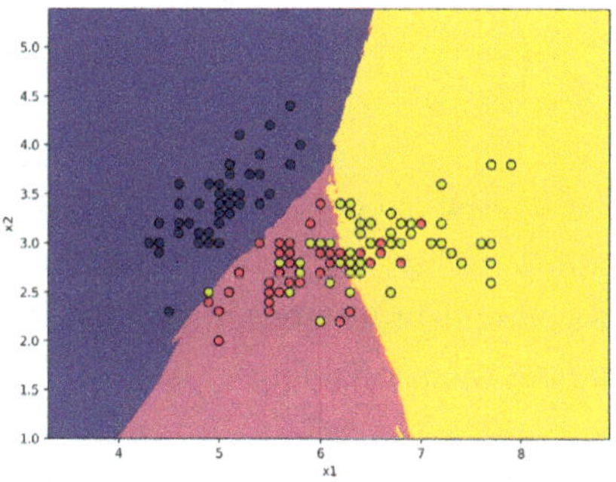

As you can see, higher values of k result in a more general model, evident from the large, smooth decision boundaries. On the other hand, smaller k values create more complex, detailed boundaries that potentially capture subtle patterns in the data.

Therefore, if your model is overfitting, increase k to smooth out the boundaries. If it's underfitting, decrease k to capture more detail and find the right balance.

Naïve Bayes

Intuition

Naïve bayes is a classification algorithm rooted in probability theory. First, let's cover some core definitions:

- Random Experiment – any situation with multiple possible outcomes
- Event – a particular outcome of a random experiment

For example, "will it rain tomorrow?" can be thought of as a random experiment, and the answers "yes" and "no" as events, each with a probability of happening: $P(yes)$ and $P(no)$. The key idea is that we know the potential outcomes, but we do not know the actual result. Our strategy is to estimate the probability of each event and predict one with the highest probability.

We could make the experiment more interesting by adding a condition: "will it rain tomorrow if it rained today?" This new information likely changes the probabilities. We denote "yes" outcome using conditional probability as:

$$P(yes \mid it\ rained\ today)$$

Lastly, we can consider an "and" scenario: "will it rain tomorrow and the day after?" Here, we look at the joint probability of two events happening together. For instance, if event A is "rain tomorrow" and event B is "rain day after", the probability of both is $P(A, B)$.

This brings us to Bayes' Theorem, one of the most famous theorems in statistics. To derive it, we start with the standard formula for conditional probability:

$$P(A|B) = \frac{P(A, B)}{P(B)}$$

We can rearrange this formula to solve for the "and" case (joint probability):

$$P(A, B) = P(A|B) * P(B)$$

The trick is that "event A and event B" is equal to "event B and event A" – the order for "and" case does not matter. Therefore, we can also write the joint probability from the other perspective:

$$P(A,B) = P(B,A) = P(B|A) * P(A)$$

Now, we simply equate the two sides:

$$P(A|B) * P(B) = P(B|A) * P(A)$$

By dividing both sides by $P(B)$, we arrive at the final Bayes' Theorem formula:

$$P(A|B) = \frac{P(B|A) * P(A)}{P(B)}$$

This formula is powerful because it allows us to calculate a probability that is difficult to measure directly using probabilities that can be easily measured.

Now that we have explored the core probability concepts, we can dive into how naïve bayes utilizes them to make predictions.

Let's begin by translating our general "events" into a classification problem.

What do we have?

- A feature matrix X (the inputs)
- A target vector y (the classes)

What do we want?

- For a new observation with feature vector x
- Predict the class y

In other words, we ask: "What is the class of this observation if these are its features?". This translates to measuring probability of each possible class given the feature vector – $P(y|x)$, then selecting class with highest probability as the prediction.

Let's apply Bayes' Theorem to compute conditional probability:

$$P(y|x) = \frac{P(x|y) * P(y)}{P(x)}$$

Now that we have our final formula in-place, let's explore how we can use it to make predictions.

In a binary classification problem (class 0 vs. class 1), we calculate two probabilities for a new observation:

- Probability of class 0:

$$P(y = 0|x) = \frac{P(x|y=0) * P(y=0)}{P(x)}$$

- Probability of class 1:

$$P(y = 1|x) = \frac{P(x|y=1) * P(y=1)}{P(x)}$$

Notice something interesting? The denominator $P(x)$ – the probability of observing that specific feature vector is exactly the same in both equations. Since we only care about comparing the two values to see which is higher, we can simply ignore the denominator.

This leaves us with simply comparing two probabilities to decide which class is more likely to be the true target for this observation:

Select class 0 if this probability:

$$P(x|y = 0) * P(y = 0)$$

Is higher than this:

$$P(x|y = 1) * P(y = 1)$$

Both probabilities can be computed from our dataset – we will explore how in the next section. For multiclass classification with r possible classes, the procedure is identical: compute the probability for each of the r classes and select the highest.

In essence, naïve bayes uses Bayes' Theorem to compute conditional probability of each possible class given features of the new observations and selects class with the highest probability as the prediction.

Formalization

We have our formula, but we still need to find actual numbers for $P(y)$ and $P(x|y)$. This is what the algorithm "learns" from the training data. Let's explore these probabilities one by one.

The prior probability – $P(y)$. This is the probability of observing a particular class in general. It is simply the proportion of times that class appears in the training set. For instance, if our dataset has 1,000 users and 600 of them bought a subscription (class 1), then:

$$P(y = 1) = \frac{600}{1000} = 0.6$$

This means that, without knowing anything else about them, we estimate a new user has a 60% chance of buying a subscription.

The conditional probability – $P(x|y)$. This is the probability of observing a particular set of feature values given class of an observation. First, x is not a scalar – it's a vector of features:

$$x = [x_1, x_2, \dots, x_m]$$

To solve this, the algorithm makes a "naïve" assumption – it assumes all features are independent. This means the value of one feature doesn't influence the values of other features.

For example, in our subscription dataset, this assumes that a user's age doesn't affect their salary, and salary doesn't affect their location. While this is rarely true, the assumption makes the problem solvable and surprisingly, naïve bayes often works well despite it.

Under this assumption, we can calculate the probability of the whole vector by simply multiplying the probabilities of each individual feature:

$$P(x|y) = P(x_1|y) * P(x_2|y) * \dots * P(x_m|y)$$

Instead of computing one complex joint probability, we compute m simple individual probabilities and combine them. How we calculate these individual probabilities depends on whether the features are categorical or continuous – we'll explore both cases next, starting with the categorical case.

Categorical

Say x_1 represents the continent a user lives on. Since there are a limited number of continents (7), this is a categorical feature. As always in ML, we encode them as numbers: Europe: 0, Asia: 1, etc.

Our goal is to find $P(x_1|y)$ – the probability of a user being from a specific continent given their subscription status.

For example, say out of 1,000 users there are 600 subscribers ($y = 1$) in total. Out of 600 subscribers 150 are from Europe ($x_1 = 0$). The probability is simply the frequency count.

If a person is subscribed, probability of them being from Europe is:

$$P(x_1 = 0|y = 1) = \frac{150}{600} = \frac{1}{4} = 0.25$$

We repeat this for every feature value and every class. For any categorical feature, we simply count how many times each value appears for a specific class and divide by the total number of observations in that class.

Continuous

Say x_3 represents user's annual salary in thousands of dollars. Let's see why we can't use same approach with continuous features.

Suppose out of 600 subscribers, 60 people have a salary of $190k, but only 10 people have a salary of $191k.

Would we expect users with 190K and 191K to behave similarly? Yes, because the difference is negligible but what does that look like if we use same approach as for categorical features?

$$P(x_3 = 190|y = 1) = \frac{60}{600} = \frac{1}{10} = 0.1$$

$$P(x_3 = 191|y = 1) = \frac{10}{600} = \frac{1}{60} \approx 0.017$$

We get 10% vs 1.7%. This suggests a massive difference in likelihood, even though the salaries are nearly identical.

Worse, what if a new user has a salary of $192k, and no one in our training set has that exact salary?

The counting method would give a probability of 0%. This would crash our model, as multiplying by zero makes the entire probability zero.

Conclude: Similar continuous values should have similar probability of happening given the same class of the observation. Therefore, we need another way to estimate them.

Let's begin by plotting salary data for subscribed users along with how often each one appears in the training dataset – count histogram.

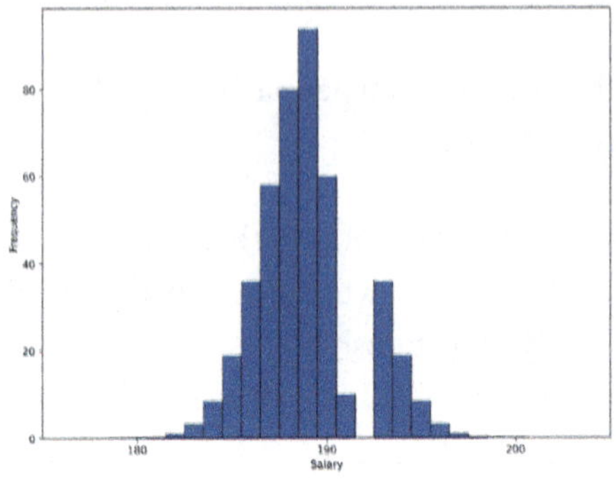

Notice that $190k appears 60 times, $191k appears 10 times, and $192k appears 0 times. This isn't because people earning $192k avoid subscriptions – it's simply chance variation from having only 600 subscribers in our dataset. We can't rely on raw sample counts to perfectly represent all potential subscribers.

We assume that similar continuous values should have similar probabilities of occurring. To achieve this, we model the data using a normal (Gaussian) distribution.

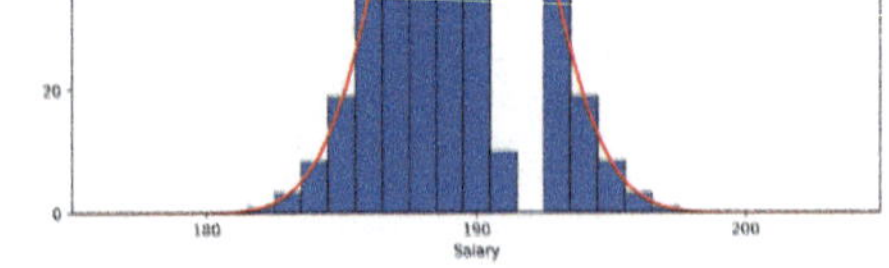

The red line represents what we would expect the salary distribution of our subscribed users to be if the sample size was large enough.

We still technically divide frequency by the total, but this time the frequency is determined by the height of the red curve, not by counting dots in the training set.

Let's look at how this fixes our previous problem. By checking the height of the curve at specific points, we get the following probabilities:

$$P(x_3 = 190|y = 1) = \frac{94}{600} \approx 0.16$$

$$P(x_3 = 191|y = 1) = \frac{80}{600} \approx 0.13$$

$$P(x_3 = 192|y = 1) = \frac{58}{600} \approx 0.1$$

Since these salaries are so close to one another, probabilities of 16%, 13%, and 10% are much more reasonable than 10%, 1%, and 0%.

Note: In this case, salary is clearly suitable for a normal distribution. This isn't always true for every feature, but the normal distribution is the standard default assumption in naïve bayes because it is robust and works well for most natural phenomena.

We computed probabilities above by looking at the red curve on the graph but in practice it is done using a formula.

First, we calculate the mean and standard deviation from the feature values for each class (for example, from all salaries of subscribed users). We use these sample statistics as estimates for our normal distribution parameters mean μ and standard deviation σ.

Then, we fit a normal distribution (bell curve) using these two numbers. To find the probability for any new salary value s, we plug it into the normal distribution formula:

$$P(x_3 = s|y) = \frac{1}{\sqrt{2\pi\sigma^2}} e^{-\frac{(s-\mu)^2}{2\sigma^2}}$$

There is no need to memorize or derive this formula. Just understand its purpose – it is the mathematical tool that draws the red curve. In this case we just use it to get a probability for salary s, assuming feature values follow a normal distribution.

Similarly, we approximate all conditional probabilities for continuous features through the normal distribution.

Now that we know how to compute $P(y)$ and $P(x|y)$ for both categorical and continuous features – let's put it all into our final formula for conditional probability of a class:

$$P(y|x) = P(x|y) * P(y) = P(x_1|y) * \dots * P(x_m|y) * P(y)$$

We are multiplying many probabilities together. Since probabilities are always between 0 and 1 (e.g. $0.5 * 0.007 * 0.01 = 0.000035$), the result rapidly becomes a tiny number. If you have 50 features, the result will very likely be rounded up to 0 by a programming language.

Therefore, as a final step we apply a transformation that keeps the relative difference while preventing the result from diminishing – natural log transformation. Logarithms have a beautiful property that converts multiplication into addition:

$$ln(a * b) = ln\, a + ln\, b$$

When we apply natural log to both sides, instead of multiplication, we sum up transformed probabilities, preventing them from vanishing.

Note that relative difference is preserved, that is if $P(y = 0|x) > P(y = 1|x)$ then $\ln P(y = 0|x) > \ln P(y = 1|x)$ and vise verca.

The final formula to compute likelihood in naïve bayes is:

$$ln\, P(y|x) = ln\, P(y) + \sum_{j=1}^{m} ln\, P(x_j|y)$$

For a single new observation with r possible classes (indexed 0 to r-1), we calculate this score for every class. The prediction is simply the class with the maximum score:

$$y_{pred} = max[ln\,P(y = 0|x), \ldots, ln\,P(y = r - 1|x)]$$

Congratulations! You now understand the complete naïve bayes classifier from start to finish.

Implementation

Naïve bayes has no hyperparameters and thus doesn't need initialization method – we jump straight into training. We begin by initializing instance variables for features and targets.

```
import numpy as np
from scipy.stats import norm

class CustomNB():

    def fit(self, X, y):

        self.X = X
        self.y = y
        n, m = self.X.shape
```

First, we identify categorical features (those with 20 or fewer unique values) and extract the unique classes:

```
        self.is_cat = np.array([len(np.unique(self.X[:, j])) <= 20
for j in range(m)])

        X_cont = self.X[:, ~self.is_cat]

        self.classes = np.unique(self.y)
        self.r = len(self.classes)
```

Next, we initialize storage for what the algorithm learns: $P(y)$ for each class, mean and standard deviation (parameters of normal distribution) for each continuous feature per class:

```
        self.P_y = np.zeros(self.r)
        self.mean = np.zeros((self.r, X_cont.shape[1]))
        self.std = np.zeros((self.r, X_cont.shape[1]))
```

Now we compute these values. For each class, we calculate the mean and standard deviation of continuous features, plus the prior probability $P(y)$:

```
        for class_idx, class_value in enumerate(self.classes):

            X_class_cont = X_cont[y == class_value]

            self.mean[class_idx, :] = X_class_cont.mean(axis=0)
            self.std[class_idx, :] = X_class_cont.std(axis=0)

            self.P_y[class_idx] = np.sum(self.y == class_value)/n
```

Similarly to k-NN we use helper method to make one prediction at a time. Inside the loop, we sum up $\ln P(y)$ and $\ln P(x|y)$ to get the final score $\ln P(y|x)$ for each class. Then, we find index of the class with highest $\ln P(y|x)$, that is "log_prob" and return encoded value of that class.

```
    def predict(self, X):

        return np.array([self._predict(x) for x in X])

    def _predict(self, x):

        log_probs = []

        for class_idx in range(self.r):

            log_prob = np.log(self.P_y[class_idx])

            log_prob +=
np.sum(np.log(self._compute_P_x_y(class_idx, x)))

            log_probs.append(log_prob)

        return self.classes[np.argmax(log_probs)]
```

Above we used a helper method to compute $P(x|y)$ for each feature vector and class, let's define it.

First, we separate categorical and continuous features from the initial vector. Then we extract all categorical features of a certain class from our dataset and get the number of observations for that class.

```
    def _compute_P_x_y(self, class_idx, x):

        x_cat = x[self.is_cat]
        x_cont = x[~self.is_cat]

        X_class = self.X[self.y == self.classes[class_idx]]
        X_class_cat = X_class[:, self.is_cat]
        n_class = X_class.shape[0]
```

Next, we compute $P(x|y)$ for the current class for all categorical features. For each categorical feature it is simply frequency of the feature value among the class divided by the total number of observations from that class.

```
        P_cat = []

        for j, value in enumerate(x_cat):

            freq = np.sum(X_class_cat[:, j] == value)
            P_cat.append(freq / n_class)
```

Then we compute $P(x|y)$ for all continuous features for the current class. Here we selected pre-computed mean and standard deviation across all continuous features for our current class. We use those statistics to get probability from normal distribution for each continuous feature value (recall our assumption).

Finally, we concatenate probabilities of categorical and continuous features to get the final $P(x|y)$ for the current class.

```
        mean = self.mean[class_idx]
        std = self.std[class_idx]
        P_cont = norm.pdf(x_cont, loc=mean, scale=std)

        return np.concatenate([P_cat, P_cont])
```

That's it for naïve bayes – the main part is computing conditional probabilities for each possible class and then selecting class with the highest probability.

Test

Let's import dependencies and load the data.

```
from data_loader import Dataset
from sklearn.naive_bayes import GaussianNB
from sklearn.metrics import accuracy_score

dataset_m = Dataset("multiclass classification")
X_train_m, X_test_m, y_train_m, y_test_m =
dataset_m.load_split_data()

dataset_b = Dataset("binary classification")
X_train_b, X_test_b, y_train_b, y_test_b =
dataset_b.load_split_data()
```

Train and test our custom implementation.

```
custom_model_m = CustomNB()
custom_model_m.fit(X_train_m, y_train_m)
y_pred_custom_m = custom_model_m.predict(X_test_m)
print(f"Custom Multiclass Classification Accuracy:
{accuracy_score(y_test_m, y_pred_custom_m):.3f}")

custom_model_b = CustomNB()
custom_model_b.fit(X_train_b, y_train_b)
y_pred_custom_b = custom_model_b.predict(X_test_b)
print(f"Custom Binary Classification Accuracy:
{accuracy_score(y_test_b, y_pred_custom_b):.3f}")

Custom Multiclass Classification Accuracy: 0.933
Custom Binary Classification Accuracy: 1.000
```

Train and test Scikit-learn's implementation.

```
sklearn_model_m = GaussianNB()
sklearn_model_m.fit(X_train_m, y_train_m)
y_pred_sklearn_m = sklearn_model_m.predict(X_test_m)
print(f"Scikit-learn Multiclass Classification Accuracy:
{accuracy_score(y_test_m, y_pred_sklearn_m):.3f}")

sklearn_model_b = GaussianNB()
sklearn_model_b.fit(X_train_b, y_train_b)
y_pred_sklearn_b = sklearn_model_b.predict(X_test_b)
print(f"Scikit-learn Binary Classification Accuracy:
{accuracy_score(y_test_b, y_pred_sklearn_b):.3f}")

Scikit-learn Multiclass Classification Accuracy: 0.967
Scikit-learn Binary Classification Accuracy: 1.000
```

Scikit-learn's class is called "GaussianNB" because when we compute probability of a feature given class of the observation, it assumes data follows Gaussian (normal) distribution. Unlike our implementation, this assumption is applied to both continuous and categorical features. There are other classes offered by Scikit-learn that assume other distributions – we will explore in the next section.

Almost identical performance verifies correctness of our implementation!

Tips

Naïve bayes is usually a great choice for classification problems with many features and a limited number of samples. The reason is that it uses a probabilistic approach that determines feature importance by design, making it less likely for unimportant features to spoil the results. Since it focuses on likelihoods, you don't need a massive dataset; as long as your samples are representative of the population, they are sufficient to approximate the probabilities.

The main limitation lies in the strong assumption that all features are conditionally independent given the class. This can become a problem when features have strong linear relationship. We have already seen this issue arise in regression models, and the same solution applies here – we can use VIF to identify and remove or merge those features before training the model.

There are multiple variations of naïve bayes that are built upon a different assumption about the distribution of features conditioned on the class. In our implementation, we used ratios to derive the distribution for categorical features and a Gaussian approximation for continuous features.

In practice, however, all features conditioned on the class are usually assumed to follow the same distribution. For instance, Scikit-learn offers "GaussianNB", "MultinomialNB", and "BernoulliNB" classes, each assuming a different distribution. While the Gaussian variant is the most common, the best version of naïve bayes depends on your data. Therefore, the best practice is to check the distribution and select the method that suits your data best. If the distribution assumption is significantly violated, model performance may suffer.

Let's visualize the decision boundary that naïve bayes creates for the same dataset we used for k-NN to build intuition about how it behaves:

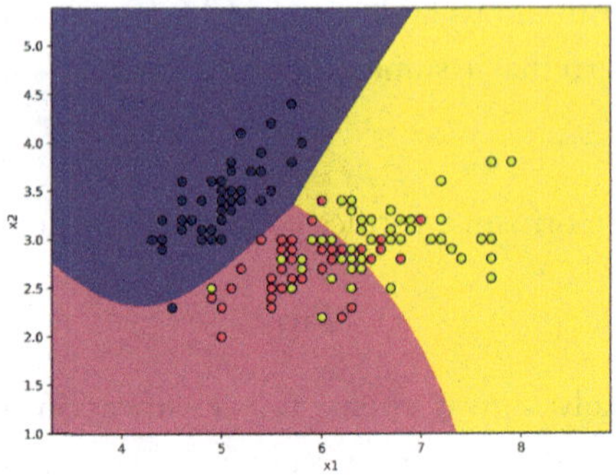

To conclude, this is a simple yet very powerful classification algorithm that performs relatively well even with small amounts of high-dimensional data.

Tree Algorithms

How do humans make decisions? Most of the time, we follow a rule or a set of rules to navigate our daily lives. Consider these examples:

- "If it rains, I will bring an umbrella and not otherwise."
- "If there is at least a 50% discount and the item looks fresh, I will buy it and not otherwise."
- "If the traffic is clear, I will drive to work; if there's moderate traffic, I will take the bus; if there's heavy traffic, I will work from home."

Tree-based algorithms are a family of machine learning models that mirror this exact logic. Every example above can be framed as an ML problem and a solution, let's explore them one by one.

- Feature: Binary indication of whether it rains (0 for no and 1 for yes)
- Target: Binary indication of whether the person will bring an umbrella (0 for no and 1 for yes)

The solution:

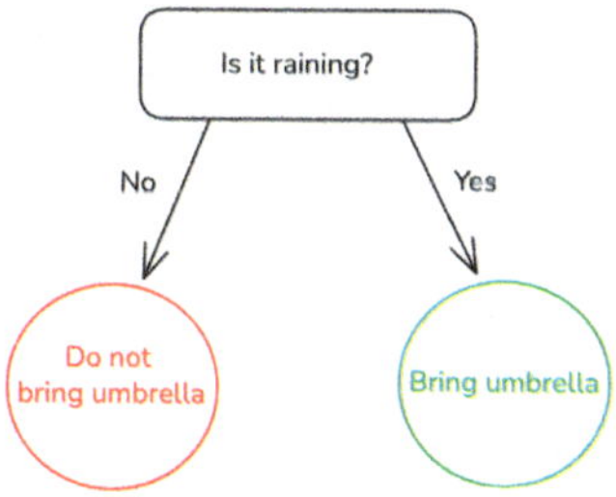

- Features: Discount on the item expressed as % (value between 0 and 100), binary indication of whether the item looks fresh (0 or 1).
- Target: Binary induction of whether a person will buy the item (0 or 1).

The solution:

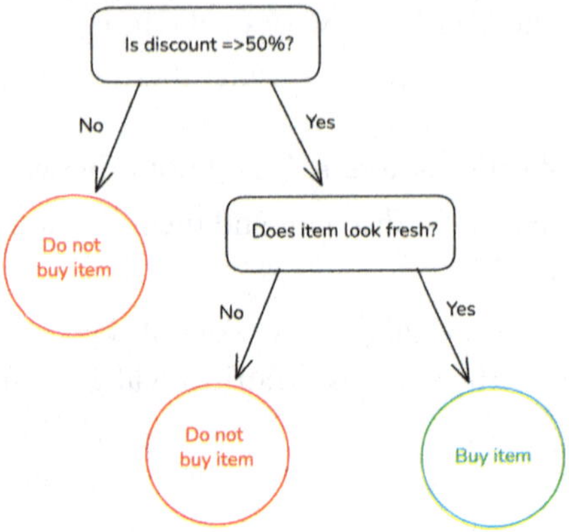

- Feature: Traffic level (e.g. 0 for clear, 1 for moderate, 2 for heavy)
- Target: Mode of transport (e.g. 0 for drive, 1 for bus, 2 for work from home)

The solution:

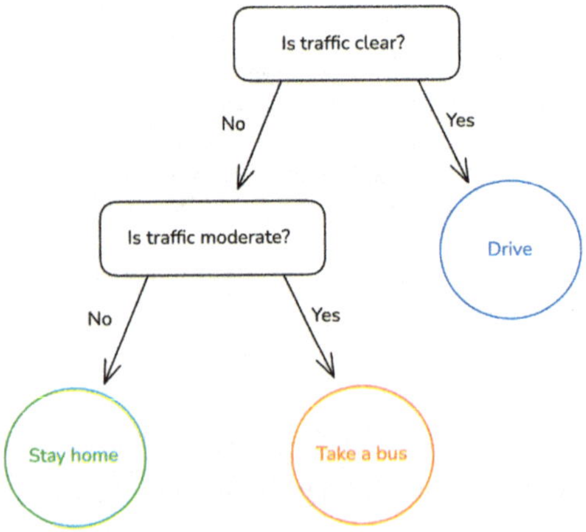

In all of these examples, the rules were defined for a single individual – but they can be applied as general rules to predict the behaviour of others in our population of interest.

The core objective of this algorithm family is to learn the specific sequence of rules that results in the most accurate predictions. While our examples are simple, real-world problems often involve thousands of complex combinations of decision rules that would be impossible for a human to calculate manually.

Why tree?

It is called a "tree" because the structure of these decisions looks like an upside-down tree.

- The root – the very first split at the top of the structure, representing the most important decision rule
- Nodes – intermediate points where a decision is made, and the data is split again
- The leaves – boxes at the bottom that provide the final outcomes (the predictions)

Tree-based algorithms combine interpretability, flexibility, and strong performance on structured data, making them workhorses of modern ML and a common choice in production systems.

Decision Tree

Intuition

Decision tree is the most fundamental algorithm of the tree family. The core idea is to build a tree of decisions by making one best decision at a time. We've already explored how humans intuitively build decision trees in their minds for day-to-day tasks, but we haven't discussed how machines can learn those rules. Let's understand that now.

Consider a binary classification problem: predicting whether a person will buy an item. We've already seen a complete decision tree, but let's see how it's built from scratch.

Imagine we have a dataset of 7 users with two features: discount percentage when the user sees the item, and whether the item looks fresh. In our training dataset, 3 users didn't buy the item and 4 did, represented by red and green dots respectively:

We want to make one best decision at a time, but what defines "best"? The decision that splits data such that most observations of the same class fall on the same side. The feature values for our observations look as follows:

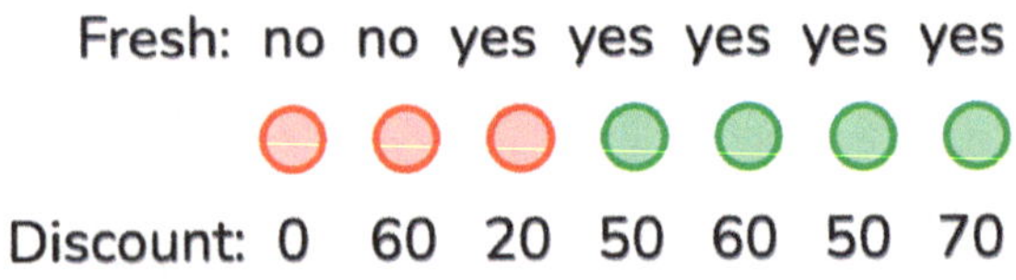

To find the best decision, we take one feature at a time, try every possible value within that feature as a threshold, and record how good each split is. Let's begin!

For feature "Discount":

- if we select ">= 0", all 7 data points go right and none go left – this decision adds no value.
- if we select ">= 60", 1 red and 2 green go right, 2 red and 2 green go to the left. We'd need to move at least 3 points to get perfect accuracy (2 green to the left and 1 red to the right).
- If we select ">= 20", 2 red, 4 green go right and 1 red goes left. We'd need to move at least 2 points to get perfect accuracy (2 red to the left).
- If we select ">= 50", 1 red, 4 green go right and 2 red go left. We'd need to move at least 1 point to get perfect accuracy (1 red to the left).

For feature "Fresh":

- If we select "==yes", 1 red, 4 green go right and 2 red go left. We'd need to move at least 1 point to get perfect accuracy (1 red to the right).
- If we select "==no" we'd get the exact same situation but reversed.

We conclude that "Discount >= 50" and "Fresh == yes" are decisions that require us to move the least number of points to get perfect accuracy. Therefore, either of them is the best first decision. Let's select "Discount >= 50" since we discovered it first.

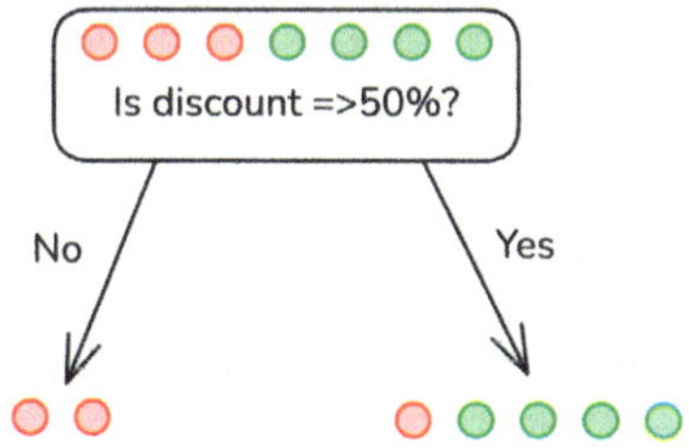

Now we repeat the procedure for both sides of the tree:

- Left side: We have 2 red points – perfectly classified already, nothing more to do.
- Right side: We have 1 red and 4 green points – the classification is not perfect yet. Therefore, we repeat the process where we try each value of

every feature as a threshold and record quality of the split, just like we did for the first decision.
After checking all possibilities, we find that "Fresh == yes" splits the data such that 1 red point goes left and 4 green ones go right.

The perfect accuracy (or purity) has been achieved – let's visualize the final decision tree:

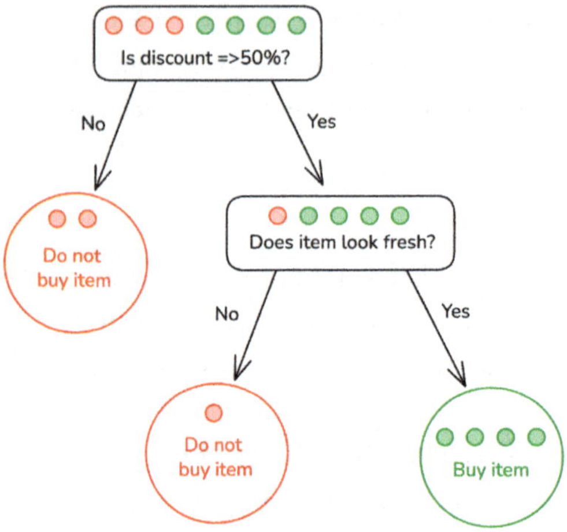

Now that we trained the tree, we can remove the training data points from the visual and use the sequential rules that we have derived for inference.

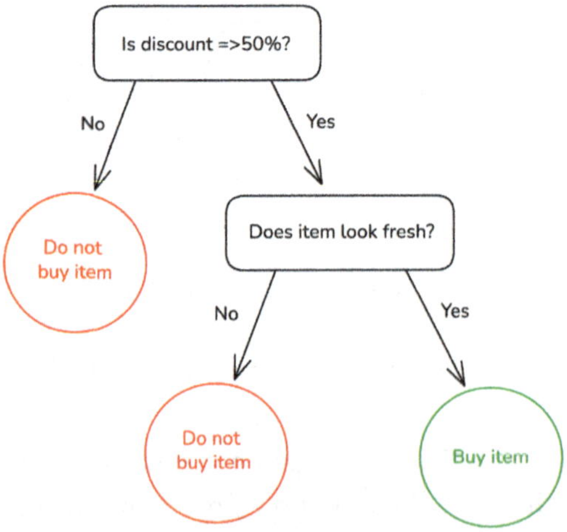

Say a new customer will see the item at 80% discount but it doesn't look fresh. Here's how they'd be classified:

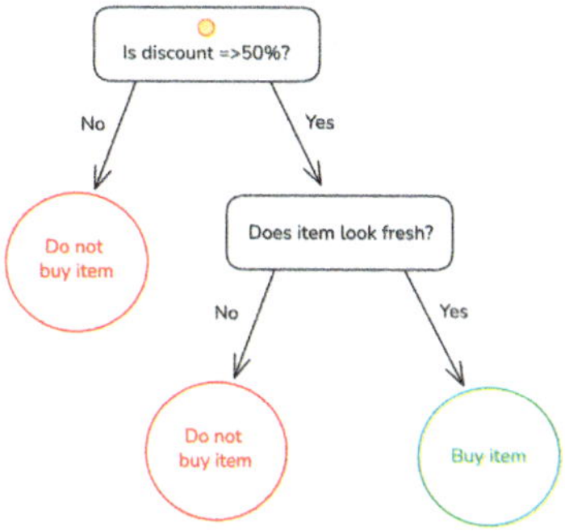

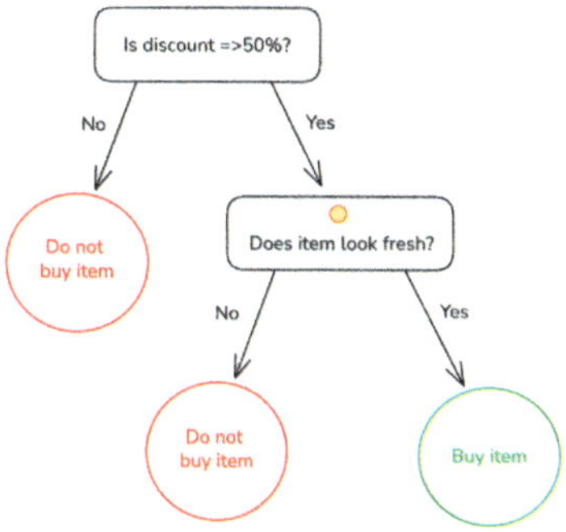

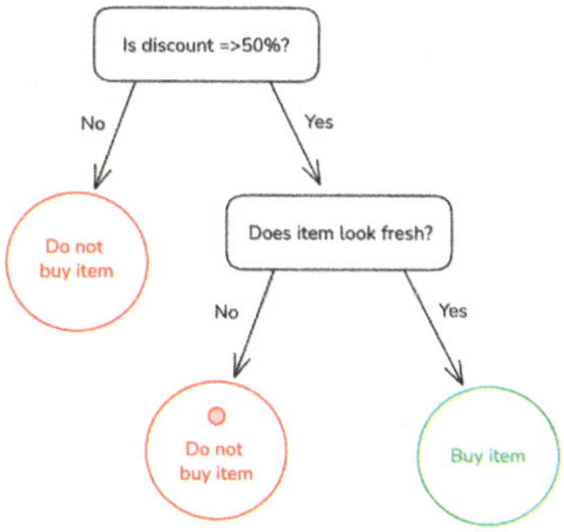

We conclude that according to our decision tree, the person wouldn't buy the item.

The core concept of making decisions that maximize split quality applies to all problem types. In the next section, we will explore how to formally define "quality" for different problem types and other practical considerations for making this algorithm work well in the real world.

Formalization

First, let's introduce some terminology. Every box in a decision tree is called a node. There are two types: decision nodes (rectangles) and leaf nodes (circles).

What information does each node store?

Decision nodes contain:

- Feature identifier and threshold used to split the data
- Quality of the split
- Pointers to left and right child nodes

For example, here's the first decision node from our earlier example with its data highlighted:

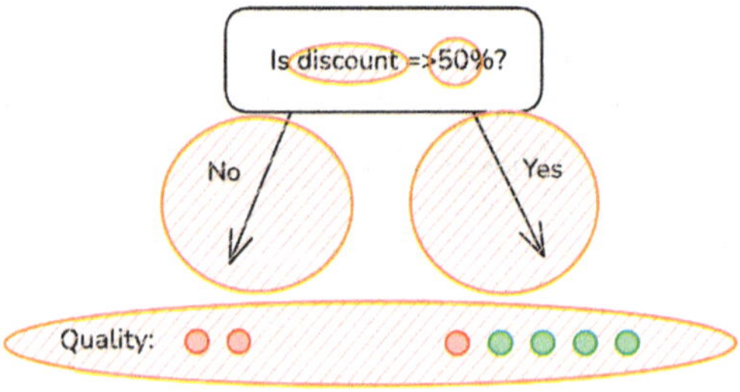

Leaf nodes only need to store their predicted value. Here's a leaf node with its data:

Think of each node as a separate unit that contains some information that either takes us one step closer to make the prediction or helps us make the decision.

In our example above, we achieved perfect leaf nodes – all data points were of the same class. Is this realistic for large real-world datasets? Not really. There's always noise in the data, which we don't want to model (otherwise we'd overfit). Therefore, we need better stopping rules – conditions under which we conclude that training is done.

We stop growing the tree when:

- Trivial case: The best possible decision doesn't add any value to the current set of decisions, in other words split quality metric is at 0 or less.
- Avoid overfitting: A node contains too little data to split reliably. Imagine we grew a huge tree for a dataset of 10,000 points, and one node contains just 10 data points – 1 of class 0 and 9 of class 1. Should we split further? No. We aim to create generalizable rules that apply to the whole population. A leaf node with 1 data point (out of 10,000) doesn't represent a reliable pattern. Instead, we stop at the node with 10 data points and label it as class 1 (the most common class).
- Avoid overfitting and save compute: Tree grows too large. Imagine a case when the best possible decision adds little value, and nodes still contain enough data to by-pass the second rule. We are not interested in weak decision rules and wasting compute time and resources in vain. Thus, we introduce a threshold that limits the maximum number of layers a decision tree may have – in other words, a cap on the length of the longest decision path.

The trivial case stopping rule is always the same, while the other two can be controlled by hyperparameters: minimum samples to split and maximum depth. These are the only two hyperparameters for decision trees.

Now let's explore how to measure quality of a split – in other words benefit of a decision. This metric is slightly different for classification and regression task.

For classification tasks, our goal is to create the purest leaf nodes possible. A node is considered "pure" if it contains observations primarily from a single class. In other words, we want our nodes to be as certain as possible about the class of the data points inside them.

To achieve this, we first need a metric to measure the uncertainty (or impurity) of a node.

First, we'll define a metric to measure uncertainty of a node. Suppose a node contains n data points with n_0 of class 0, n_1 of class 1, etc. For a dataset with r possible classes the following is true: $n_0 + n_1 + \cdots + n_r = n$.

The proportion of points belonging to class k is defined as:

$$p_k = \frac{n_k}{n}$$

We use a metric called Entropy to measure the uncertainty of this node. For r possible classes, it is defined as:

$$E = -\sum_{k=0}^{r} p_k * log_2(p_k)$$

The lower the entropy, the purer (more certain) a node is – each node aims to minimize it.

Let's break down the intuition:

- p_k is the proportion of data points in the node belonging to class k
- $log_2\, p_k$ tells us how much "uncertainty" that class contributes

If p_k is close to 1 (the node is almost entirely this class), then $log_2(1) = 0$. This contributes zero uncertainty.

If p_k is around 0.5 (the node is a mix 50-50), then $log_2(0.5) = -1$. This contributes maximum uncertainty.

Since the log of a probability (0 to 1) is always negative, the sum would be negative. We negate the entire formula (the minus sign at the front) to make Entropy a positive number.

Conclude: Entropy is a measure of impurity – we need to minimize it to maximize purity of a node. The best possible entropy is 0, the higher – the worse.

To make the best decision, we compute the benefit of every possible decision and select the most beneficial one. Now that we can measure node purity using entropy, let's see how to measure a decision's benefit.

First, think of nodes as parents and children. During training, a parent node's decision determines what data goes to its left and right child nodes.

> Note: The root node has no parent, and leaf nodes have no children.

What makes a decision valuable? One that substantially splits data into two relatively pure nodes. We need a benefit metric accounting for both the amount of data in each child node and their purity.

Let p_l and p_r denote the proportions of points going to the left and right child nodes. If our current (parent) node contains 10,000 points and a decision sends 4,000 left and 6,000 right, then:

- $p_l = \frac{4,000}{10,000} = 0.4$
- $p_r = \frac{6,000}{10,000} = 0.6$

We use these to weight the purity of each child node:

$$p_l * E(child_l) + p_r * E(child_r)$$

But we're not just interested in the purity of child nodes – we want to measure their benefit. How much purer does our tree become from this decision?

We subtract the weighted child purity from the parent's purity, called Information Gain:

$$IG = E(parent) - (p_l * E(child_l) + p_r * E(child_r))$$

Information gain gives us the actual benefit of a potential decision. To select the best decision, we compute information gain for every possible split and choose the one with the highest value. If the benefit is 0 or less, we conclude that our current node is a leaf and label it with the most common class.

The only change for regression problem is in the way we measure purity. It still means "how similar are the values in that node", but instead of measuring by class, we measure variation of continuous values using variance – squared standard deviation.

$$Var(node) = \frac{1}{n} * \sum_{i=1}^{n} (x_i - \bar{x})^2$$

This measures spread of target values within a node. It computes the mean value in a node, then measures how far each value is from the mean on average. The lower the variance – the more similar observations are within the node – the purer it is.

The benefit metric is now called variance reduction:

$$VR = Var(parent) - (p_l * Var(child_l) + p_r * Var(child_r))$$

Finally, instead of predicting the most common class, regression leaf nodes predict the mean value of their observations. Once a stopping condition is met for a node, we take the mean of all observations it contains. The mean computed during training becomes the predicted value for any new observation that ends up in that node during inference.

Conclude: For training, we make one best decision at a time by computing the potential benefit of every possible decision and selecting the most beneficial one. We repeat this for every node until one of three stopping conditions is met:

1. No decisions are beneficial
2. Too few observations to split
3. The tree has grown too large

For classification, each node gets assigned a value of the most common class among the observations that ended up there during training. For regression, instead of the most common class we assign the mean value.

Implementation

First, let's define the Node class. Remember, we treat every node as a separate unit with specific properties. A leaf node stores only its predicted value (most common class or average). A decision node stores the feature, threshold, benefit, and pointers to its left and right children.

```
import numpy as np

class Node():

    def __init__(self, feature_idx=None, threshold=None,
left=None, right=None, benefit=None, value=None):

        self.feature_idx = feature_idx
        self.threshold = threshold
        self.left = left
        self.right = right
        self.benefit = benefit

        self.value = value
```

To create a decision node, we specify the first five parameters. To create a leaf node, we only specify "value".

Next, let's define a helper function to compute entropy for classification:

```
def _entropy(y):

    class_labels = np.unique(y)
    entropy = 0

    for k in class_labels:

        p_k = len(y[y == k]) / len(y)
        entropy += p_k * np.log2(p_k)

    return -entropy
```

This takes the target values of all data points in a node, sums each class's contribution to uncertainty, and returns it as a positive number.

Now we define the decision tree class with two hyperparameters representing our stopping rules. We also initialize root – the starting point of our tree. Just like a real tree, we can reach any leaf by starting at the root.

```
class CustomDecisionTree():

    def __init__(self, min_samples_split=5, max_depth=5):

        self.root = None

        self.min_samples_split = min_samples_split
        self.max_depth = max_depth
```

Next, grow the tree using our training data. First, we identify the problem type: classification if there are 20 or fewer unique labels, regression otherwise. This determines how we measure benefit and what leaf nodes predict.

Training is equivalent to building the tree, so our "fit" method calls a helper that returns the root of the complete tree.

```
    def fit(self, X, y):

        if len(set(y)) <= 20:
            self.problem_type = "classification"
        else:
            self.problem_type = "regression"

        dataset = np.concatenate((X, y.reshape(-1, 1)), axis=1)

        self.root = self._build_tree(dataset)
```

Now let's build the tree. This method is recursive – it creates a node, and if that node needs children, it calls itself to build them. This way the tree keeps growing until every path reaches a leaf. Eventually, the method returns the root of the tree.

```
    def _build_tree(self, dataset, curr_depth=0):

        X, y = dataset[:, :-1], dataset[:, -1]

        num_samples, num_features = np.shape(X)

        if num_samples >= self.min_samples_split and curr_depth <=
self.max_depth:

            best_decision = self._get_best_decision(dataset,
num_features)

            if best_decision["benefit"] > 0:

                child_l =
self._build_tree(best_decision["dataset_left"], curr_depth + 1)
                child_r =
self._build_tree(best_decision["dataset_right"], curr_depth + 1)

                return Node(best_decision["feature_idx"],
best_decision["threshold"], child_l, child_r,
best_decision["benefit"])

        leaf_value = self._calculate_leaf_value(y)

        return Node(value = leaf_value)
```

How it works:

1. Check if we should stop (not enough data or tree too deep).
2. If not, find the best way to split the data. To find the best possible decision we use a helper method that returns a dictionary with all information a new decision node needs:

    - Benefit of the decision
    - Data going to left child
    - Data going to right child
    - Feature index used
    - Threshold value used

3. Check if that split is helpful (benefit > 0).

4. If yes, build left and right sides of the tree by calling same "_build_tree" method on them.
5. If any stopping condition is met, create a leaf node.

This repeats for every node until the entire tree is built!

Next, we define a helper method to find the best decision.

```
    def _get_best_decision(self, dataset, num_features, k=10):

        best_decision = {}

        max_benefit = -float("inf")

        for feature_idx in range(num_features):

            feature_values = dataset[:, feature_idx]
            possible_thresholds = np.unique(feature_values)

            for threshold in possible_thresholds[::k]:

                dataset_left, dataset_right = self._split(dataset,
feature_idx, threshold)

                if len(dataset_left) > 0 and len(dataset_right) >
0:

                    y, y_left, y_right = dataset[:, -1],
dataset_left[:, -1], dataset_right[:, -1]

                    curr_benefit = self._compute_benefit(y,
y_left, y_right)

                    if curr_benefit > max_benefit:
                        best_decision["feature_idx"] = feature_idx
                        best_decision["threshold"] = threshold
                        best_decision["dataset_left"] =
dataset_left
                        best_decision["dataset_right"] =
dataset_right
                        best_decision["benefit"] = curr_benefit
                        max_benefit = curr_benefit

        return best_decision
```

We iterate over every feature-threshold combination (using every 10th threshold to save time). For each combination:

1. Split the data using a helper method

2. Check that both sides have data (a split that keeps everything on one side is useless)
3. Compute the benefit of this split
4. If it's the best so far, save all its details

Finally, return the dictionary storing the best decision.

Next, we define helper methods that split the data into left and right subtrees based on provided feature and threshold value.

```
    def _split(self, dataset, feature_idx, threshold):

        dataset_left = np.array([row for row in dataset if
row[feature_idx] <= threshold])
        dataset_right = np.array([row for row in dataset if
row[feature_idx] > threshold])

        return dataset_left, dataset_right
```

Then define helper methods to compute benefit of a decision and leaf node value depending on the problem type.

```
    def _compute_benefit(self, parent, child_l, child_r):

        p_l = len(child_l) / len(parent)
        p_r = len(child_r) / len(parent)

        if self.problem_type == "classification":
            return _entropy(parent) - (p_l * _entropy(child_l) +
p_r * _entropy(child_r))
        else:
            return np.var(parent) - (p_l * np.var(child_l) + p_r *
np.var(child_r))

    def _calculate_leaf_value(self, y):

        if self.problem_type == "classification":
            y = list(y)
            return max(y, key=y.count)
        else:
            return np.mean(y)
```

Now that we've built the tree, let's use it for making predictions. Since each observation must travel down the tree individually, we make one prediction at a time.

For each observation, we start at the root:

1. Check if we're at a leaf – if yes, return its value as the prediction
2. If not, we're at a decision node – use its feature-threshold rule to go left or right
3. Apply the same method to the next node down
4. Continue until we reach a leaf – its value becomes our prediction

```
    def predict(self, X):

        predictions = [self._predict_for_observ(x, self.root) for
x in X]

        return predictions

    def _predict_for_observ(self, x, tree):

        if tree.value is not None:
            return tree.value

        feature_val = x[tree.feature_idx]

        if feature_val <= tree.threshold:
            return self._predict_for_observ(x, tree.left)

        else:
            return self._predict_for_observ(x, tree.right)
```

Test

As usual, we load the data and import necessary dependencies.

```
from data_loader import Dataset
from sklearn.tree import DecisionTreeClassifier,
DecisionTreeRegressor
from sklearn.metrics import accuracy_score, mean_squared_error

dataset_m = Dataset("multiclass classification")
X_train_m, X_test_m, y_train_m, y_test_m =
dataset_m.load_split_data()

dataset_b = Dataset("binary classification")
X_train_b, X_test_b, y_train_b, y_test_b =
dataset_b.load_split_data()

dataset_r = Dataset("regression")
X_train_r, X_test_r, y_train_r, y_test_r =
dataset_r.load_split_data()
```

Let's train and test our models!

```
custom_model_m = CustomDecisionTree()
custom_model_m.fit(X_train_m, y_train_m)
y_pred_custom_m = custom_model_m.predict(X_test_m)
print(f"Custom Multiclass Classification Accuracy:
{accuracy_score(y_test_m, y_pred_custom_m):.3f}")

custom_model_b = CustomDecisionTree()
custom_model_b.fit(X_train_b, y_train_b)
y_pred_custom_b = custom_model_b.predict(X_test_b)
print(f"Custom Binary Classification Accuracy:
{accuracy_score(y_test_b, y_pred_custom_b):.3f}")

custom_model_r = CustomDecisionTree()
custom_model_r.fit(X_train_r, y_train_r)
y_pred_custom_r = custom_model_r.predict(X_test_r)
print(f"Custom Regression MSE: {mean_squared_error(y_test_r,
y_pred_custom_r):.3f}")

Custom Multiclass Classification Accuracy: 0.933
Custom Binary Classification Accuracy: 0.971
Custom Regression MSE: 0.494
```

This is another instance when Scikit-learn offers two separate classes for different problem types.

```
sklearn_model_m = DecisionTreeClassifier()
sklearn_model_m.fit(X_train_m, y_train_m)
y_pred_sklearn_m = sklearn_model_m.predict(X_test_m)
print(f"Scikit-learn Multiclass Classification Accuracy:
{accuracy_score(y_test_m, y_pred_sklearn_m):.3f}")

sklearn_model_b = DecisionTreeClassifier()
sklearn_model_b.fit(X_train_b, y_train_b)
y_pred_sklearn_b = sklearn_model_b.predict(X_test_b)
print(f"Scikit-learn Binary Classification Accuracy:
{accuracy_score(y_test_b, y_pred_sklearn_b):.3f}")

sklearn_model_r = DecisionTreeRegressor()
sklearn_model_r.fit(X_train_r, y_train_r)
y_pred_sklearn_r = sklearn_model_r.predict(X_test_r)
print(f"Scikit-learn Regression MSE: {mean_squared_error(y_test_r,
y_pred_sklearn_r):.3f}")

Scikit-learn Multiclass Classification Accuracy: 0.967
Scikit-learn Binary Classification Accuracy: 0.949
Scikit-learn Regression MSE: 0.477
```

Identical performs indicates our implementation is correct.

Tips

In practice, decision trees alone tend to overfit and can be unstable. We usually prefer more sophisticated tree methods that combine multiple trees, which we will explore next!

Ensemble Learning Algorithms

Ensemble methods are all about combining multiple models to make better predictions. Instead of relying on a single model to capture everything about the data, we train a group of models and let them work together. The idea is that even if each model isn't perfect on its own, together they can cover for each other's weaknesses and produce a stronger, more stable final prediction. This makes ensembles not only more accurate, but also more resistant to overfitting.

There are two main ways to build ensembles. One approach is to mix different types of models, for example, combining a decision tree, a logistic regression, and a naïve bayes. This setup is very flexible, but usually depends heavily on the specific dataset and requires lots of experimentation. So instead, we'll focus on a more structured and widely used approach: combining many models of the same kind – usually decision trees. These models may be simple individually, often called weak learners, but when combined in the right way, they become a very strong predictor.

Now, depending on how we combine these models, ensembles can be split into two types: parallel and sequential. In parallel ensemble methods, all the models are trained at the same time. They don't depend on each other – each one makes its own predictions independently, and in the end, we average or vote across them to get a final result. The goal here is to smooth out individual errors and make the overall prediction more stable. In contrast, sequential ensemble methods train models one after another. Each new model focuses on the mistakes made by the previous one, trying to fix them. Over time, the ensemble becomes better and better at handling difficult examples, because each model learns from what came before it.

In the next sections, we'll dive into these well-established ensemble methods and see how they work in practice. Just remember: the power of an ensemble comes from combining many small decisions into one strong and reliable prediction.

Random Forest

Intuition

In essence we simply train multiple decision trees and let each one make a prediction. For classification problem our final prediction becomes the most common class among predictions of individual decision trees. For regression, final result is the average value of individual predictions of all trees. Many trees form a forest!

Consider that given the same dataset, decision tree will always create the same set of rules because there's no randomness about this algorithm. Therefore, it would make no sense to train many trees on same data – they all would produce same predictions.

That's where the random part of the forest comes in! We train each tree in the forest on a slightly modified version of the original dataset. Random forest is a parallel ensemble learning algorithm, meaning it's made out of decision trees that are independent of one another, allowing them to run simultaneously.

Formalization

First, we make several new datasets by randomly picking data points from the original training set. Each of these new datasets is of the same size as the original, but we sample with replacement. This means the same data point can be picked more than once, while others might not be picked at all.

This process is called bootstrap sampling, and we create one such dataset for every tree we plan to train. Even though all the datasets are built from the same original data, the small differences between them help each tree learn slightly different patterns. This adds variety to the model and makes the final predictions more stable and reliable. For a random forest that consists of 4 decision trees this could look as follows.

The original dataset:

	ID	Feature	Target
0	1	6	11
1	2	7	12
2	3	8	13
3	4	9	14
4	5	10	15

Sampled datasets:

	ID	Feature	Target
0	4	9	14
1	5	10	15
2	1	6	11
3	5	10	15
4	3	8	13

	ID	Feature	Target
0	5	10	15
1	1	6	11
2	5	10	15
3	4	9	14
4	4	9	14

	ID	Feature	Target
0	2	7	12
1	3	8	13
2	2	7	12
3	5	10	15
4	2	7	12

	ID	Feature	Target
0	3	8	13
1	3	8	13
2	4	9	14
3	3	8	13
4	1	6	11

Another way we add variety is by limiting the number of features considered at each split. At every node in the tree, instead of searching across all features for the best split, we randomly sample a subset of features and only consider those. This means that even within a single tree, different splits are made using different combinations of features. As a result, each tree learns a more diverse and unique view of the data, which further reduces the chance of overfitting and helps the ensemble make more balanced decisions.

Implementation

Since we already built decision trees ourselves – we can freely use Scikit-learn's implementation for convenience.

```
import numpy as np
from sklearn.tree import DecisionTreeClassifier,
DecisionTreeRegressor
```

Let's first define a helper function that generates bootstrapped samples for training each tree.

```
def _generate_sample(X, y):

    num_samples = X.shape[0]

    idxs = np.random.choice(num_samples, num_samples,
replace=True)

    return X[idxs], y[idxs]
```

This method generates bootstrapped samples that we will use to train each tree in our forest.

Now we define the random forest class with two additional parameters: the number of trees to train and the maximum number of features randomly considered at each split. We also initialize "forest" instance variable to store all trained decision trees.

```
class CustomRandomForest():

    def __init__(self, num_trees=10, max_features=5,
min_samples_split=5, max_depth=12):

        self.forest = []

        self.num_trees = num_trees
        self.max_features = max_features

        self.min_samples_split = min_samples_split
        self.max_depth = max_depth
```

Next, we define the training method. First, we determine whether it's a classification or regression problem.

```
    def fit(self, X, y):

        if len(set(y)) <= 20:
            self.problem_type = "classification"
        else:
            self.problem_type = "regression"
```

Then we loop through and create each decision tree, training it on a different bootstrapped sample generated by our helper function. We specify that the number of features randomly chosen for each split with "max_features" parameter. Finally, we store each trained tree in the "forest" list.

```
        for _ in range(self.num_trees):

            if self.problem_type == "classification":

                tree = DecisionTreeClassifier(
                    min_samples_split=self.min_samples_split,
                    max_depth=self.max_depth,
                    max_features=self.max_features
                )

            else:

                tree = DecisionTreeRegressor(
                min_samples_split=self.min_samples_split,
                max_depth=self.max_depth,
                max_features=self.max_features
            )

            X_sample, y_sample = _generate_sample(X, y)

            tree.fit(X_sample, y_sample)

            self.forest.append(tree)
```

Now that the model is trained, it's time to make predictions. We create a list to store each tree's predictions. Each tree takes in original feature matrix and returns its predictions, which we collect and aggregate using a helper method.

```
    def predict(self, X):

        tree_preds = np.array([tree.predict(X) for tree in
self.forest])
        predictions = [self._predict(tree_pred) for tree_pred in
tree_preds.T]

        return np.array(predictions)
```

The helper method aggregates predictions from all trees in the forest to produce a final output. For classification, it returns the most common predicted class across all trees; for regression, it returns the average. This same helper is used to make final prediction for each data point based on predictions of all trees in the forest.

```
    def _predict(self, y):

        if self.problem_type == "classification":
            y = list(y)
            return max(y, key=y.count)
        else:
            return np.mean(y)
```

Test

Now we perform all the usual steps to verify correctness of our implementation.

```
from data_loader import Dataset
from sklearn.ensemble import RandomForestClassifier,
RandomForestRegressor
from sklearn.metrics import accuracy_score, mean_squared_error

dataset_m = Dataset("multiclass classification")
X_train_m, X_test_m, y_train_m, y_test_m =
dataset_m.load_split_data()

dataset_b = Dataset("binary classification")
X_train_b, X_test_b, y_train_b, y_test_b =
dataset_b.load_split_data()

dataset_r = Dataset("regression")
X_train_r, X_test_r, y_train_r, y_test_r =
dataset_r.load_split_data()

custom_model_m = CustomRandomForest()
custom_model_m.fit(X_train_m, y_train_m)
y_pred_custom_m = custom_model_m.predict(X_test_m)
print(f"Custom Multiclass Classification Accuracy:
{accuracy_score(y_test_m, y_pred_custom_m):.3f}")

custom_model_b = CustomRandomForest()
custom_model_b.fit(X_train_b, y_train_b)
y_pred_custom_b = custom_model_b.predict(X_test_b)
print(f"Custom Binary Classification Accuracy:
{accuracy_score(y_test_b, y_pred_custom_b):.3f}")
```

```
custom_model_r = CustomRandomForest()
custom_model_r.fit(X_train_r, y_train_r)
y_pred_custom_r = custom_model_r.predict(X_test_r)
print(f"Custom Regression MSE: {mean_squared_error(y_test_r,
y_pred_custom_r):.3f}")

Custom Multiclass Classification Accuracy: 0.967
Custom Binary Classification Accuracy: 0.993
Custom Regression MSE: 0.278
```

Scikit-learn's implementation divides random forest into two classes depending on the problem type.

```
sklearn_model_m = RandomForestClassifier()
sklearn_model_m.fit(X_train_m, y_train_m)
y_pred_sklearn_m = sklearn_model_m.predict(X_test_m)
print(f"Scikit-learn Multiclass Classification Accuracy:
{accuracy_score(y_test_m, y_pred_sklearn_m):.3f}")

sklearn_model_b = RandomForestClassifier()
sklearn_model_b.fit(X_train_b, y_train_b)
y_pred_sklearn_b = sklearn_model_b.predict(X_test_b)
print(f"Scikit-learn Binary Classification Accuracy:
{accuracy_score(y_test_b, y_pred_sklearn_b):.3f}")

sklearn_model_r = RandomForestRegressor()
sklearn_model_r.fit(X_train_r, y_train_r)
y_pred_sklearn_r = sklearn_model_r.predict(X_test_r)
print(f"Scikit-learn Regression MSE: {mean_squared_error(y_test_r,
y_pred_sklearn_r):.3f}")

Scikit-learn Multiclass Classification Accuracy: 0.967
Scikit-learn Binary Classification Accuracy: 0.993
Scikit-learn Regression MSE: 0.239
```

The almost identical performance verifies our implementation, and the results align with our expectation – in most cases, random forest outperforms a single tree.

Tips

Random forest is incredibly versatile and forgiving. One of its greatest strengths is the ability to handle a massive number of features with minimal preprocessing. Additionally, it's very interpretable – random forest ranks features by importance, which helps you identify the most relevant variables.

To keep random forest model efficient and manageable, you can tune these hyperparameters:

- "num_trees": The total number of trees in your forest, more is usually better but takes longer to train
- "max_depth": Limits how deep each individual tree can grow to prevent them from becoming overly complex
- "max_features": Controls how many randomly selected features each tree considers at every split, which can speed up training

Finally, remember that while the averaging effect makes random forest robust to outliers and resistant to overfitting, it isn't bulletproof. If you see perfect training accuracy but poor test performance, your trees are likely over-tuned to your training data. You can fix this by simplifying the trees – limiting their depth or decreasing the number of features each tree considers.

Gradient Boosting

Intuition

Now that we've covered the most common parallel ensemble method – random forest, let's move on to sequential approaches, starting with gradient boosting.

The main distinction:

- In parallel methods, each tree is built independently
- In sequential methods, trees are built one after another, with each new tree trained to correct the mistakes made by the previous ones

The core idea behind boosting is simple: We start with a small decision tree, identify where it went wrong, and then train the next tree to focus more on those errors. This process repeats for a set number of rounds, and with each new tree, the overall model improves. Because the trees learn from one another's mistakes, the final model is often much more accurate than any single tree or even a forest of independent trees.

Alright, we simply train trees such that each new one learns from the mistakes of the previous, but what exactly does it use to correct those mistakes?

It uses gradient of the cost function. Just like in linear regression, we calculate the gradient to determine how to adjust our predictions in the right direction. These gradients guide each new tree, helping it reduce the overall error step by step.

Gradient boosting gets its name from how it's trained – the algorithm leverages gradient of the cost function so that each new tree can improve or "boost" the overall model.

Formalization

The general concept is shared for both regression and classification problems. We start by making a very simple general prediction that minimizes cost function. In other words, we come up with a single value that is closest to all targets within training dataset, denoted as F_0.

How do we determine the single value that is closest to all target values in the training data?

Define cost function that measures "closeness" and find one value that minimizes it. Fortunately, we have already defined appropriate cost functions for linear and logistic regression, which we will reuse here.

For regression:

$$J = \frac{1}{n} * \sum_{i=1}^{n} \left(y_{pred_i} - y_{actual_i}\right)^2$$

A single value y_{pred} that minimizes this function is the mean of all actual targets. Therefore, we define initial predictions as:

$$F_0 = \frac{1}{n} * \sum_{i=1}^{n} y_{actual_i} = \bar{y}$$

Our initial prediction for regression problems is the mean target of the training dataset.

For binary classification:

$$J = -\frac{1}{n} * \sum_{i=1}^{n} y_{actual_i} * log\left(y_{pred_i}\right) + \left(1 - y_{actual_i}\right) * log\left(1 - y_{pred_i}\right)$$

How did we arrive at the probability prediction y_{pred_i}?

Recall that in logistic regression, to get a prediction, we apply the sigmoid function to the output of a linear model to squash that value between 0 and 1. We follow that same logic here. Instead of searching directly for the optimal y_{pred_i}, we find a "raw" model output F_0 that results in the optimal y_{pred_i} once transformed by the sigmoid function.

By following this logic, we represent the relationship as:

$$y_{pred} = \frac{1}{1 + e^{-F_0}}$$

Naturally, the optimal probability for an observation belonging to class 1 is the proportion of values in our dataset that belong to class 1. Given there are n total observations in a dataset and n_1 of them belong to class 1, optimal first prediction becomes:

$$y_{pred} = \frac{n_1}{n}$$

Conclude that this is the best single-valued prediction we can make. Now, let's find F_0 that makes this come true. We know that :

$$y_{pred} = \frac{1}{1 + e^{-F_0}}$$

By substituting y_{pred} we get:

$$\frac{1}{1 + e^{-F_0}} = \frac{n_1}{n}$$

Taking the reciprocal of both sides:

$$1 + e^{-F_0} = \frac{n}{n_1}$$

Subtract 1 from both sides:

$$e^{-F_0} = \frac{n}{n_1} - 1 = \frac{n - n_1}{n_1}$$

Apply ln to both sides to get rid of the exponent:

$$-F_0 = ln\left(\frac{n - n_1}{n_1}\right)$$

Multiply both sides by -1:

$$F_0 = ln\left(\frac{n_1}{n - n_1}\right)$$

Given that we deal with binary classification problem, we know that $n_0 + n_1 = n$. Therefore, $n - n_1 = n_0$ and we can rewrite the final formula as:

$$F_0 = ln\left(\frac{n_1}{n_0}\right)$$

That's our optimal first raw model prediction for a binary classification problem.

Up to this point, we've focused on making the best possible initial prediction – one that is, on average, as close as possible to all actual targets. By minimizing the average error right from the start, we reduce the amount of "correction work" future decision trees need to do. After all, if the starting point is already close, each tree only needs to make small, targeted adjustments, making learning more efficient overall.

Now that we've established this initial guess, let's explore how each subsequent decision tree improves upon it. Remember, each new tree is designed to learn just one correction pattern at a time. The overall cost isn't minimized all at once – rather, it's gradually reduced by learning and fixing these patterns of error step by step.

Let's denote this process step-by-step. We call each new Decision Tree a weak learner and denote their predictions by $wl_1, wl_2, \dots, wl_k$.We call the initial prediction F_0. Each time we add a new weak learner, we update the prediction:

After the first weak learner:

$$F_1 = F_0 + wl_1$$

After the h-th weak learner:

$$F_h = F_{h-1} + wl_h$$

But this naturally raises a question:

How does each new weak learner know how to adjust the previous prediction?

Just like in linear or logistic regression, the gradient of the loss function tells us how far off we are, and in what direction to move to reduce the cost.

Even though loss functions for regression and binary classification are different, their gradients with respect to the prediction are the same:

$$\frac{dl}{dy_{pred}} = y_{pred} - y_{actual}$$

You may have noticed that this gradient formula looks slightly different from what we saw before.

Recall in linear and logistic regression, we computed gradients and updated weights directly to reduce the cost. We used a numerical method to compute gradient because y_{pred} was described by an equation but now y_{pred} is a sequence of decision trees. Hence, it is impossible to compute $\frac{dl}{dy_{pred}}$ with a formula. How do we compute the gradient then?

We estimate it using a decision tree – this is the key!

Each new tree predicts the value of the gradient – this information guides the next change to reduce the loss. In other words, the tree learns where the model is making mistakes, and how big those mistakes are. Then, estimated gradient is used to adjust prediction of the overall model.

> Note: just as in linear and logistic regression, we use the negative gradient to update the model. The same applies here, we directly train each weak learner to predict the negative gradient (simply gradient with negative sign).

Finally, to ensure robustness, we include a learning rate (same as with gradient descent) to control the step size when updating predictions with the gradient. With learning rate in-place our update formula becomes:

$$F_h = F_{h-1} + \alpha * wl_h$$

Where wl_h is a decision tree that estimates negative gradient of the cost with respect to the prediction, meaning it simply has a target of:

$$-\frac{dl}{dy_{pred}} = y_{actual} - y_{pred}$$

Conclude: In gradient descent, each iteration uses a formula to compute the gradient and update the model to reduce the cost. In gradient boosting, each iteration trains a decision tree to estimate the gradient, then uses that estimated gradient to reduce the loss, indirectly minimizing the cost function step by step.

We can formalize the training algorithm as:

1. Compute F_0 using the formula

   For regression:

$$F_0 = \frac{1}{n} * \sum_{i=1}^{n} y_{actual_i} = \bar{y}$$

   For binary classification:

$$F_0 = ln\left(\frac{n_1}{n_0}\right)$$

   Where n_0 and n_1 represent number of observations of class 0 and class 1 respectively.

2. Initialize our model with the starting prediction:

$$F_{h-1} = F_0$$

3. For a set number of iterations:

- Define the target for a weak learner. For both regression and binary classification, negative gradient is the target:

$$y_{actual} - y_{pred}$$

Where y_{pred} is different for each problem type. Recall, while for regression raw model output is the prediction, for binary classification we transform it with sigmoid to get probability. Therefore, predictions are computed as follows.

For regression:

$$y_{predicted} = F_{h-1}$$

For binary classification:

$$y_{predicted} = \frac{1}{1 + e^{-F_{h-1}}}$$

- Train a decision tree to predict negative gradient.

Regardless of the problem type, gradient is a continuous value. Therefore, our weak learner is always a decision tree regressor – also called a weak learner denoted as wl_h.

- Update the model by adding prediction of the weak learner we just trained, scaled by learning rate:

$$F_h = F_{h-1} + \alpha * wl_h$$

This F_h represents the current overall raw prediction of our model after the h-th iteration.

Once training is complete, what exactly have we learned?

Initial prediction F_0 and a weak learner for each iteration of the algorithm $wl_1, wl_2, \dots, wl_k$.

How do we leverage that to make a prediction for a new observation?

1. Take initial prediction F_0 that we learned during training
2. Set it as our current prediction of the overall model $F_{h-1} = F_0$
3. For a set number of iterations k:
   - Take an already trained weak learner wl_h and make it predict errors of the current state of the model F_{h-1} – in other words, gradient of the cost
   - Add prediction of wl_h scaled by learning rate to the overall model:

$$F_h = F_{h-1} + \alpha * wl_h$$

After k iterations, our model is done and can be represented as:

$$F_k = F_{k-1} + \alpha * wl_k$$

If we expand F_{k-1} we can write same formula as:

$$F_k = (F_{k-2} + \alpha * wl_{k-1}) + \alpha * wl_k$$

Let's now also expand F_{k-2}:

$$F_k = ((F_{k-3} + \alpha * wl_{k-2}) + \alpha * wl_{k-1}) + \alpha * wl_k$$

By removing the brackets, we get:

$$F_k = F_{k-3} + \alpha * wl_{k-2} + \alpha * wl_{k-1} + \alpha * wl_k$$

Also equivalent to:

$$F_k = F_{k-3} + \alpha * (wl_{k-2} + wl_{k-1} + wl_k)$$

As we keep expanding previous states of the model the pattern repeats. This way we can represent our model through what we learned during training, – F_0 and $wl_1, wl_2, \dots, wl_k$. We can represent final raw model as:

$$F_k = F_0 + \alpha * \sum_{h=1}^{k} wl_h$$

To recap: F_0 is the initial prediction – a single value chosen to be, on average as close as possible to the training targets. Each weak learner wl_h captures and corrects a systematic error over a subset of data points and their contributions are scaled by the learning rate α to improve robustness and reduce overfitting.

The final model prediction for any new input is given by the following formula.

For regression:

$$y_{pred} = F_k$$

For binary classification:

$$y_{pred} = \frac{1}{1 + e^{-F_k}}$$

As in logistic regression, the sigmoid function converts the raw model output into a probability, which is the preferred output format for a binary classification problem. Just as before, we can then interpret that probability – the most common way is to predict class 1 for all probabilities of 0.5 or higher and class 0 otherwise.

Implementation

Note we will only import decision tree regressor because regardless of the problem type – our weak learner will predict negative gradient, which is a continuous value.

```
import numpy as np
from sklearn.tree import DecisionTreeRegressor
```

We define our gradient boosting class where the first parameter is responsible for the number of weak learners (or iterations), then we have learning rate and maximum depth of each weak learner – decision tree.

```
class CustomGradientBoosting():

    def __init__(self, n_estimators=300, learning_rate=0.1,
max_depth=16):

        self.n_estimators = n_estimators
        self.learning_rate = learning_rate
        self.max_depth = max_depth
```

Now we get to training the model. First, we identify the problem type, then we initialize the prediction with a helper method and begin the loop.

```
    def fit(self, X, y):

        if len(set(y)) == 2:
            self.problem_type = "binary classification"
        else:
            self.problem_type = "regression"

        self.wls = []
        self.F_0 = self._compute_F0(y)

        F_h = self.F_0
```

On each iteration we define the target (negative gradient) and train weak learner to predict negative gradient based on features. Then, we update our current model with the new weak learner prediction scaled by learning rate and store the weak learner for later inference.

```
        for _ in range(self.n_estimators):

            wl = DecisionTreeRegressor(max_depth=self.max_depth)

            wl_target = self._get_wl_target(y, F_h)

            wl.fit(X, wl_target)

            F_h += self.learning_rate * wl.predict(X)

            self.wls.append(wl)
```

Next up, we define method to compute the initial prediction F_0. Depending on the problem type, we choose an appropriate formula.

```
    def _compute_F0(self, y):

        if self.problem_type == "binary classification":
            return np.log(sum(y == 1) / sum(y == 0))
        else:
            return np.mean(y)
```

Another helper method is used to define target for each weak learner.

```
    def _get_wl_target(self, y, F_h):

        if self.problem_type == "binary classification":
            y_pred = 1 / (1 + np.exp(-F_h))

        else:
            y_pred = F_h

        return y - y_pred
```

Now we get to the prediction method. First, we compute the raw model output using the final formula for inference.

For binary classification, we apply the sigmoid function to obtain predicted probabilities, then assign class 1 to those above 0.5 and class 0 otherwise. For regression, we simply return the raw model output as the final prediction.

```
    def predict(self, X):

        F_k = self.F_0 + self.learning_rate *
np.sum([wl.predict(X) for wl in self.wls], axis=0)

        if self.problem_type == "binary classification":

            y_pred = 1 / (1 + np.exp(-F_k))

            y_pred = np.array([1 if i >= 0.5 else 0 for i in
y_pred])

        else:
            y_pred = F_k

        return y_pred
```

Test

Let's load and split the data.

```
from data_loader import Dataset
from sklearn.ensemble import GradientBoostingClassifier,
GradientBoostingRegressor
from sklearn.metrics import accuracy_score, mean_squared_error

dataset_b = Dataset("binary classification")
X_train_b, X_test_b, y_train_b, y_test_b =
dataset_b.load_split_data()

dataset_r = Dataset("regression")
X_train_r, X_test_r, y_train_r, y_test_r =
dataset_r.load_split_data()
```

Train and test our custom model.

```
custom_model_b = CustomGradientBoosting()
custom_model_b.fit(X_train_b, y_train_b)
y_pred_custom_b = custom_model_b.predict(X_test_b)
print(f"Custom Binary Classification Accuracy:
{accuracy_score(y_test_b, y_pred_custom_b):.3f}")

custom_model_r = CustomGradientBoosting()
custom_model_r.fit(X_train_r, y_train_r)
y_pred_custom_r = custom_model_r.predict(X_test_r)
print(f"Custom Regression MSE: {mean_squared_error(y_test_r,
y_pred_custom_r):.3f}")

Custom Binary Classification Accuracy: 0.949
Custom Regression MSE: 0.288
```

Scikit-learn's implementation as usual provides two separate class for regression and classification.

```
sklearn_model_b = GradientBoostingClassifier()
sklearn_model_b.fit(X_train_b, y_train_b)
y_pred_sklearn_b = sklearn_model_b.predict(X_test_b)
print(f"Scikit-learn Binary Classification Accuracy:
{accuracy_score(y_test_b, y_pred_sklearn_b):.3f}")

sklearn_model_r = GradientBoostingRegressor()
sklearn_model_r.fit(X_train_r, y_train_r)
y_pred_sklearn_r = sklearn_model_r.predict(X_test_r)
print(f"Scikit-learn Regression MSE: {mean_squared_error(y_test_r,
y_pred_sklearn_r):.3f}")

Scikit-learn Binary Classification Accuracy: 0.993
Scikit-learn Regression MSE: 0.298
```

Similar performance verifies correctness of our implementation.

Tips

Gradient Boosting is a very powerful algorithm – it can capture complex patterns and deliver high accuracy even with relatively shallow trees. But with that power comes sensitivity. It's more prone to overfitting than random forest, especially on noisy or messy data, so regularization becomes important. Tuning parameters "n_estimators", "learning_rate" and "max_depth" is key to keeping the model generalizable. Often, using a smaller learning rate with more trees works better than the reverse, even if it takes longer to train.

Since it leverages gradients, it's more sensitive to data preprocessing. Scaling features like we do for linear or logistic regression can sometimes help but is usually not required. It's also more affected by extreme values, so if they are not relevant to your problem, it's a good idea to remove them.

The next chapter covers the most robust tree-based ML algorithm – one that fixes nearly all the shortcomings of gradient boosting while keeping the same core idea. This chapter sets you up for success in the next one!

Extreme Gradient Boosting (XGBoost)

Intuition

Name speaks for itself – it's an improved version of gradient boosting that is capable of learning more complex patterns in a very robust way. It also requires less data preprocessing as it can handle missing values and addresses overfitting while keeping the training time down.

Sounds like a dream, right?

In practice, it is considered to be a magic wound of ML with a common saying: "just use XGBoost" for most real-world ML problems.

On a high level, the formula stays the same as for Gradient Boosting. We compute initial prediction just like before, then on each iteration train a weak learner and add its corrections scaled by learning rate to the current prediction.

So, what's different for XGBoost?

We simply change the weak learner and its target.

In standard gradient boosting, the weak learner's primary role is to fix the errors of the current model state during each iteration. The underlying concept is that by iteratively correcting these immediate errors, the model will gradually improve, eventually leading to a good overall fit.

However, this approach has a limitation. By focusing primarily on immediate error reduction at each step, the algorithm does not always take the most efficient path to optimize the overall cost function of the entire model. In other words, greedily fixing specific error patterns one by one does not guarantee that each update is the most optimal step toward the global minimum cost.

Consequently, this indirect influence on the full cost function does not ensure an optimal final model. To truly maximize performance and achieve the best fit, XGBoost takes a more robust and direct approach. Instead of merely making a single step towards the minimum based on the gradient, each weak learner calculates the optimal adjustment required to minimize the total objective. Additionally, the cost function is not simply an average loss; it incorporates regularization terms that control model complexity to prevent overfitting.

Formalization

The final formula, training and inference in XGBoost are absolutely the same as in gradient boosting. Let's recall the procedure:

1. Make the initial prediction F_0, as close as possible to all data points
2. For a set number of iterations k:
   - Train weak learner wl_h to improve the overall model
   - Append weak learner's output scaled by learning rate to the current model:

$$F_h = F_{h-1} + \alpha * wl_h$$

Finally, after k iterations, we can express the raw model output as:

$$F_k = F_0 + \alpha * \sum_{h=1}^{k} wl_h$$

The difference is that XGBoost's weak learners are smarter but how?

Weak learner employed by XGBoost is a variation of a tree that we will call XGB tree. Let's think about what defines a tree, say what differentiates a decision tree classifier from decision tree regressor?

- Target value – what we aim to predict. For decision tree classifier it is a categorical outcome and for regressor it is a continuous value (e.g. in gradient boosting it was negative gradient of the loss).
- Splitting rule or the way we measure benefit of a decision. For a decision tree classifier it's informational gain and for regressor it's variance reduction. Benefit of a decision quantifies what we prioritize in our tree, for classifier it was proportion of observation that belong to one class, while for regressor it was variance of targets in a node.

- Calculating leaf node values. For a decision tree classifier, leaf node value is the most common class and for regressor it's the mean of targets in that leaf.

In order to understand XGBoost – we simply need to define XGB tree and to do that we just need to address three points defined above – equivalently answer the following three key questions:

- What to predict? (The target values)
- How to know a decision is the "best"? (The splitting rule)
- How to compute outputs? (The leaf values)

The core idea is that XGB trees are "perfect" because each weak learner directly minimizes overall cost instead of just fixing the last error pattern. How do we make it "perfect"?

We use the overall cost to answer each of the three questions in an optimal way. Therefore, let's begin be defining the overall cost for XGBoost on a high level:

$$J = average\ loss + regularization$$

Similarly to what we have seen with regression models that employ L1, L2 or elastic net regularization to prevent overfitting – cost function of XGBoost consists of two parts. The first part accounts for performance and the second part for complexity of the model, minimization of such objective results into a robust model that fits just right!

Formula for this looks as follows:

$$J = \frac{1}{n} * \sum_{i=1}^{n} l(y_{pred_i}, y_{actual_i}) + \sum_{h=1}^{k} \Omega(wl_h)$$

Where:

- Loss l – measures accuracy (MSE for regression, log-loss for classification)

- Penalty $\Omega(wl_h)$ – measures complexity of a weak learner and is defined as:

$$\Omega(wl_h) = \gamma * T + \frac{1}{2} * \lambda * \sum_{j=1}^{T} \omega_j^2$$

- T – the number of leaves, penalized by γ to keep trees small
- ω_j – value in leaf j, penalized by λ to keep outputs reasonable

Conclude: The cost is average loss plus the total complexity of all weak learners. It makes sense because our goal is to make model that is as accurate as possible all while preserving simplicity.

Now we will use this cost to derive everything that makes up an XGB tree – equivalently answer the three key questions.

We train one tree at a time in sequential order – each tree only needs to focus on things it can change. All other trees that were trained before it are constant, meaning they cannot be changed. When we define objective for a current tree, there's no point in including terms that do not depend on that tree.

When it comes to the overall cost function, parts that do not depend on the new tree are $\frac{1}{n}$ and complexities of all other trees that were trained before it. By removing those, we get the objective that every weak learner will aim to minimize:

$$J_{XGB\ tree} = \sum_{i=1}^{n} l\left(y_{pred_i}, y_{actual_i}\right) + \Omega(wl_h)$$

Objective for every tree translates to: "How much will this tree reduce loss?" + "How simple is it?" – exactly how we want to measure "goodness" of every tree.

Next step is to derive what value of the new tree (or weak learner) would minimize this objective $J_{XGB\ tree}$.

We have already done something like this, recall gradient descent. First, we computed gradient of the cost (hill). Then, we initialized parameter values (person). Finally, we guided the person towards bottom of the hill. Bottom of the hill was indicated by flat surface, which is mathematically manifested as slope of tangent line being 0 for every parameter or gradient equal to 0. Conclude that gradient of objective being approximately 0 means we reached bottom of the hill, and our objective is minimized.

This time instead of gradually tweaking parameter value to eventually approach gradient of 0, we directly set gradient to 0 and see what value of parameter makes it true. This direct computation can only be done with a tractable objective – one that is directly solvable in a single step (which doesn't always work for linear and logistic regression – that's why we used gradient descent in those cases).

One problem right now is that our tree objective is not tractable because of the loss l. Therefore, we approximate loss with an equation that will allow us to directly find the optimal parameter values.

Think of it this way: Initially, we have a hill that blocks our person's view of the bottom, making it impossible to reach it directly. We replace it with a similar hill that allows the person to see the bottom and descend in a single step. This replacement allows us to directly compute the approximately optimal value of the new tree.

Recap: We want to find value of a new tree that would minimize $J_{XGB\ Tree}$ but it's impossible to do so because objective is not tractable. Therefore, to directly find the optimal value for a new tree we use math to make the objective tractable while being approximately equal to original $J_{XGB\ tree}$.

Note: While a prediction of linear or logistic regression is quantifiable by learnable parameters (weights and bias), tree's prediction can only be quantified by its leaf nodes that represent all possible predictions it may make. Therefore, when we say tree values – we refer to the leaf nodes of that tree, denoted by $\omega_1, \omega_2, \dots, \omega_T$.

Conclude: Finding optimal tree value means finding leaves $\omega_1, \omega_2, \ldots, \omega_T$ that minimize the tree objective. With the help of approximation, we will be able to find the optimal leaf values directly.

Let's jump straight into the final form of the tree objective after applying the approximation:

$$J_{XGB\ tree} = \sum_{j=1}^{T}\left(G_j * \omega_j + \frac{1}{2} * (H_j + \lambda) * \omega_j^2\right) + \gamma * T$$

> Note: It's not meant to be intuitive – we used math to approximate the original $J_{XGB\ Tree}$ into a hill with a clear bottom – allowing our person to get there in one step. In other words, the form of the tree objective allows us to find $\omega_1, \omega_2, \ldots, \omega_T$ that minimize the tree objective.

There's no point in memorizing it – we only need to understand each term and why it makes sense. Let's unpack how this objective balances performance and simplicity of a tree:

- G_j – shows the push needed in leaf j. If G_j is big – we need big push, meaning at this point the leaf value is far from optimal.
- H_j – shows how confident we are in that push. If H_j is large it means curvature is strong; therefore, we are certain that G_j represents surface well.
- ω_j – the actual leaf value.
- λ – keeps ω_j from becoming extreme, avoiding overfitting.
- γ – penalizes adding leaves to keep the tree simple.
- T – the number of leaves; bigger T means more complexity.

Now we will calculate G_j and H_j. Recall, loss function is dependent on a problem type – MSE for regression and log-loss for binary classification. Either one measures how far off the prediction is from the actual target for a single data point.

Additionally, let's recall the notation:

- F_{h-1} – our current overall model on iteration h
- $F_{h-1}(x_i)$ – a prediction of the current model for an observation i
- $l(F_{h-1}(x_i), y_{actual_i})$ – a loss function value for an observation i at the current state of the model – we will equivalently denote it as l

With this in mind:

- g_i– derivative of the loss with respect to the prediction at point i. It gives us the direction and magnitude of change that would reduce loss for that point:

$$g_i = \frac{dl}{dF_{h-1}(x_i)}$$

- h_i – second order derivative of the loss with respect to the prediction at point i. It tells us how quickly that direction changes (curvature). This quantity is calculated as derivative of the derivative:

$$h_i = \frac{d^2 l}{dF_{h-1}^2(x_i)} = \frac{dg_i}{dF_{h-1}(x_i)}$$

Then for a leaf node j:

$$G_j = \sum_{i \in j} g_i$$

$$H_j = \sum_{i \in j} h_i$$

- G_j can be thought of as the total slope for all data points that end up in the leaf j
- H_j can be thought of as the total curvature for all data points that end up in the leaf j, which tells us how quickly the surface changes overall

This way, every term in the tree's objective has a clear role:

- The G_j, H_j part says how good this leaf's predictions are for the data it holds
- The λ, γ, T part says don't make the tree too big or messy

This concludes the final formula for the tree objective $J_{XGB\ Tree}$.

Think about this: First we defined objective for overall model (cost). In order to train the model, we need to train individual trees one by one – so we defined objective for each tree. In turn, training a tree means finding optimal value for its leaf nodes – so we need to define objective for each leaf node.

How do we ensure that the more detailed objective directly represents the overall objective – the cost?

For the tree objective $J_{XGB\ tree}$, we took the overall objective J and extracted the part that only depended on a single tree that is being trained. Similarly, to define the leaf objective $J_{leaf\ j}$ we take the tree objective $J_{XGB\ tree}$ and extract the part that only depends on the current leaf node. Let's take one more look at our final tree objective:

$$J_{XGB\ tree} = \sum_{j=1}^{T} \left(G_j * \omega_j + \frac{1}{2} * (H_j + \lambda) * \omega_j^2 \right) + \gamma * T$$

> Note: This objective is a sum of individual contributions from each leaf j, plus the overall $\gamma * T$ penalty for the total number of leaves in the tree.

We can conceptually represent it as:

$$J_{XGB\ tree} = \sum_{j=1}^{T} (leaf\ j\ objective) + regularization$$

The part of this equation that applies specifically to a single leaf j is:

$$J_{leaf\ j} = G_j * \omega_j + \frac{1}{2} * (H_j + \lambda) * \omega_j^2$$

Each leaf only cares about how it influences the tree because at the time we are making the best decision in a node, the rest of the tree stays constant. Therefore, equation above represents the objective function each leaf node aims to minimize.

Note that we had to drop $\gamma * T$ for each leaf's objective because it's a property of the entire tree, not the leaf. However, we'll still consider it when finding the best decision.

Conclude the flow so far:

1. Define objective for overall model (the cost)
2. Derive objective for an XGB tree (trees make up the overall model)
3. Derive objective for a leaf (leaves make up an XGB tree)

We've been breaking this down layer by layer to get to what really matters. Think of it like building a car:

- The car – XGBoost model
- The parts (engine, wheels, etc.) – individual XGB trees
- The smallest components (bolts, pistons, etc.) – leaves

To build the car, you need the parts; to build the parts, you start with the smallest components. The optimal leaf values ω_j are those smallest components that fit together to form an XGB tree, and eventually the entire XGBoost.

Recall that we used approximation to make $J_{XGB\ tree}$ tractable – in other words, a hill that allows our person to directly reach the bottom. The objective for every leaf was derived from the tree objective; therefore, it holds the same property.

With a well-defined objective function, we can determine the exact optimal weight for any given leaf. Essentially, we are asking: what value of the leaf ω_j will minimize our error?

To find this "bottom of the hill" where the cost is the lowest, we calculate the derivative of the objective function with respect to ω_j and set it to zero.

$$\frac{dJ_{leaf\ j}}{d\omega_j} = G_j + (H_j + \lambda) * \omega_j = 0$$

By solving this equation for ω_j, we derive a powerful formula for the optimal leaf value:

$$\omega_j = -\frac{G_j}{H_j + \lambda}$$

This result is significant because it directly addresses the core requirements of building a tree. Recall that to fully define any decision tree, we must answer three fundamental questions:

1. What to predict? (The target values)
2. How to know a decision is the "best"? (The splitting rule)
3. How to compute outputs? (The leaf values)

The formula we just derived provides a definitive answer to the third question. Unlike simpler trees that might just use the average value of the data in a leaf, XGB tree calculates the precise optimal output – just like a person who reaches bottom of the hill in one direct step.

This formula allows us to calculate the optimal value for every leaf in the tree simultaneously. You can think of the tree as a "team" of leaves, where each leaf is responsible for minimizing the error on its specific subset of data. By using this formula, every leaf finds "bottom of its own hill". Because these local hills are mathematically derived directly from the global objective function, when every leaf optimizes its own output, the tree as a whole achieves its maximum potential. This guarantees that the entire model takes the most optimal step possible toward minimizing the total cost.

With the leaf values (Question 3) now solved, the next logical step is to answer Question 2 – the splitting rule.

As with all trees, XGB tree leaf outputs depend on which data points end up in those leaves. Therefore, we need to ensure the most optimal data points reach each leaf. To do this, we define a splitting rule that directly minimizes the tree objective.

Conceptually, the general form of a splitting rule (or measure of benefit) for any tree can be described as:

$$Benefit = Objective\ before\ split - Objective\ after\ split$$

Previously this benefit was measured by informational gain (IG) or variance reduction (VR). IG measured how class proportions changed after a split, while VR measured how variance changed. This time, we measure how much the contribution to the tree objective changes given a split, while also accounting for the fact that the tree's complexity grows with each split.

Conclude: Classical trees asked "How will this split affect leaf node purity?" XGB trees ask "How will this split affect the tree objective?" This results in more effective decisions because they're tailored to directly boost overall model performance, rather than achieving it indirectly.

Recall leaf objective is computed as:

$$J_{leaf\ j} = G_j * \omega_j + \frac{1}{2} * \left(H_j + \lambda\right) * \omega_j^2$$

We can compute the optimal contribution of a leaf node to the objective by substituting the optimal value for a leaf node – ω_j.

$$\omega_j = -\frac{G_j}{H_j + \lambda}$$

After substituting ω_j into $J_{leaf\ j}$ formula, we get the final form that measures contribution of a single leaf node towards the tree objective:

$$J_{node\ j} = -\frac{1}{2} * \frac{G_j^2}{H_j + \lambda}$$

Recall that out tree objective has regularization term that we had to drop for the leaf objective – now we bring it back. Each time we make a decision we want to weight the fact that our tree grows more complex if the decision is made.

With this in mind let's complete each part of benefit metric one by one. Our objective before split is the leaf objective for the parent plus regularized depth of the tree:

$$Objective\ before\ split = J_{parent} + \gamma * T$$

Where T is number of leaf nodes before split and $J_{leaf\ parent}$ measure contribution of a parent node to the tree objective.

Next, we compute the total contribution of the child leaf nodes to the tree objective plus regularized depth of the tree + 1 (because if decision is made tree will have 1 more leaf):

$$Objective\ after\ split = (J_{child\ L} + J_{child\ R}) + \gamma * (T + 1)$$

The final formula to measure benefit of a decision becomes:

$$Benefit = J_{parent} - (J_{child\ L} + J_{child\ R}) - \gamma$$

This answers Question 2 – the best decision is the one that maximizes benefit defined above.

We've already answered points 2 and 3, which correspond to the splitting rule and leaf output calculation. The answer to point 1 – "what's the target of a weak learner?" naturally flows from these.

Recall that in gradient boosting, each weak learner aims to predict the negative gradient, or current error of the overall model, expressed as $y_{pred} - y_{actual}$. When training a weak learner, we passed parameters:

- Features: X
- Target: $y_{pred} - y_{actual}$

With the goal of predicting the error based on feature matrix.

XGB trees work differently. They're already designed to directly minimize the overall objective of the model – this is embedded in how they make splits and compute leaf values. Therefore, the target is implicit: it's a mathematically derived "optimal" value rather than an explicit target variable.

However, to calculate a leaf value, we need G_j and H_j – first and second order derivative of loss with respect to the current prediction. Since this computation involves loss function, it requires y_{actual} (targets) and y_{pred} (the current model prediction).

A common point of confusion: Usually "fit" method takes features and target as parameters and model tries to predict target based on features. In this case XGB Trees don't have a target, instead they just use current prediction of the overall model and targets to help them compute "perfect" prediction that minimizes overall cost. To conclude – XGB tree doesn't have a target, instead:

1. Derived the XGBoost objective (the cost)
2. Derived the XGB tree objective from the XGBoost objective
3. Derived the leaf objective from the XGB tree objective
4. Computed the optimal leaf output using the leaf objective
5. Derived the splitting rule (or measure of benefit) from the leaf objective and the optimal leaf value

Now we can formalize XGB trees by answering three questions that fully defined any decision tree:

1. What to predict? (The target value). There is no explicit target. The tree directly optimizes the overall model objective through its splitting and leaf calculation rules, rather than predicting a separate target variable.

2. How to know a decision is the "best"? (The splitting rule). Benefit is measured by how much a split improves the overall objective. We compare the parent's contribution to the tree objective versus the children's, while penalizing the increased complexity to keep trees simple:

$$Benefit = J_{parent} - (J_{child\ L} + J_{child\ R}) - \gamma$$

   Where $J_{leaf\ j}$ measures contribution to the tree objective of a node as a leaf and γ is the penalty for growing one more leaf.

3. How to compute outputs? (The leaf values). The leaf value ω_j is derived by directly finding the bottom of the hill created by $J_{leaf\ j}$:

$$\omega_j = -\frac{G_j}{H_j + \lambda}$$

With the core mechanics of XGB trees now in place, we're ready for the final major improvement – one that rethinks when we stop growing the tree.

Previously, with standard decision trees, we stopped growing as soon as the next best split failed to improve the objective (its benefit was negative). But feature relationships aren't always so simple. A split that offers no immediate benefit can unlock a subsequent split that's enormously valuable. Just like in real life – a decision that seems pointless right now can open a door you couldn't have anticipated.

So how do you know which path will lead to the best outcome down the line? Rationally speaking, it's impossible to know in real life. But algorithms can explore hypothetical scenarios and choose the one that leads to the best result.

In XGBoost, this is exactly what each XGB tree does. First, it makes the best possible decisions regardless of whether they individually offer immediate value. The tree grows until it hits a hard limit, which is:

- Maximum depth was reached. To prevent trees from growing too large as usual, we use "max_depth" parameter.

- Further split results in weak leaves. To prevent creating leaves that are too small or weak – we use "min_child_weight" (e.g. min_child_weight=1 means a new child leaf is only created if H_j in that leaf meets the threshold; otherwise, the split is rejected).

Once these stopping conditions are met, the tree is fully grown. At this point, we assess which hypothetical scenarios led to a meaningful improvement and which did not.

For this we evaluate the benefit of every split that created leaf nodes (the final decision). If a split was beneficial, meaning the path it led to was worth taking – we keep it. If not, we undo it. When a split is removed, its two child leaves disappear and their parent becomes the new leaf node, which means there's now a new set of final splits to evaluate. We repeat this process: keeping beneficial splits, undoing wasteful ones – until no dead-end decisions remain.

The result is a tree made entirely of decision paths that eventually prove their worth – capturing deeper, non-obvious patterns that classical decision trees miss by solely relying on immediate benefit.

To summarize: We grow every XGB tree to the maximum depth and minimum child weight, then scan the final decisions, removing any splits that led nowhere, until every remaining path in the tree is justified – a process called pruning.

This concludes the main components that make up XGB trees – the key components that make XGBoost so powerful.

Now that we understand why XGB trees are so effective and how they're designed to be optimal, we can use this knowledge to formulate the final training and inference procedures for XGBoost.

Training:

1. Compute the initial estimate F_0 that is as close to all training targets as possible
2. Set the initial prediction as the current $F_{h-1} = F_0$
3. For a set number of iterations k:
   - Train a weak learner (XGB tree) – wl_h.
   - Add the new weak learner scaled by learning rate to the current model:

$$F_h = F_{h-1} + \alpha * wl_h$$

   - Update the current prediction y_{pred}

     For regression:

$$y_{pred} = F_h(X)$$

     For binary classification:

$$y_{pred} = \frac{1}{1 + e^{-F_h(X)}}$$

Once all weak learners have been trained, our model is done and we move on to inference – how to make predictions for new observations.

Inference:

1. Take the initial estimate F_0 we learned during training
2. Set the initial prediction as the current one $F_{h-1} = F_0$
3. For a set number of iterations k:
   - Take an already trained weak learner wl_h and use it to predict the optimal correction based on the current predictions and targets

- Add prediction of wl_h scaled by learning rate to the overall prediction:

$$F_h = F_{h-1} + \alpha * wl_h$$

- Update the current y_{pred}

  For regression:

$$y_{pred} = F_h(X)$$

  For binary classification:

$$y_{pred} = \frac{1}{1 + e^{-F_h(X)}}$$

With this procedure in mind, we can summarize inference with this formula:

$$F_k = F_0 + \alpha * \sum_{h=1}^{k} wl_h$$

Where the final predictions for input X are computed as follows.

For regression:

$$y_{pred} = F_k(X)$$

For binary classification:

$$y_{pred} = \frac{1}{1 + e^{-F_k(X)}}$$

This was the core idea of XGBoost. There are a couple more enhancements introduced in this model to make it even more robust, fast and flexible. Let's unpack them one by one along with hyperparameters.

XGBoost, like random forest, can add randomness by training each tree on only part of the data – helping prevent overfitting and speeding up the training process. There're multiple ways to determine what data each weak learner is trained on:

- To select the proportion of all rows every weak learner will be trained on – use "subsample" (e.g. subsample=0.8 means each tree will be trained on 80% of randomly selected training rows).
- To select the proportion of all features every weak learner will be trained on (once for the whole tree) – use "colsample_bytree" (e.g. colsample_bytree=0.7 means each tree will be trained on 70% of randomly selected feature columns)
- To select the proportion of features separately at each tree depth – use "colsample_bylevel" (e.g. colsample_bylevel=0.9 means that at every depth, splits will consider only 90% of randomly selected features from the subset already chosen by colsample_bytree)
- To select the proportion of features for each split – use "colsample_bynode" (e.g. colsample_bynode=0.5 means for every split decision, only 50% of features are randomly chosen to evaluate)

This way the algorithm fully leverages all the information to minimize overall cost, preventing stronger patterns from overpowering more subtle but potentially important ones.

Additionally, it makes no sense to keep adding weak learners if they don't improve the overall model performance. For that reason, we use "early_stopping_rounds" hyperparameter (e.g. early_stopping_rounds=10 stops training if the overall objective hasn't improved for 10 consecutive rounds, keeping the best iteration).

These parameters together prevent trees from fitting noise (weak learner-level) and stop the training process when the objective stops improving (model-level).

Next, XGBoost handles missing values in a smart way. Some features may have missing entries, and during training, when XGBoost considers a split on such a feature, it temporarily sends all missing data points to the left and then to the right, calculates the $Benefit$ for both cases, and chooses the side that provides the most benefit. During inference, any data point with a missing value for that feature simply follows the default side learned during training. This technique is called sparsity-aware split finding.

Let's recall how XGBoost incorporates regularization, along with the parameter controlling each term:

- Penalty on leaf values – controlled by "lambda" (λ), which keeps individual leaf predictions reasonable
- Penalty on the overall prediction contribution of a weak learner – controlled by "alpha" (α), which discourages a single tree from making overly large adjustments to the model
- Penalty on the number of leaves – controlled by "gamma" (γ), which promotes simplicity of every tree

Lastly, XGBoost was designed to be extremely efficient, using parallel processing wherever possible. One of the most time-consuming tasks is to find the best split for each node – traditionally we had to evaluate every threshold in each feature column one by one. XGBoost solves this by evaluating multiple features simultaneously across available processing cores. Combined with efficient data structures, this makes XGBoost exceptionally fast in practice.

The final recap: XGBoost is an efficient implementation of gradient boosting with optimized trees as weak learners.

Why are XGB trees optimal?

- Each tree directly minimizes the overall objective with built-in regularization, balancing performance and model simplicity
- Smart sampling and stopping rules to further address overfitting
- Missing values are handled automatically through learned split directions
- Non-obvious feature interactions are captured by growing trees to their full extent, then pruning to retain only the splits that meaningfully improve predictions

Congratulations! This is often considered the most practical ML algorithm for tabular data!

Implementation

First, we define XGBoost class that takes all hyperparameters as input and stores them in instance variables along with list to store all weak learners and corresponding features each one is trained on – just like gradient boosting.

```
import numpy as np

class CustomXGBoost():

    def __init__(self,
                 n_estimators=100,
                 subsample=0.8,
                 colsample_bytree=0.8,
                 learning_rate=0.5,
                 reg_lambda=1.5,
                 gamma=0.05,
                 max_depth=3,
                 min_child_weight=5):

        self.wls = []
        self.feature_idxs = []

        self.n_estimators = n_estimators

        self.subsample = subsample
        self.colsample_bytree = colsample_bytree

        self.learning_rate = learning_rate
        self.reg_lambda = reg_lambda
        self.gamma = gamma

        self.max_depth = max_depth
        self.min_child_weight = min_child_weight
```

Next, let's define "fit" method to train the overall model. We start by identifying the problem type, computing the initial prediction using a helper method, and setting it as the current prediction. Note that "full_like" creates a vector filled with F_0, matching the length of y.

```
    def fit(self, X, y):

        if len(set(y)) == 2:
            self.problem_type = "binary classification"
        else:
            self.problem_type = "regression"

        self.F_0 = self._compute_F0(y)
        F_h = np.full_like(y, self.F_0, dtype="float")
```

Then for each iteration, we:

1. Compute y_{pred} from the current F_h using a helper method
2. Generate a bootstrapped sample with random feature selection
3. Train a new XGB tree on the sampled data
4. Update F_h by adding the scaled predictions from the new tree
5. Store the trained tree and its feature indices for later use during inference

```
        for _ in range(self.n_estimators):

            y_pred = self._compute_y_pred(F_h)

            X_sample, y_sample, y_pred_sample, feature_idxs = 
self._generate_sample(X, y, y_pred)

            wl = XGBTree(self.max_depth,self.min_child_weight,
                         self.gamma, self.reg_lambda)

            wl.fit(X_sample, y_sample, y_pred_sample)

            F_h += self.learning_rate * wl.predict(X[:, 
feature_idxs])

            self.wls.append(wl)
            self.feature_idxs.append(feature_idxs)
```

Let's now define each helper method we used above.

The initial prediction is computed the same way as for gradient boosting.

```
    def _compute_F0(self, y):

        if self.problem_type == "binary classification":
            return np.log(sum(y == 1) / sum(y == 0))
        else:
            return np.mean(y)
```

The samples and features to train each weak learner on are randomly selected using "subsample" and "colsample_bytree" hyperparameters respectively.

```
    def _generate_sample(self, X, y, y_pred):

        n, m = X.shape

        m_new = int(self.colsample_bytree * m)
        col_idxs = np.random.choice(m, m_new)

        n_new = int(self.subsample * n)
        row_idxs = np.random.choice(n, n_new)

        return X[row_idxs][:, col_idxs], y[row_idxs],
y_pred[row_idxs], col_idxs
```

Finally, we define "predict" method for inference. The raw model output leverages our general formula that sums up the initial prediction with prediction of each weak learner scaled by learning rate. Then, the raw model output is transformed into the final prediction using a helper method.

```
    def predict(self, X):

        F_k = self.F_0 + self.learning_rate *
np.sum([wl.predict(X[:, idxs]) for wl, idxs in zip(self.wls,
self.feature_idxs)], axis = 0)

        y_pred = self._compute_y_pred(F_k, prob = False)

        return y_pred
```

The following helper method transforms the raw model output according to the problem type.

```
    def _compute_y_pred(self, F_h, prob=True):

        if self.problem_type == "binary classification":
            y_pred = 1 / (1 + np.exp(- F_h))

            if not prob:
                y_pred = np.array([1 if i >= 0.5 else 0 for i in
y_pred])
        else:
            y_pred = F_h

        return y_pred
```

Now it's time to define XGB Tree. In terms of structure, it's actually the same kind of tree as the ones we previously built. The only differences are:

- The way we compute benefit of a decision
- Values in leaf nodes
- One more stopping condition

Let's begin by defining Node class – exactly the same as for any other tree. As before, it can either contain information about a decision or a leaf node value.

```
class Node():

    def __init__(self, feature_idx=None, threshold=None,
left=None, right=None, benefit=None, value=None):

        self.feature_idx = feature_idx
        self.threshold = threshold
        self.left = left
        self.right = right
        self.benefit = benefit

        self.value = value
```

Now, we get to the tree class itself. First, we initialize root along with all the tree-level hyperparameters.

```
class XGBTree():

    def __init__(self, max_depth, min_child_weight, gamma,
reg_lambda):

        self.root = None

        self.max_depth = max_depth
        self.min_child_weight = min_child_weight

        self.gamma = gamma
        self.reg_lambda = reg_lambda
```

Previously, we computed split benefit and leaf values directly from X and y. However, XGB trees only need G_j and H_j – the sums of g_i and h_i for observations in node j. Therefore, instead of passing all the data around, we compute g_i and h_i for all observations at once, then access the relevant ones for each node using indices.

In this same method, we initialize indices for each data point to track which node it belongs to during the tree-building process.

```
def fit(self, X, y, y_pred):

    self.X = X
    self.y = y

    self.all_g_i = self._compute_all_g_i(y, y_pred)
    self.all_h_i = self._compute_all_h_i(y, y_pred)

    dataset_idxs = np.arange(len(y))

    self.root = self._build_tree(dataset_idxs)
```

> Note: Instead of physically splitting the dataset during the process – we use indices to track data in each node and eventually compute leaf values.

Let's define the helper methods used to compute g_i and h_i. For regression with MSE loss, the second derivative is constant (ones). For binary classification with log loss, it depends on the current predictions.

```
def _compute_all_g_i(self, y, y_pred):

    return y_pred - y

def _compute_all_h_i(self, y, y_pred):

    if len(np.unique(y)) == 2:
        return y_pred * (1 - y_pred)
    else:
        return np.ones_like(y)
```

Now we get to building the tree.

For simplicity, rather than implementing full pruning, we will stop splitting when the benefit is zero – this captures the core idea without adding unnecessary complexity.

Therefore, in our implementation we grow a tree until:

- The maximum depth is reached
- The minimum child weight constraint is violated (ensures child nodes contain enough information and aren't just modeling noise)

- The best split provides no benefit

Recall that growing a tree means identifying the best decision (using helper method), then if conditions hold – we create a decision node that splits the data. Then we call the same method on the child nodes. Once a stopping condition is met, we compute and return leaf nodes.

```
    def _build_tree(self, dataset_idxs, curr_depth=0):

        if curr_depth < self.max_depth:

            best_decision = self._get_best_decision(dataset_idxs)

            if best_decision and best_decision["benefit"] > 0 and
best_decision["child_weight"] > self.min_child_weight:

                child_l =
self._build_tree(best_decision["dataset_left_idxs"], curr_depth +
1)
                child_r =
self._build_tree(best_decision["dataset_right_idxs"], curr_depth +
1)

                return Node(best_decision["feature_idx"],
best_decision["threshold"], child_l, child_r,
best_decision["benefit"])

        leaf_value = self._compute_leaf_value(dataset_idxs)

        return Node(value = leaf_value)
```

Let's define the helper method used to compute optimal leaf node values. We compute G_j and H_j using the indices of observations in the leaf, then apply the optimal leaf value formula.

```
    def _compute_leaf_value(self, idxs):

        G_j = self.all_g_i[idxs].sum()
        H_j = self.all_h_i[idxs].sum()

        return -G_j / (H_j + self.reg_lambda)
```

Next, we define the helper method used to find the best decision. We evaluate every feature-threshold pair and store the one with the highest benefit. We also track child weight to ensure the split creates meaningful children.

```
    def _get_best_decision(self, dataset_idxs, k=10):

        best_decision = {}

        max_benefit = -float("inf")

        num_features = self.X[dataset_idxs].shape[1]

        for feature_idx in range(num_features):

            feature_values = self.X[dataset_idxs, feature_idx]
            possible_thresholds = np.unique(feature_values)

            for threshold in possible_thresholds[::k]:

                dataset_left_idxs, dataset_right_idxs =
self._split(dataset_idxs, feature_idx, threshold)

                if len(dataset_left_idxs) > 0 and
len(dataset_right_idxs) > 0:

                    curr_benefit =
self._compute_benefit(dataset_idxs, dataset_left_idxs,
dataset_right_idxs)

                    curr_child_weight =
self._compute_weight(dataset_left_idxs, dataset_right_idxs)

                    if curr_benefit > max_benefit:
                        best_decision["feature_idx"] = feature_idx
                        best_decision["threshold"] = threshold
                        best_decision["dataset_left_idxs"] =
dataset_left_idxs
                        best_decision["dataset_right_idxs"] =
dataset_right_idxs
                        best_decision["benefit"] = curr_benefit
                        max_benefit = curr_benefit

                        best_decision["child_weight"] =
curr_child_weight

        return best_decision
```

The helper method used to split indices based on a feature-threshold pair.

```
    def _split(self, dataset_idxs, feature_idx, threshold):

        feature_values = self.X[dataset_idxs, feature_idx]

        is_left = feature_values <= threshold

        dataset_left_idxs = dataset_idxs[is_left]
        dataset_right_idxs = dataset_idxs[~is_left]

        return dataset_left_idxs, dataset_right_idxs
```

One of the stopping conditions was to have meaningful child nodes. Child weight is H_j in a node. We compute it for both children and return the minimum. Since both must pass the minimum weight check, we only need the smaller one.

```
    def _compute_weight(self, l_idxs, r_idxs):

        H_l = self.all_h_i[l_idxs].sum()
        H_r = self.all_h_i[r_idxs].sum()

        return min(H_l, H_r)
```

Now we implement the helper method to measure benefit of a decision used to make the best decision – the splitting rule.

```
    def _compute_benefit(self, parent_idxs, l_idxs, r_idxs):

        G_parent = self.all_g_i[parent_idxs].sum()
        G_l = self.all_g_i[l_idxs].sum()
        G_r = self.all_g_i[r_idxs].sum()

        H_parent = self.all_h_i[parent_idxs].sum()
        H_l = self.all_h_i[l_idxs].sum()
        H_r = self.all_h_i[r_idxs].sum()

        J_parent = self._compute_leaf_objective(G_parent,
H_parent)
        J_l = self._compute_leaf_objective(G_l, H_l)
        J_r = self._compute_leaf_objective(G_r, H_r)

        return J_parent - (J_l + J_r) - self.gamma
```

Note: This is a lot of code – it's best to come back to the "Formalization" section and map each piece of code to theory.

At this point, we get to the prediction part for a single XGB tree. As usual, we make the prediction for one observation at a time. Each observation walks down the tree using information in decision nodes until it reaches a leaf, which contains the prediction.

```
    def predict(self, X):

        predictions = [self._predict(x, self.root) for x in X]

        return np.array(predictions)

    def _predict(self, x, tree):

        if tree.value is not None:
            return tree.value

        feature_val = x[tree.feature_idx]

        if feature_val <= tree.threshold:
            return self._predict(x, tree.left)

        else:
            return self._predict(x, tree.right)
```

This implementation captures all key algorithmic components of XGBoost. We have omitted some features that add complexity without changing core concepts.

Missing value handling: You understand the concept (learned split directions), and XGBoost handles this automatically in practice.

Additional sampling levels: We have implemented row and column sampling at the tree level. XGBoost also supports:

- "colsample_bynode" – randomly sample features for each split
- "colsample_bylevel" – different feature subsets per tree depth

These follow the same principles we've covered.

Computational optimizations: We focused on the ML part, whereas XGBoost comes with substantial engineering enhancements:

- Parallel preprocessing for speed
- Early stopping ("early_stopping_rounds") – stops training when no improvement is observed

Note: We've presented the code from higher to lower abstraction levels for conceptual clarity. When implementing in a Jupyter Notebook, reverse the order – define "Node", "XGBTree" and finally "XGBoost" so each class can reference the ones defined before it.

This was a big section, it is natural to read it through multiple times and re-structure the order of the code to get a better hold of the concepts.

Test

XGBoost is not offered by Scikit-learn – we import it from a dedicated library created specifically for this model by its original authors – XGBoost.

```
from data_loader import Dataset
from xgboost import XGBClassifier, XGBRegressor
from sklearn.metrics import accuracy_score, mean_squared_error

dataset_b = Dataset("binary classification")
X_train_b, X_test_b, y_train_b, y_test_b =
dataset_b.load_split_data()

dataset_r = Dataset("regression")
X_train_r, X_test_r, y_train_r, y_test_r =
dataset_r.load_split_data()
```

Since XGBoost has many hyperparameters, a common convention is to store them in a dictionary and pass the dictionary as input to keep the code clean.

First, we specify the number of estimators. Next come two sampling hyperparameters that control randomness at the tree level. We then have three regularization terms that prevent overfitting across both the model and individual weak learners. Finally, two hyperparameters ensure each weak learner remains robust and well-formed.

Let's define the dictionary of hyperparameters.

```
params = {
    "n_estimators": 100,

    "subsample": 0.8,
    "colsample_bytree": 0.8,

    "learning_rate": 0.5,
    "reg_lambda": 1.5,
    "gamma": 0.05,

    "max_depth": 3,
    "min_child_weight": 5
}
```

Now, let's train and test our implementation.

```
custom_model_b = CustomXGBoost(**params)
custom_model_b.fit(X_train_b, y_train_b)
y_pred_custom_b = custom_model_b.predict(X_test_b)
print(f"Custom Binary Classification Accuracy:
{accuracy_score(y_test_b, y_pred_custom_b):.3f}")

custom_model_r = CustomXGBoost(**params)
custom_model_r.fit(X_train_r, y_train_r)
y_pred_custom_r = custom_model_r.predict(X_test_r)
print(f"Custom Regression MSE: {mean_squared_error(y_test_r,
y_pred_custom_r):.3f}")

Custom Binary Classification Accuracy: 0.956
Custom Regression MSE: 0.288
```

Note: The "**" operator unpacks the dictionary, converting each key-value pair into a keyword argument. This pattern serves as a cleaner alternative to passing long lists of arguments, allowing for better organization without changing the underlying logic.

Next up is XGBoost library implementation with separate classes dedicated for regression and classification tasks.

```
xgboost_model_b = XGBClassifier(**params)
xgboost_model_b.fit(X_train_b, y_train_b)
y_pred_xgboost_b = xgboost_model_b.predict(X_test_b)
print(f"XGBoost Binary Classification Accuracy:
{accuracy_score(y_test_b, y_pred_xgboost_b):.3f}")
```

```
xgboost_model_r = XGBRegressor(**params)
xgboost_model_r.fit(X_train_r, y_train_r)
y_pred_xgboost_r = xgboost_model_r.predict(X_test_r)
print(f"XGBoost Regression MSE: {mean_squared_error(y_test_r,
y_pred_xgboost_r):.3f}")

XGBoost Binary Classification Accuracy: 0.993
XGBoost Regression MSE: 0.253
```

This verifies correctness of our implementation.

Tips

XGBoost is extremely powerful and robust with the right choice of hyperparameters. Fortunately, you have the deepest possible understanding of every core hyperparameter – now we will put it all together for recap.

> Note: This algorithm applies to all problem types, with multiclass classification extending naturally from the binary case. Hyperparameter values are very case dependent – the following ranges are meant to give you a broad idea of what's considered reasonable. We will break down hyperparameters into groups by what aspects of the model they control.

The overall model complexity. "n_estimators" and "learning_rate" go together and account for how many weak learners there's in total and how much each one affects the overall prediction respectively. For more robust model select a sufficiently large number of weak learners (100-500) and smaller learning rate (0.01-0.1).

In case the model hasn't seen improvement in a specified number of consecutive iterations (also called boosting rounds) – it stops adding weak learners. The hyperparameter to control the number of such rounds is "early_stopping_rounds" with a reasonable value range of (5-20).

Weak learner complexity. "max_depth" is responsible for the maximum number of levels each weak learner may have, a reasonable range is (3-8). "min_child_weight" controls the minimum amount of uncertainty in a node to continue splitting, this is expressed by the sum of second order derivatives with a range around (1-10).

"subsample" and "colsample_bytree" cover fraction of randomly selected columns and rows to train every tree respectively, (0.8-1) is a reasonable range for both of them.

"reg_lambda" is a regularization strength parameters, controlling L2 regularization strength with common range of (0-10). "gamma" is another regularization parameter the minimum loss reduction required to make a split with common ranges of (0-5).

Additional hyperparameters. Let's finalize this section with some practical hyperparameters which we haven't seen yet. The ones listed here were not part of the original XGBoost implementation but rather added later on as useful extensions.

"alpha" is L1 regularization term with a reasonable range of (0-1), it is useful for dataset with many features where some might be irrelevant.

"scale_pos_weight" is designed to handle class imbalance in binary classification problems. When a dataset has more observations that belong to one of the classes, by default model can overconcentrate on the majority class – this hyperparameter addresses that issue. It increases the importance of the minority class during training, helping the model learn decision boundaries that are not biased toward the majority class. A common approach is to set it to the ratio of class 0 to class 1 samples.

Congratulations on learning about the "magic weapon" of ML from the ground up!

Neural Network

Intuition

There is a widespread perception that neural networks are incredibly complicated. Here's the good news – they're complicated to interpret, not to understand. To clarify this, let's distinguish between what is under our control as ML practitioners and what is not.

What is under our control is making the best use of an ML algorithm. This can only be achieved by understanding how the algorithm learns and makes predictions. Given everything we've covered so far, understanding how neural networks work is surprisingly straightforward.

What is outside our control is the specific patterns an algorithm learns from the data. Neural networks are often mistakenly perceived as "hard" simply because the patterns they learn are uninterpretable to humans. But this interpretability is outside our control and, frankly, irrelevant to understanding the mechanics.

In fact, this is the whole point of neural networks – they're designed to discover complex, hidden patterns that would be impossible for humans to specify manually. So, when it comes to what we actually care about as professionals, that is understanding how to use them effectively – neural networks are quite simple.

Now imagine we have a dataset with features and a target, but the relationship is too complex to model directly with classical methods. What can we do?

Recall that for linear or logistic regression to perform well, the relationship between the inputs and the target must be linear.

We can think of a neural network as a system consisting of two parts to solve this problem.:

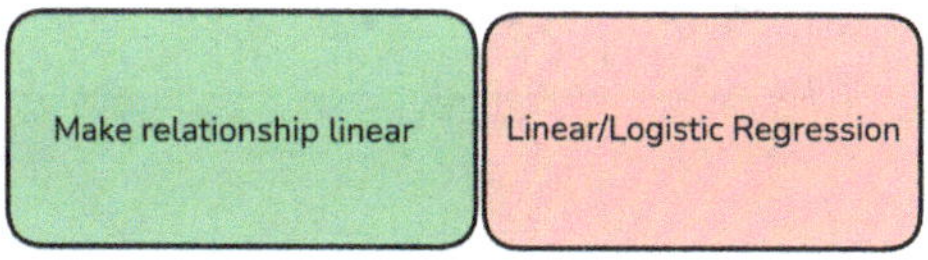

First, the neural network acts as a data transformer, processing the raw input to reshape the relationship between the features and the target into an approximately linear form. Second, once the data is transformed, the network simply applies a standard linear or logistic regression to describe that relationship.

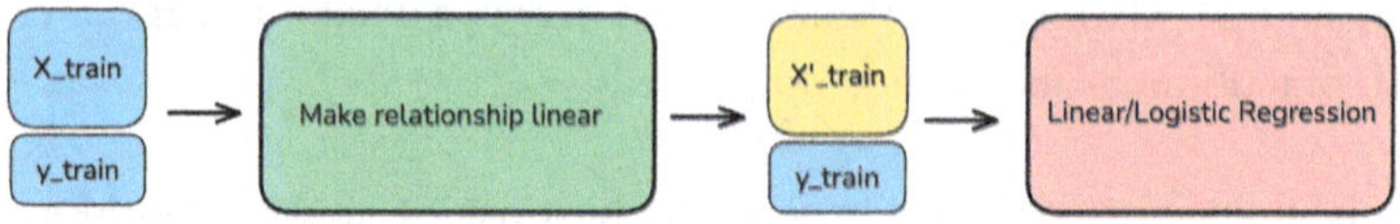

Training a neural network is iterative, just like many other algorithms we've covered. Both parts adjust their parameters on every iteration to minimize an objective.

Formalization

All there's to learn is how the green box is able to transform features such that they have approximately linear relationship with targets and how it all comes together with the red box.

Since the green box needs to transform features such that they have linear relationship with the target, we can infer that the relationship is likely non-linear in the first place.

Let's see an example of non-linear relationship between two variables x and y.

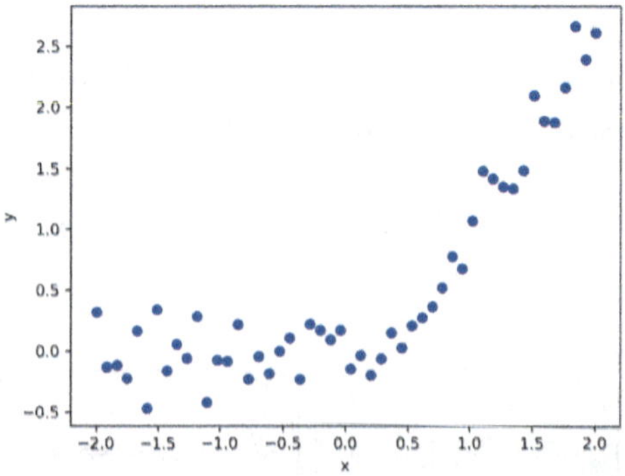

How can we describe y using just x? Let's start by trying a straight line:

$$y = \omega * x + b$$

This is just linear regression. We already know how to find optimal parameters using gradient descent with MSE (mean squared error) as our objective.

After training, we can plot the model's predictions as a red line:

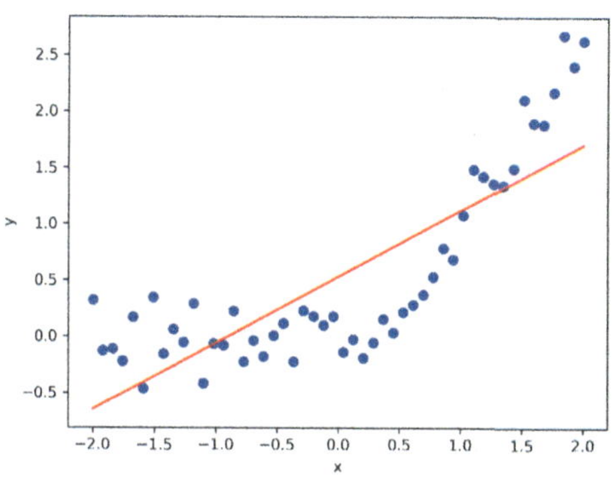

The straight line clearly doesn't capture the relationship well. How can we do better?

Conceptually, this relationship could be described by an angle – a flat line that suddenly tilts. The simplest improvement is to delay the linear regression from activating until it makes sense.

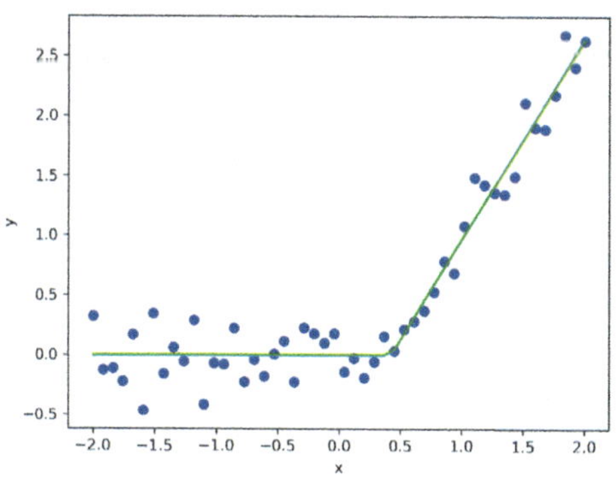

This fits our non-linear data much better!

We started with:

$$y = \omega * x + b$$

Now we add a rule: "Stay flat at zero until the linear prediction becomes positive."

Mathematically, this is:

$$y = max\ (\omega * x + b, 0)$$

This transformation keeps the line flat at 0 until the original linear model's prediction becomes positive – exactly what we need for the angular shape. To train this model, we use gradient descent with the same MSE objective as before.

Recap: The green line represents $\max\ (\omega * x + b, 0)$ with optimal parameters ω and b found through gradient descent, using MSE as the objective.

Great, we could describe an angle, but can we describe this bowl shape:

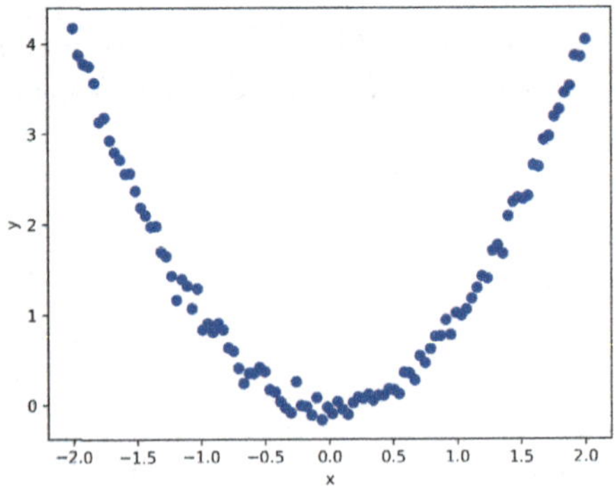

Let's try to fit our newly defined model:

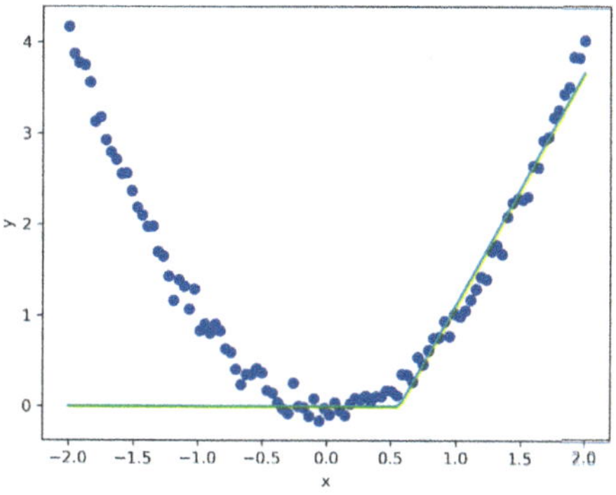

Not ideal – it fails to capture the pattern on the left. But notice this complex bowl shape could be roughly broken down into two angles. What if we added a second angle to our model?

If we fit two angles (one green, one orange) to the data, we get:

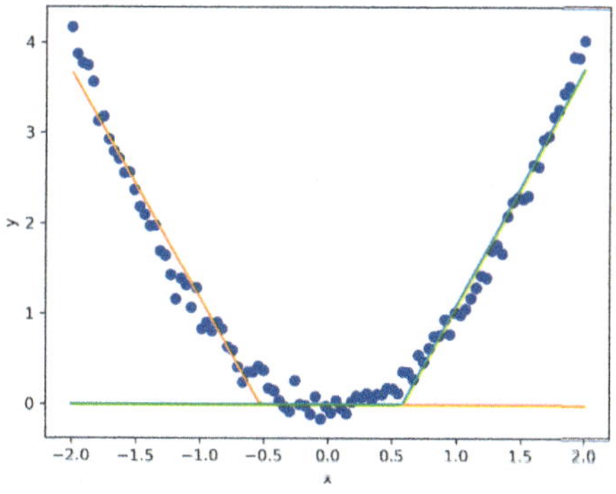

This looks promising, but it's not quite a proper model yet – for any given x, we have both a green and orange prediction. Since any input needs exactly one output, we need to combine these two angles into a final model.

Here's how it works: on the left, the green line is at 0, so adding it to orange gives us just the orange line. On the right, the orange line is at 0, so adding it to green gives us just the green line. In the middle, both lines are at 0, so their sum is 0.

By adding the green and orange lines together, we get the final model:

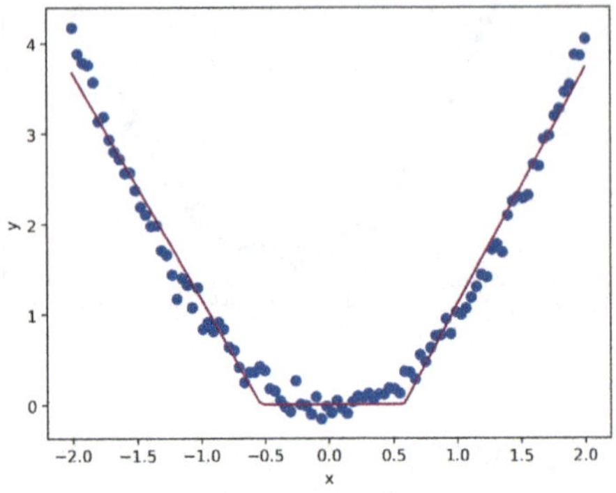

This looks like a great fit, let's formalize what we just did.

First, we define two angles, using the angle formula we already know:

$$y_1 = max\ (\omega_1 * x + b_1, 0)$$

$$y_2 = max\ (\omega_2 * x + b_2, 0)$$

Then we sum up two angles to get the bowl shape:

$$y = y_1 + y_2$$

By expanding the equation, we can express final model as:

$$y = max(\omega_1 * x + b_1, 0) + max\ (\omega_2 * x + b_2, 0)$$

In order to train this model, we use gradient descent with MSE as the objective just as we did for linear regression.

How about even more complex relationship:

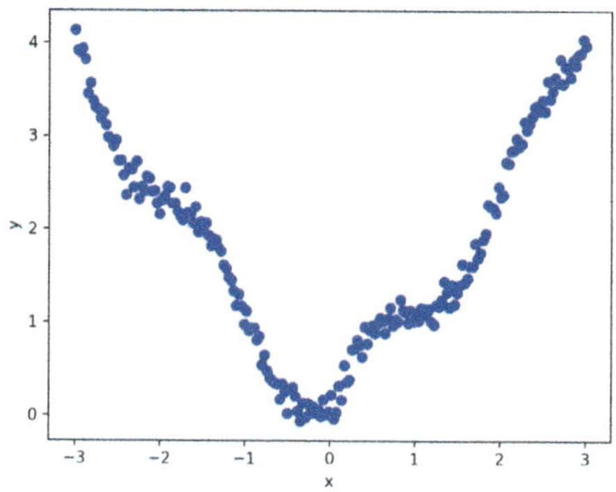

Instead of 2, let's try to fit 5 angles and sum them up, our equation is:

$$y = \sum_{h=1}^{5} max\ (\omega_h * x + b_h, 0)$$

By employing gradient descent with MSE to find optimal parameters: $[\omega_1, \omega_2, \omega_3, \omega_4, \omega_5]$ and $[b_1, b_2, b_3, b_4, b_5]$ we get the following fit:

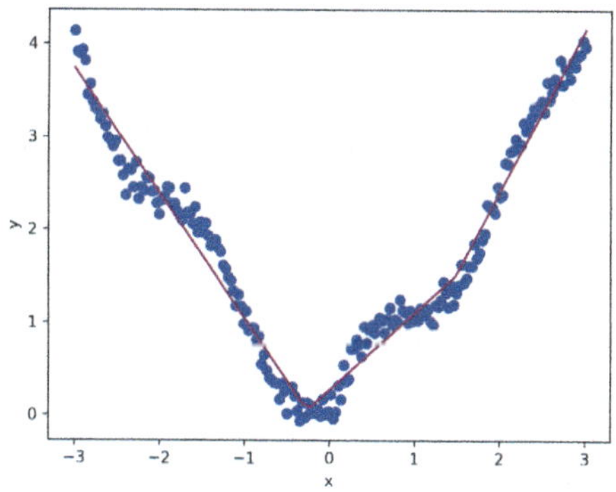

We conclude that our model is able to fit pretty complex patterns through combining "angles" in a smart way. We can think of our model as a smart arrangement of small pieces each piece represented by:

$$y = max\ (\omega * x + b, 0)$$

Each piece learns only a portion of the data it can fit well. Given each small piece handles its part – we get a strong overall model. It's like different departments in a company working together. Each specializes in one part, and together they create a well-functioning whole!

Great, we have already created a pretty good ML algorithm that can fit a complex non-linear pattern. We did so by defining an equation that depends on some parameters and learning them via gradient descent.

However, there's a problem: each angle (max function) can only output positive numbers or zero. What if our target is negative? We can't get a negative number by adding positive numbers together.

Right, so let's improve our model by allowing each piece to be scaled by a number. We've seen that model complexity depends on the number of pieces, but the principle works the same for any number. For illustration, let's stick with our two-angle model:

$$y_1 = max(\omega_1 * x + b_1, 0)$$

$$y_2 = max(\omega_2 * x + b_2, 0)$$

$$y = y_1 + y_2$$

Since both y_1 and y_2 are non-negative, y cannot be negative – this is a strong limitation. To fix this, we introduce two additional parameters (ω_3 and ω_4) that scale y_1 and y_2:

$$y = \omega_3 * y_1 + \omega_4 * y_2$$

Substituting back, our final model becomes:

$$y = \omega_3 * max(\omega_1 * x + b_1, 0) + \omega_4 * max(\omega_2 * x + b_2, 0)$$

Now ω_3 and ω_4 can be positive or negative, giving us two key benefits:

1. Flexibility for negative predictions – negative weights allow the model to output negative values
2. Weighted importance – the model can emphasize one angle over another for a better fit

As before, we use gradient descent with MSE to learn optimal parameters. Once trained, we have a very flexible model that can fit complex non-linear patterns.

But wait! This looks familiar. If we break down the final step of our model:

$$y = \omega_3 * input_1 + \omega_4 * input_2$$

This is literally linear regression without a bias term! Previously in linear regression, we assigned a weight to each feature. Now we assign a weight to each piece. Hence, we can think of each piece as a transformed feature!

Recall why we needed a bias term in linear regression – it's the value the model outputs when all features are zero, acting as a baseline. Let's add that baseline here for even more flexibility:

$$y_1 = max(\omega_1 * x + b_1, 0)$$

$$y_2 = max(\omega_2 * x + b_2, 0)$$

$$y = \omega_3 * y_1 + \omega_4 * y_2 + b_3$$

Let's map equations to the respective box they represent:

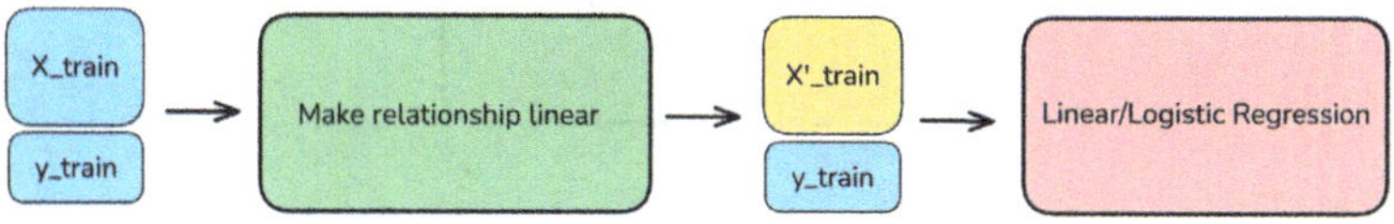

Our input is x, and we model it with:

$$y_1 = max\ (\omega_1 * x + b_1, 0)$$

$$y_2 = max\ (\omega_2 * x + b_2, 0)$$

Each piece learns a non-linear relationship and transforms it to be approximately linear. This is the green box – the transformation layer:

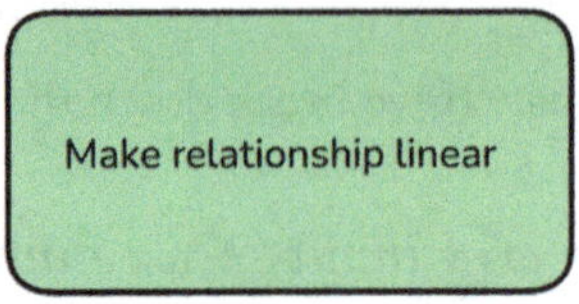

The outputs y_1 and y_2 become our new features – transformed to have an approximately linear relationship with the target. Represented by:

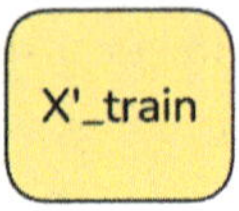

Our final model treats each transformed feature as input:

$$y = \omega_3 * y_1 + \omega_4 * y_2 + b_3$$

This is the red box – the regression layer:

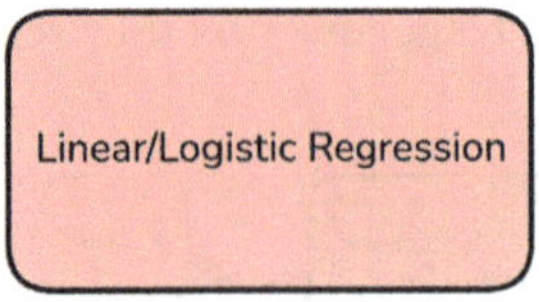

Gradient descent with MSE is applied to the complete equation:

$$y = \omega_3 * max(\omega_1 * x + b_1, 0) + \omega_4 * max(\omega_2 * x + b_2, 0) + b_3$$

The entire model trains together. On each iteration, gradient descent updates all weights $(\omega_1, \omega_2, \omega_3, \omega_4)$ and biases (b_1, b_2, b_3) simultaneously to minimize the objective.

Recap: A neural network is a collection of pieces, each learning a small non-linear pattern. When combined and scaled, these pieces can fit very complex patterns.

> Note: This example uses two pieces (y_1 and y_2), but the principle works for any number. More pieces result in more complex patterns.

Here's the same dataset fit with 2, 20, and 100 pieces:

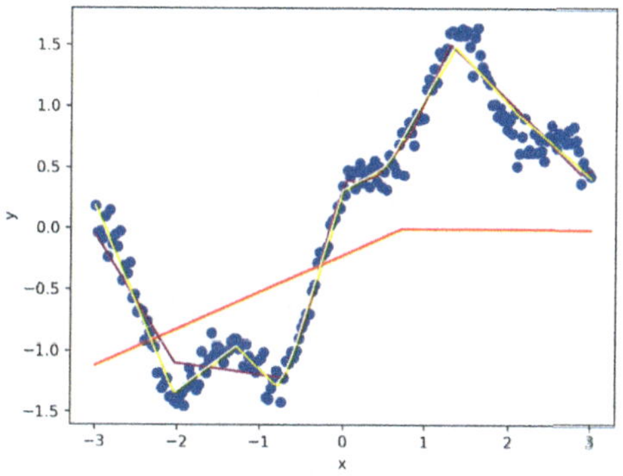

The red line is the 2-piece model, purple is 20 pieces, and yellow is 100 pieces. With many pieces, the model captures unusual patterns very well. However, more isn't always better – with noisy datasets, too many pieces can cause overfitting. We'll explore this more as we go.

So far, we've explored continuous targets, but the extension to binary classification is straightforward. Let's return to our two-piece example:

$$y_1 = max\ (\omega_1 * x + b_1, 0)$$

$$y_2 = max\ (\omega_2 * x + b_2, 0)$$

$$y_{raw} = \omega_3 * y_1 + \omega_4 * y_2 + b_3$$

Or all in a single equation:

$$y_{raw} = \omega_3 * max(\omega_1 * x + b_1, 0) + \omega_4 * max(\omega_2 * x + b_2, 0) + b_3$$

We make the same two changes as going from linear to logistic regression: apply sigmoid to the output and use log-loss as the objective.

The final form for binary classification:

$$y_1 = max\ (\omega_1 * x + b_1, 0)$$

$$y_2 = max\ (\omega_2 * x + b_2, 0)$$

$$y_{raw} = \omega_3 * y_1 + \omega_4 * y_2 + b_3$$

$$y_{pred} = \frac{1}{1 + e^{-y_{raw}}}$$

Recap: So far, we have gradually developed a model that combines arbitrary number of pieces to fit very complex relationships for both regression and binary classification problems. To train it, we use gradient descent with an objective that depends on the problem type (MSE for regression, log-loss for binary classification). Essentially, it's the same process as linear or logistic regression – just a different equation for making predictions!

Let's visualize our model conceptually:

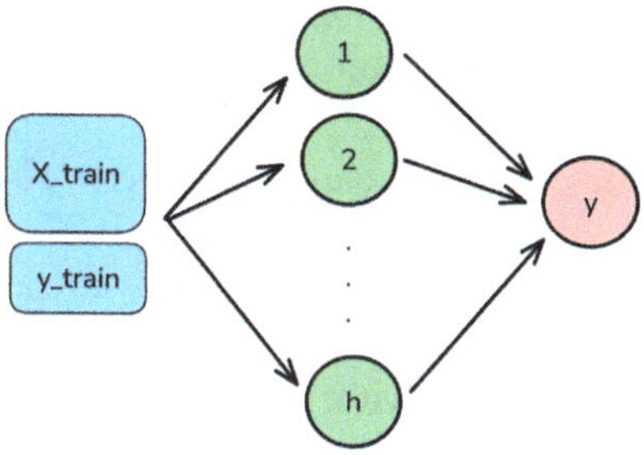

Each green circle represents a single piece, formally defined as:

$$y_1 = max\ (\omega_1 * x + b_1, 0)$$

$$y_2 = max\ (\omega_2 * x + b_2, 0)$$

$$\vdots$$

$$y_h = max\ (\omega_h * x + b_h, 0)$$

The red circle represents the final linear equation:

$$y_{raw} = \omega_{h+1} * y_1 + \omega_{h+2} * y_2 + \cdots + \omega_{h+h} * y_h + b_{h+1}$$

As before, the raw output is our prediction for regression. For binary classification, we apply sigmoid at the end to get a probability.

For regression:

$$y_{pred} = y_{raw}$$

For binary classification:

$$y_{pred} = \frac{1}{1 + e^{-y_{raw}}}$$

The blue boxes represent training data. Feature x defines our model, and y_{actual} is used by gradient descent.

Now that we have defined the equation, let's put it all together:

1. Initialize all parameters ($\omega_1, \ldots, \omega_{h+h}$ and $b_1, \ldots, b_{h+1}$) to be random numbers
2. For a set number of iterations:

   - Compute the prediction with:

$$y_1 = max\ (\omega_1 * x + b_1, 0)$$

$$y_2 = max\ (\omega_2 * x + b_2, 0)$$

$$\vdots$$

$$y_h = max\ (\omega_h * x + b_h, 0)$$

$$y_{raw} = \omega_{h+1} * y_1 + \omega_{h+2} * y_2 + \cdots + \omega_{h+h} * y_h + b_{h+1}$$

For regression:

$$y_{pred} = y_{raw}$$

For binary classification:

$$y_{predicted} = \frac{1}{1 + e^{-y_{raw}}}$$

- Compute the cost function value – average loss (MSE or log-loss):

$$J = \frac{1}{n} * \sum_{i=1}^{n} l(y_{pred_i}, y_{actual_i})$$

- Compute gradient of the cost – slope of the tangent line with respect to every parameter:

$$\left(\frac{dJ}{d\omega_1}, \frac{dJ}{d\omega_2}, \dots, \frac{dJ}{d\omega_{h+h}}\right)$$

$$\left(\frac{dJ}{db_1}, \frac{dJ}{db_2}, \dots, \frac{dJ}{db_h}\right)$$

Recall: Each parameter determines position of our person on the hill, and this gradient tells our person the direction and steepness so they can step toward the bottom (decrease the cost).

- Update all parameters using gradient:

$$\omega_1 = \omega_1 - \alpha * \frac{dJ}{d\omega_1}$$

$$\omega_2 = \omega_2 - \alpha * \frac{dJ}{d\omega_2}$$

$$\vdots$$

$$\omega_{h+h} = \omega_{h+h} - \alpha * \frac{dJ}{d\omega_{h+h}}$$

$$b_1 = b_2 - \alpha * \frac{dJ}{db_1}$$

$$b_2 = b_2 - \alpha * \frac{dJ}{db_2}$$

$$\vdots$$

$$b_{h+1} = b_{h+1} - \alpha * \frac{dJ}{db_{h+1}}$$

> Note: We have $h + 1$ biases (h for green circles plus one for the final model) and $2 * h$ weights (h to compute each green circle, plus h more in the final model to weight each circle).

That's it! Our training is done. Now we have a model that combines small pieces that each learn a non-linear pattern in a smart way. It's time to reveal their names.

Each green circle is a neuron, here's one of them:

Every one of them has the same form. The difference is that they learn different parameters because each one focuses only on a small, distinct pattern in the data.

One or more neurons that take same inputs and their outputs go to the same place form a layer:

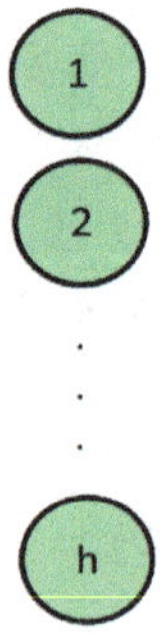

So far, we can conclude the following:

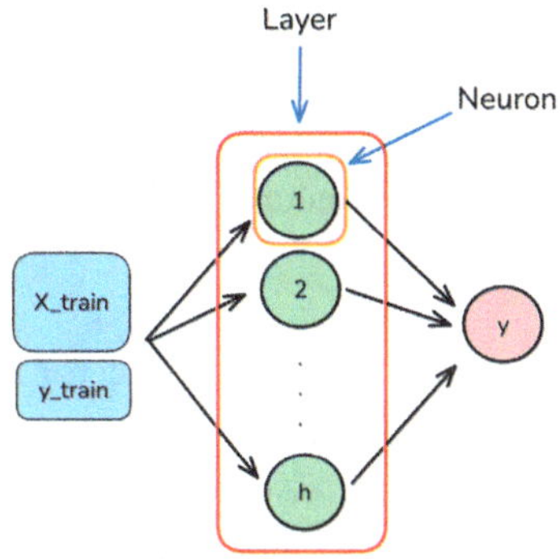

While green and red circles have different forms (the red circle doesn't go through the max transformation), the red circle still has learnable parameters, so it's also considered a neuron. Additionally, green and red neurons have different inputs, and their outputs go to different places, which means they are on different layers.

The red neuron produces the final model output, so its layer is called the output layer. We never see the outputs of the green neurons directly, so we call it a hidden layer.

Final diagram with terminology:

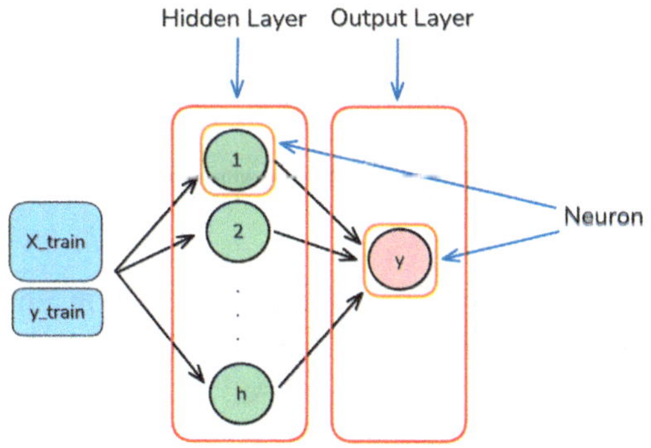

Blue arrows denote terminology (differentiating from black arrows showing data flow). The red rectangle represents a layer, and orange squares highlight example neurons.

Conclude: Each circle is a neuron, one or more neurons with the same inputs form a layer. The whole model is a neural network – a network that connects individual neurons.

So far, we've used datasets with only 1 feature (vector x) because our examples relied on plots. Fortunately, everything extends to any number of features represented by matrix X. All neurons on hidden layers remain the same – this change only slightly affects their general form.

Since every feature (column) needs its own weight, instead of a single weight we have a vector of weights matching the number of features inside each neuron.

With this in mind, we expand the model to datasets with arbitrary number of features:

$$y_1 = max\,(X \cdot \omega_1 + b_1, 0)$$

$$y_2 = max\,(X \cdot \omega_2 + b_2, 0)$$

$$\vdots$$

$$y_h = max\,(X \cdot \omega_h + b_h, 0)$$

$$y_{raw} = \omega_{h+1} * y_1 + \omega_{h+2} * y_2 + \cdots + \omega_{h+h} * y_h + b_{h+1}$$

As before, for regression, we leave the raw prediction untouched and for binary classification it gets transformed by sigmoid:

$$y_{pred} = \frac{1}{1 + e^{-y_{raw}}}$$

Instead of multiplication, we simply have a dot product between the feature matrix and vector of weights inside each neuron.

Let's see how this model fits non-linear binary classification dataset with two features:

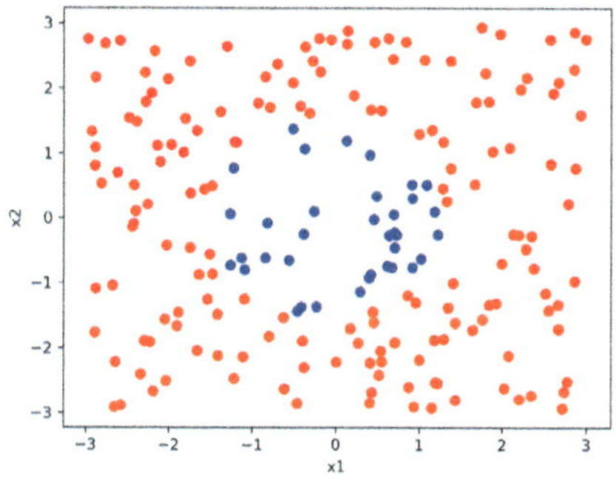

> Note: The color determines class of an observation. Logistic regression could never fit this non-linear pattern – we can't even plot a meaningful decision boundary.

Here's what our 20-piece model can do:

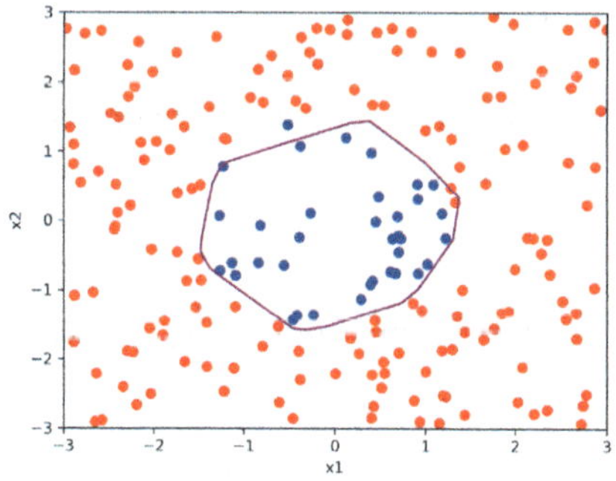

It does an excellent job separating two classes!

Great – now we can fit a neural network with an arbitrary number of neurons to a dataset with any number features to solve regression and binary classification problems.

We've discovered that all green neurons have identical form, and we can add as many as we want (represented by h). More neurons means more "angles", which translates to learning more complex patterns. But is this sophisticated enough?

For some problems with very complicated patterns and lots of data with many features (text, images, etc.), one hidden layer isn't complex enough. To learn even more complicated patterns, we can add another hidden layer:

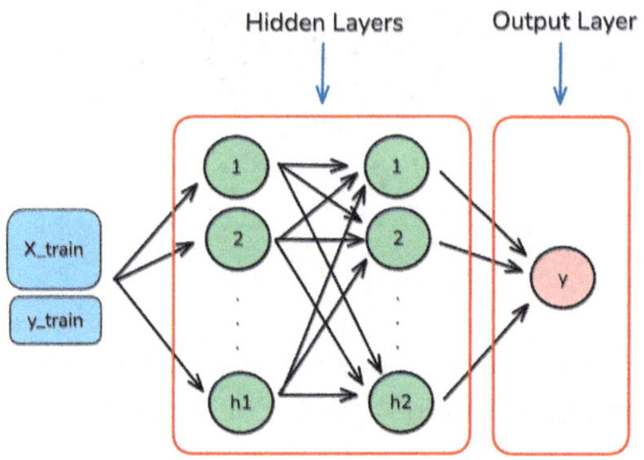

Now we have two hidden layers of arbitrary sizes (h_1 and h_2) plus the output layer. Every neuron on the second hidden layer takes outputs from all neurons of the first layer as inputs.

In practice, if the first hidden layer has h_1 neurons, every neuron on the second hidden layer takes h_1 inputs and treats them as features. Layer 3 would take h_2 inputs, and so on.

We can extend our neural network even further – we can have as many hidden layers as we like (say k layers). Here's the general form:

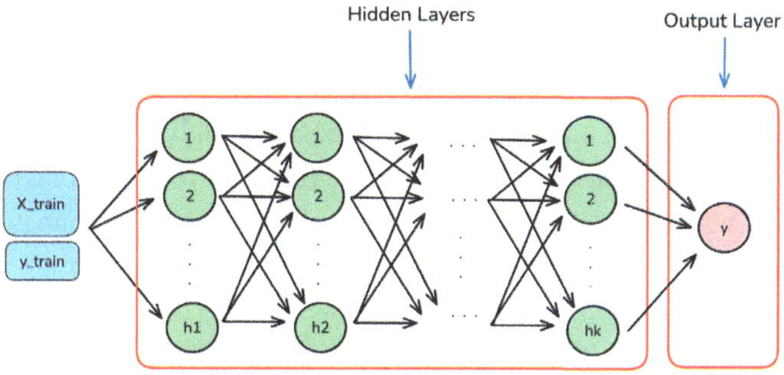

This sums up our initial intuition about boxes:

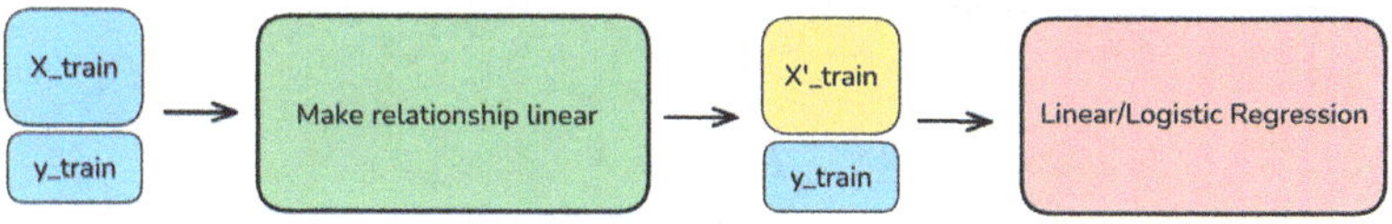

Hidden layers learn complicated, non-linear patterns. Results from the last hidden layer are treated as features by the output layer, which is a simple linear model.

Let's think about what kind of neurons we have seen so far and see if we can observe a common pattern. For this purpose, will use general form of X as what neuron treats as features, ω as a vector of weights and b as the bias term.

Neuron on a hidden layer:

$$max\ (X \cdot \omega + b, 0)$$

Neuron on the output layer for regression:

$$X \bullet \omega + b$$

Neuron on the output layer for binary classification:

$$\frac{1}{1 + e^{-(X \cdot \omega + b)}}$$

Note all of them feature equation of general linear model $X \bullet \omega + b$. We can generalize a neuron as a linear model that goes through some transformation. In this case, transformation is simply some function that is applied on top of the original linear model. Let's formalize and learn names of transformations we apply to each kind of neuron we have learned.

For a hidden layer the transformation is called ReLU and can be expressed as:

$$f(x) = max\ (x, 0)$$

The transformation on the output layer for regression:

$$f(x) = x$$

This is a simple linear function, which doesn't change the input at all.

The transformation on the output layer for binary classification:

$$f(x) = \frac{1}{1 + e^{-(x)}}$$

This is sigmoid function that transforms raw model output into a probability.

With this in mind, we can stop differentiating neurons by color at all and slightly change our perspective. From now on we know that all neurons are absolutely the same, they just get transformed by different functions. If we represent any transformation by a purple rectangle, we can visualize arbitrary neural network as follows:

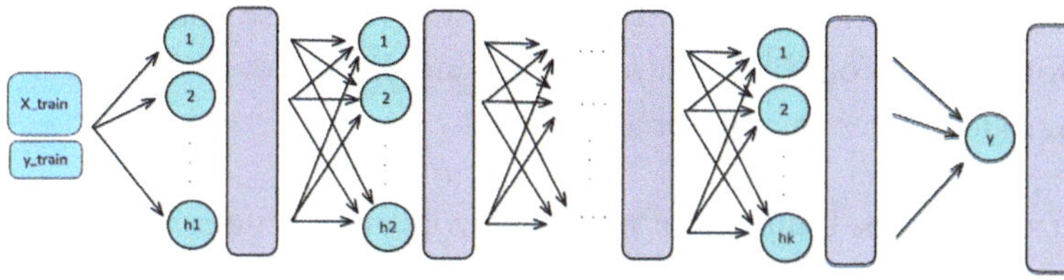

Say we denote ReLU transformation by yellow colour, linear transformation (same as no transformation) by white colour and sigmoid transformation by pink colour. We can represent a neural network for different problem types as follows:

For regression:

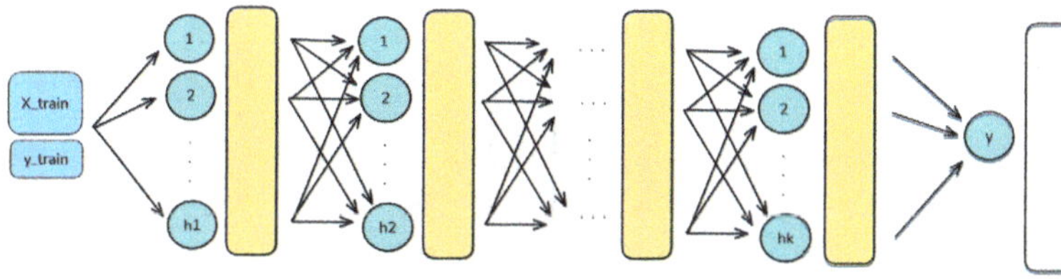

For binary classification:

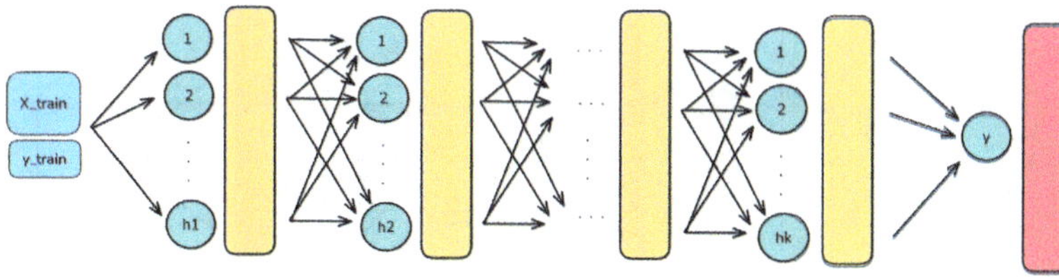

Pretty simple, each neuron is a linear model – they're all the same. Since every neuron is a like, every layer is also the same – the only differences the number of neurons and the transformation a layer of neurons goes through.

Let's recall, what was so special about ReLU represented by the yellow box? Well, it allowed linear model to fit non-linear patterns, namely "angles". That's it – there's nothing else. Therefore, we can use other non-linear transformation in our hidden layers. For example, we could also use sigmoid on any hidden layer we want or all of them!

Let's explore some examples of neural network architectures we could use to solve one problem.

For regression:

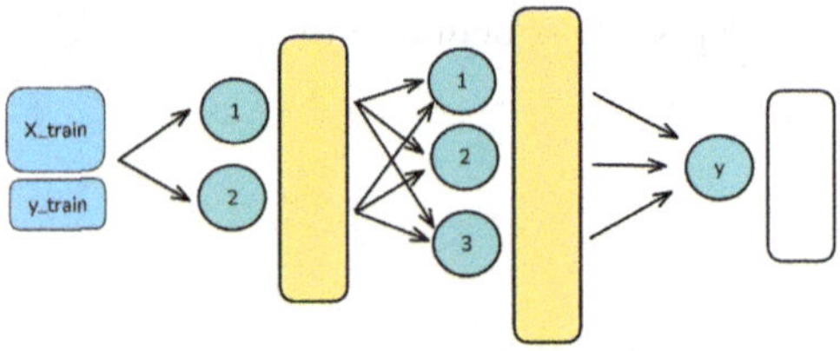

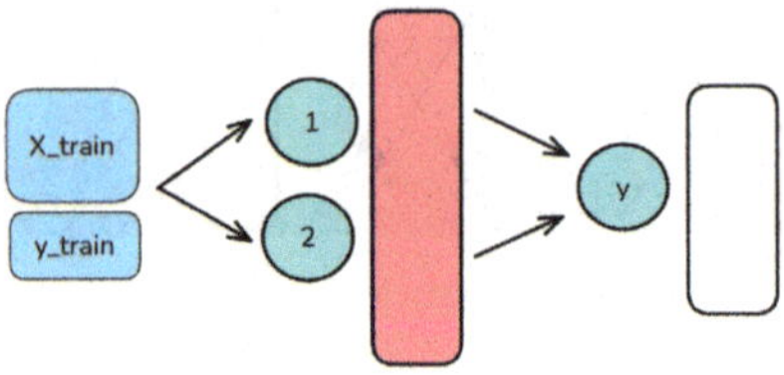

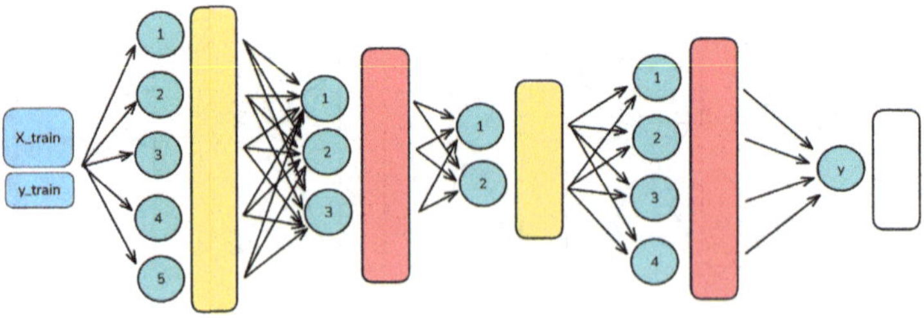

As you can observe – the only limitation for regression is that the final transformation is linear (same as no transformation at all). The number of hidden layers and the number of neurons on those layers as well as the choice of non-linear transformation after each hidden layer is completely up to us!

If we replace the white box with the pink one – all architectures above will be suitable for a binary classification task.

So far we have treated every neuron as a separate piece. But since all neurons on the same layer go through identical transformation – it would make sense to treat each layer of neurons as a single unit.

Recall every neuron is represented by a simple linear model:

$$X \cdot \omega + b$$

Where X is a matrix of either original or transformed features, ω vector of weights and b a single number that acts as a baseline. Then before applying a transformation, we can represent output of a single layer with h neurons as:

$$[X \cdot \omega_1 + b_1, X \cdot \omega_2 + b_2, \dots, X \cdot \omega_h + b_h]$$

This is just writing out each neuron's output one by one.

We could get exact same form if we stuck all weight vectors into matrix:

$$W = \begin{bmatrix} \vdots & \vdots & \vdots & \vdots \\ \omega_1 & \omega_2 & \cdots & \omega_h \\ \vdots & \vdots & \vdots & \vdots \end{bmatrix}$$

All biases into a single vector:

$$b = \begin{bmatrix} b_1 \\ b_2 \\ \vdots \\ b_h \end{bmatrix}$$

Then we can compute output of the whole layer before transformation in a single operation:

$$X \cdot W + b$$

This compact form is mathematically identical to computing each neuron's output separately, but far more convenient. After this linear step, we then apply a transformation (ReLU, sigmoid, linear, etc.) elementwise to obtain the final output of the layer.

Now let's put general form of a neural network along with formulas visually:

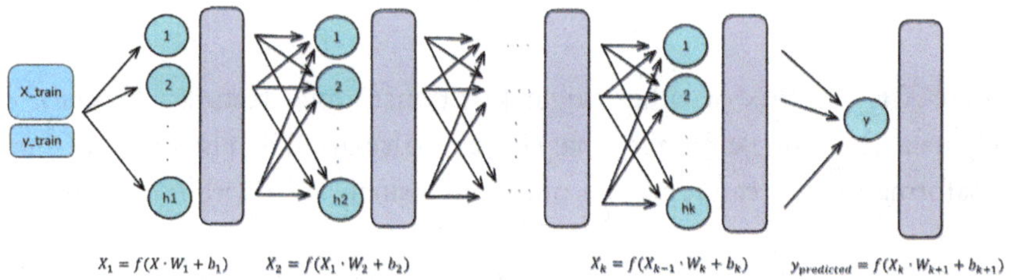

Here $f(x)$ represents purple box, which is any transformation we put layer through. As you can observe, output of every previous layer is treated as transformed matrix of features by the next layer until the prediction is made on the output layer. We can use this general framework to solve a regression or binary classification problem with Neural network of any size and form.

A binary classification example:

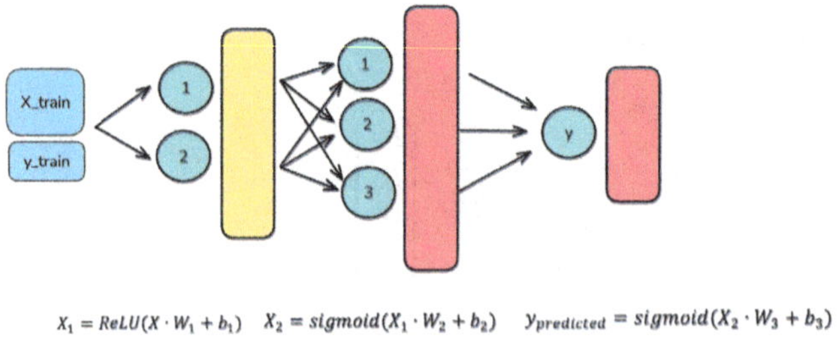

A regression example:

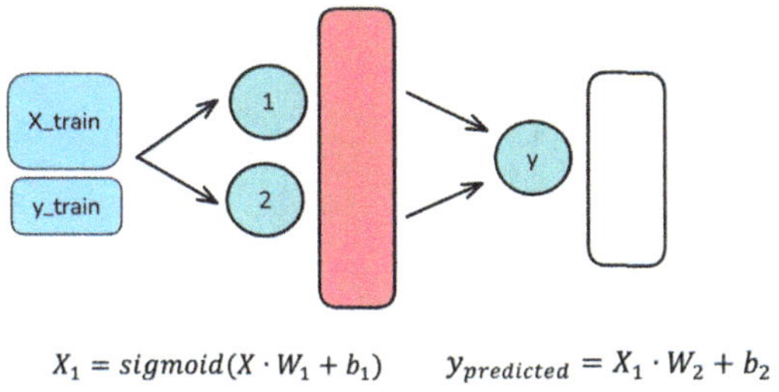

Perfect, we know how a neural network makes a prediction by putting features through a number of transformations for the linear model on the output layer to produce the final prediction. We can think of this as pulling original data forward through the network.

The last piece we need to formalize is how the neural network learns optimal parameters, that is $W_1, W_2, \dots, W_{k+1}$ and $b_1, b_2, \dots, b_{k+1}$. Well, we know it uses gradient descent, which means that first all parameters are initialized randomly. Then on each iteration the neural network passes data through each layer one by one starting from the first hidden layer and ending with the output layer to make the prediction:

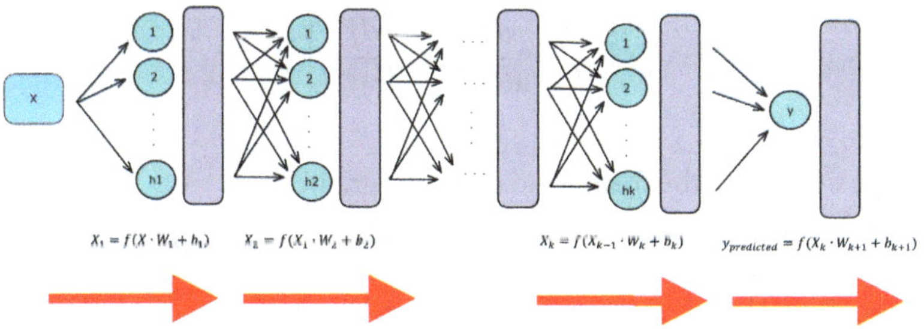

Note: y_{pred} is short for $y_{predicted}$.

Once the prediction is made, the next step is to compute our objective – the cost function to measure how close y_{pred} is to y_{actual} on average:

$$J = \frac{1}{n} * \sum_{i=1}^{n} l(y_{pred_i}, y_{actual_i})$$

Where loss depends on the problem type.

For regression:

$$l = \left(y_{pred_i} - y_{actual_i}\right)^2$$

For binary classification:

$$l = -\left[y_{actual_i} * log\left(y_{pred_i}\right) + \left(1 - y_{actual_i}\right) * log\left(1 - y_{pred_i}\right)\right]$$

Next, we compute gradient of the cost:

$$\left[\frac{dJ}{dW_1}, \frac{dJ}{dW_2}, \ldots, \frac{dJ}{dW_{k+1}}\right]$$

$$\left[\frac{dJ}{db_1}, \frac{dJ}{db_2}, \ldots, \frac{dJ}{db_{k+1}}\right]$$

Now we will derive the formula to compute gradient.

Let's think about our objective J, what parameters does it take in? Well, it measures how close the prediction is to actual target on average, so it takes in vectors y_{pred} and y_{actual}. We can write it as:

$$J(y_{pred}, y_{actual})$$

Great but what's y_{pred}? It's whatever comes out of the transformed output layer:

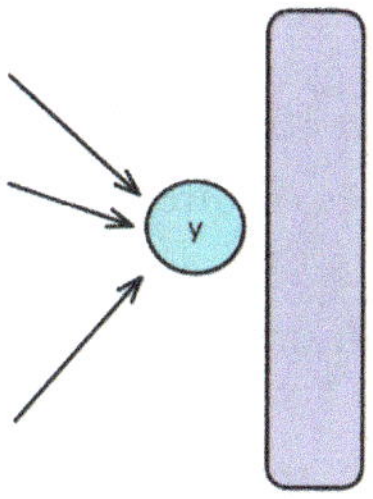

Therefore, we conclude the following sequence of events to compute J so far:

1. Weights W_{k+1} and bias b_{k+1} of the last layer are used to produce result of the last layer:

$$layer_{k+1} = X_k \cdot W_{k+1} + b_{k+1}$$

2. Output of the last layer gets transformed by a function to become the final prediction:

$$transformation_{k+1} = f(layer_{k+1})$$

   Where f is linear or sigmoid function depending on the problem type.

3. Output of the final transformation is then used to compute our objective – the cost.

$$J(transformation_{k+1}, y_{actual})$$

> Note: $transformation_{k+1}$ is equivalent to y_{pred}.

Now we need to measure how W_{k+1} and b_{k+1} affect J. Well, they don't affect it directly. First, parameters affect output of the last layer then output of that layer affects output of the final transformation which directly affects the objective.

This can be thought of as a domino effect represented by:

$$W_{k+1}, b_{k+1} \rightarrow layer_{k+1} \rightarrow transformation_{k+1} \rightarrow J$$

Therefore, we can't directly get to know how W_{k+1} and b_{k+1} affect J. We need to go through all the stages of direct effects in between.

1. How parameters affect output of the last layer:

$$\frac{d(layer_{k+1})}{dW_{k+1}}$$

$$\frac{d(layer_{k+1})}{db_{k+1}}$$

2. How output of that layer affects output of the final transformation:

$$\frac{d(transformation_{k+1})}{d(layer_{k+1})}$$

3. How output of the transformation affects the objective:

$$\frac{dJ}{d(transformation_{k+1})}$$

Fortunately, there's a way to compute any indirect effect by leveraging all direct effects in between them. Let's see how it can be done.

1. State the desired indirect effect we want to compute:

$$\frac{dJ}{dW_{k+1}}$$

$$\frac{dJ}{db_{k+1}}$$

2. Lay out every direct effect or "step" in between:

$$W_{k+1}, b_{k+1} \rightarrow layer_{k+1} \rightarrow transformation_{k+1} \rightarrow J$$

You can think of this as domino. We want to know how the first domino piece will affect the fourth:

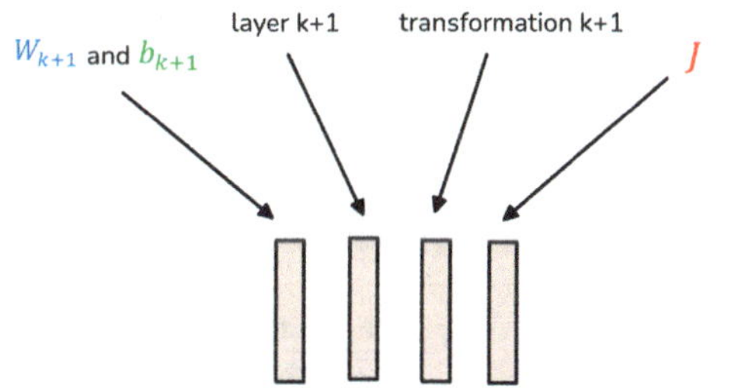

The actual effects that we observe can be represented as:

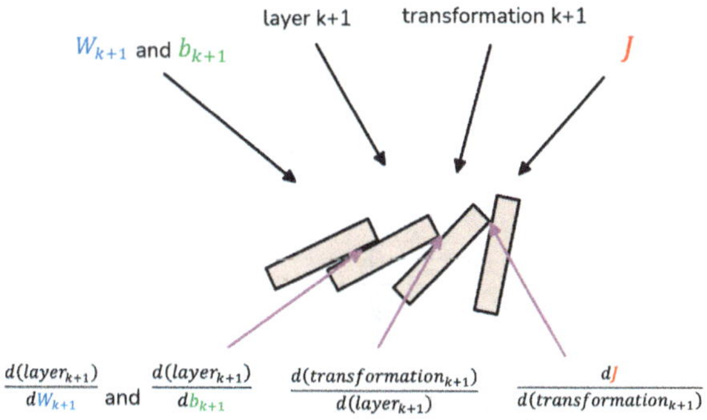

As we said, parameters affect output of the last layer (first interaction), output of the layer affects output of the transformation, which directly affects the objective.

3. Multiply each direct effect in between to get the desired indirect effect:

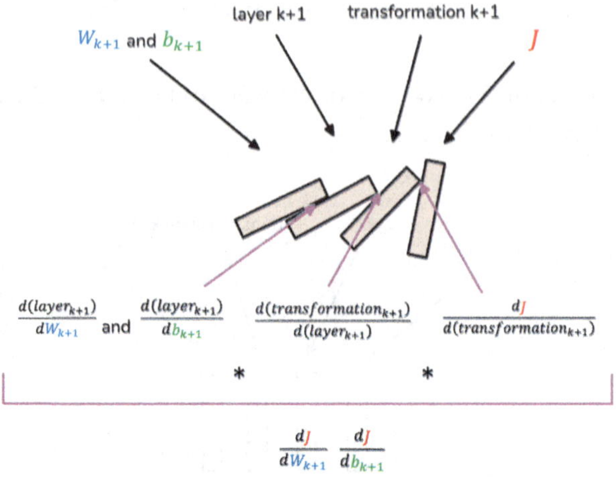

This is just a rule – in order to get the indirect effect, we have to multiply all direct effects that go in between. This means that to understand how the first domino affects the fourth, we need to multiply effect of the first on second, second on third and third on fourth.

For weights:

$$\frac{dJ}{dW_{k+1}} =$$

$$\frac{d(layer_{k+1})}{dW_{k+1}} * \frac{d(transformation_{k+1})}{d(layer_{k+1})} * \frac{dJ}{d(transformation_{k+1})}$$

For biases:

$$\frac{dJ}{db_{k+1}} =$$

$$\frac{d(layer_{k+1})}{db_{k+1}} * \frac{d(transformation_{k+1})}{d(layer_{k+1})} * \frac{dJ}{d(transformation_{k+1})}$$

Note: This domino effect can be used to compute any indirect effect and is also known as the chain rule. Weights and biases represent a single domino piece because they affect the same layer together. Therefore, the gradient computation structure is identical for both.

We've just learned how to compute gradients with respect to parameters on the output layer, which allows us to update them using gradient descent:

$$W_{k+1} = W_{k+1} - \alpha * \frac{dJ}{dW_{k+1}}$$

$$b_{k+1} = b_{k+1} - \alpha * \frac{dJ}{db_{k+1}}$$

Great – we've updated the output layer parameters. But we need to optimize all parameters in the network. So, we move backward to update W_k and b_k from the previous layer. Again, this is done by measuring how changes in these parameters affect the objective.

As we go further from the final prediction, the number of direct affects in between grows:

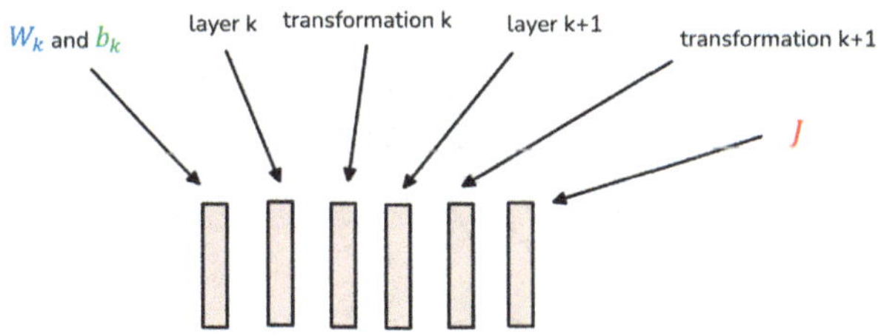

Parameters W_k and b_k affect output of the layer k, which affects output of the transformation k. Output of the transformation k can also be thought of as transformed features matrix X_k.

X_k then affects output of the layer $k + 1$ by definition:

$$X_k \cdot W_{k+1} + b_{k+1}$$

Then output of the layer $k + 1$ affects output of the final transformation $k + 1$, which directly affects the objective J.

We can represent immediate affects one by one as:

1. Parameters W_k and b_k affect output of the layer k
2. Output of the layer k affects output of the transformation k
3. Output of the transformation k can also be thought of as transformed feature matrix X_k. According to the formula for layer $k + 1$:

$$X_k \cdot W_{k+1} + b_{k+1}$$

   X_k affects output of the layer $k + 1$.

4. Output of the layer $k + 1$ affects output of the final transformation $k + 1$, which directly affects the objective J

We can represent the immediate affects one by one as:

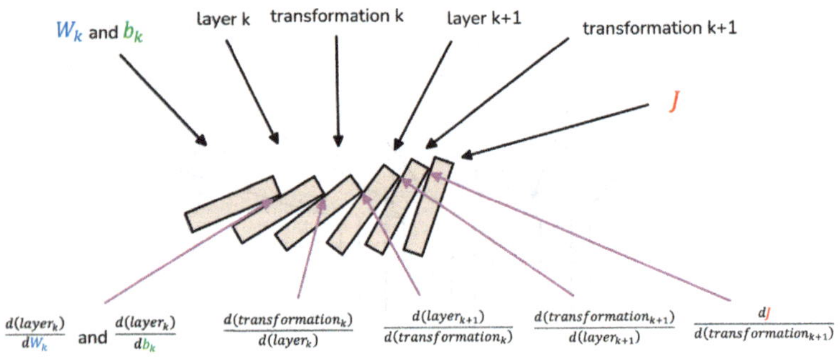

As before, it's just one domino at a time that affects the next domino. Looking at this already long sequence, we can only imagine how big it gets as the number of layers grows!

Fortunately, while computing gradient for the parameters on the output layer we already computed two things from this sequence (go back and check for yourself to make sure):

$$\frac{d(transformation_{k+1})}{d(layer_{k+1})}$$

And

$$\frac{dJ}{d(transformation_{k+1})}$$

Since we already computed all direct effects in between $layer_{k+1}$ and J, we can compute the indirect effect of $layer_{k+1}$ on J using the domino rule that we learned:

$$\frac{dJ}{d(layer_{k+1})} = \frac{d(transformation_{k+1})}{d(layer_{k+1})} * \frac{dJ}{d(transformation_{k+1})}$$

This means that for further computation we no longer care how $layer_{k+1}$ affects $transformation_{k+1}$ or how $transformation_{k+1}$ affects J. We've already computed the indirect effect of $layer_{k+1}$ on J by combining these two gradients into $\frac{dJ}{d(layer_{k+1})}$.

Therefore, we can now glue these domino pieces and treat them as one:

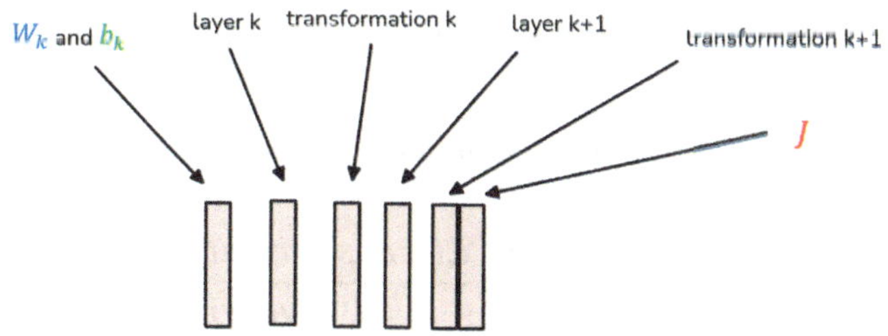

Now that we want to compute every immediate effect, we only need to consider the following affects:

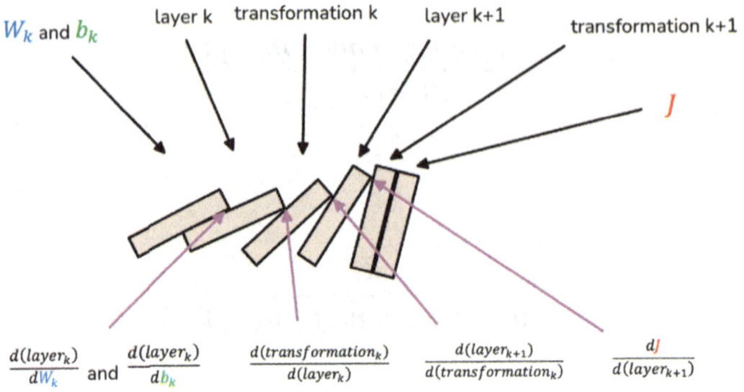

This allows us to compute gradient with respect to parameters on layer k:

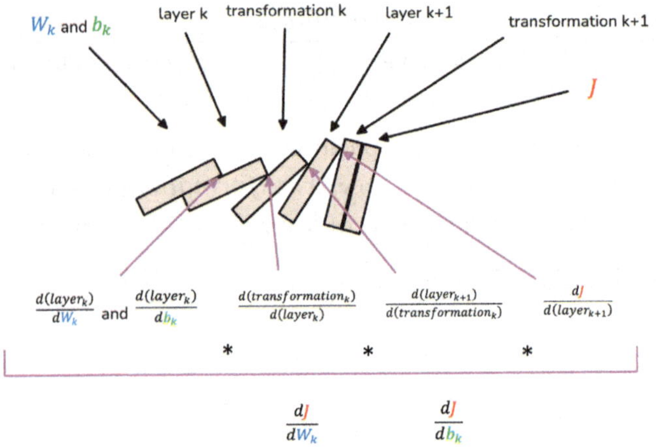

Which translates to the following computation for weights:

$$\frac{dJ}{dW_k} = \frac{d(layer_k)}{dW_k} * \frac{d(transformation_k)}{d(layer_k)} *$$

$$\frac{d(layer_{k+1})}{d(transformation_k)} * \frac{dJ}{d(layer_{k+1})}$$

And biases:

$$\frac{dJ}{db_k} = \frac{d(layer_k)}{db_k} * \frac{d(transformation_k)}{d(layer_k)} *$$

$$\frac{d(layer_{k+1})}{d(transformation_k)} * \frac{dJ}{d(layer_{k+1})}$$

> Note: This may look scary, but we simply multiply all direct effects of dominos on the picture to get the desired indirect effect.

With this computation in-place, we can update parameters on layer k:

$$W_k = W_k - \alpha * \frac{dJ}{dW_k}$$

$$b_k = b_k - \alpha * \frac{dJ}{db_k}$$

Next, we go further down the network to update parameters on the layer one before it, that is W_{k-1} and b_{k-1}. Let's visualize all the dominos:

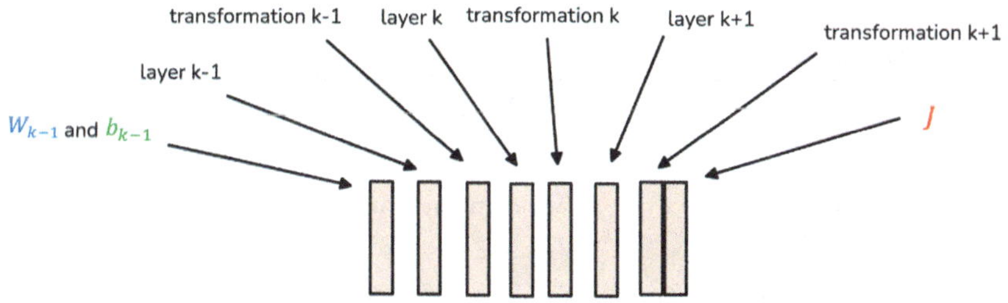

Effects are as follows:

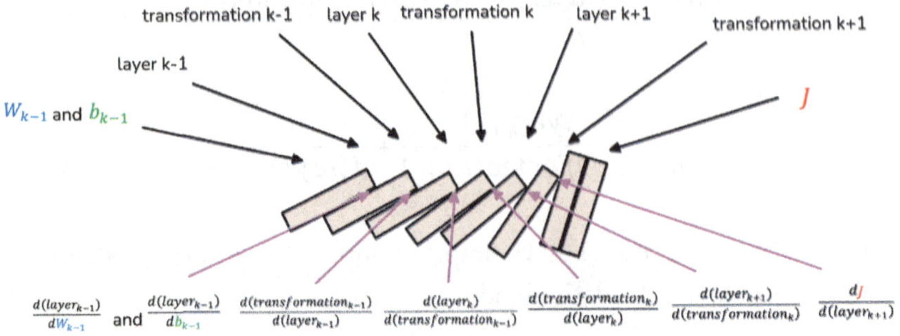

This looks like a lot of domino pieces and effects!

But wait! We already computed the following affects in the previous steps: $\frac{dJ}{d(layer_{k+1})}$, $\frac{d(layer_{k+1})}{d(transformation_k)}$ and $\frac{d(transformation_k)}{d(layer_k)}$.

This means we can use our domino rule to compute the indirect effect:

$$\frac{dJ}{d(layer_k)} =$$

$$\frac{d(transformation_k)}{d(layer_k)} * \frac{d(layer_{k+1})}{d(transformation_k)} * \frac{dJ}{d(layer_{k+1})}$$

This enables us to "glue" even more dominos at the front:

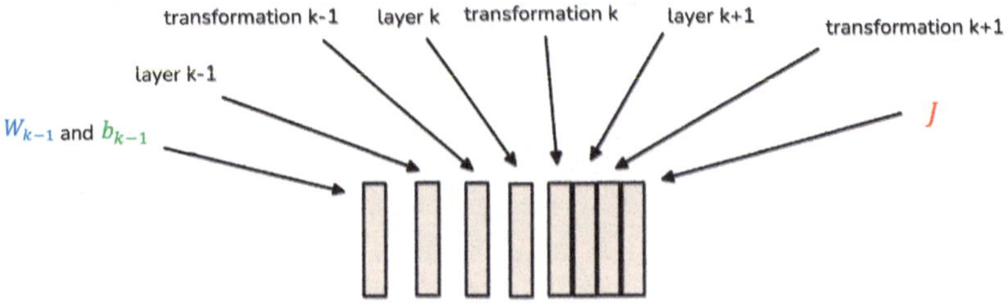

This translates to the following effects:

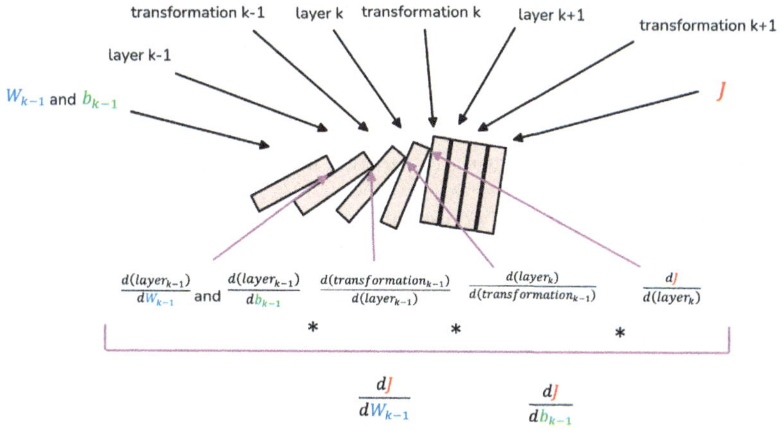

Now we can compute gradient with respect to parameters on the layer $k - 1$:

$$\frac{dJ}{dW_{k-1}} = \frac{d(layer_{k-1})}{dW_{k-1}} * \frac{d(transformation_{k-1})}{d(layer_{k-1})} * \frac{d(layer_k)}{d(transformation_{k-1})} * \frac{dJ}{d(layer_k)}$$

And

$$\frac{dJ}{db_{k-1}} = \frac{d(layer_{k-1})}{db_{k-1}} * \frac{d(transformation_{k-1})}{d(layer_{k-1})} * \frac{d(layer_k)}{d(transformation_{k-1})} * \frac{dJ}{d(layer_k)}$$

> Note: This equation has the exact same structure as the gradient with respect to W_k and b_k – the only difference is that every subscript has shifted by -1. Double-check to see for yourself!

As we move backward through the network to compute the gradient, we can spot a clear pattern: effects we have already calculated are being "glued together" at the front. If we repeat this process for all parameters, the formula structure stays exactly the same – we only need to update the subscripts to match the current layer.

Let's generalize this process for any arbitrary layer r. We need to compute $\frac{dJ}{dW_r}$ and $\frac{dJ}{db_r}$ to update W_r and b_r. To do this, we track the domino of effects step-by-step:

1. How parameters W_r and b_r affect output of the layer r?

   Recall, a layer of neurons is a simple linear model:

$$layer_r = X_{r-1} \bullet W_r + b_r$$

   Using definition of the gradient, we find how an infinitely small increase in parameters affects the layer's output to be:

$$\frac{d(layer_r)}{dW_r} = X_{r-1}$$

$$\frac{d(layer_r)}{db_r} = 1$$

2. How output of layer r affects output of transformation r?

   Next, we look at how change in the layer output affects the transformed output. Inherently, this value depends on the type of transformation in place – we focus on the most common one, which is ReLU.

   The effect is straightforward, coming from the definition $\max(x, 0)$: no effect at all if input is positive and an effect that makes the whole thing zero otherwise.

$$\frac{d(transformation_r)}{d(layer_r)}$$

The other transformations we explored are linear, which has no effect and sigmoid, whose effect is $sigmoid(x) * (1 - sigmoid(x))$ – derived from the gradient definition and simplified to this form.

3. How output of transformation r affects output of the next layer $r + 1$? Recall that the layer $r + 1$ treats output of the transformation r as its feature matrix (X_r):

$$layer_{r+1} = X_r \cdot W_{r+1} + b_{r+1}$$

Taking gradient with respect to X_r – equivalently $transformation_r$, we get:

$$\frac{d(layer_{r+1})}{d(transformation_r)} = W_{r+1}$$

4. How output of the next layer $r + 1$ affects the objective?

Finally, we need the term that connects the next layer to the final cost:

$$\frac{dJ}{d(layer_{r+1})}$$

> Note: We do not need to recompute this! This term represents the "glued domino piece" passed down to us. It was already computed during the parameter update for layer $r + 1$.

Now, we multiply three direct effects and the "glued domino" to get the total indirect effect of W_r and b_r on the objective J:

For weights:

$$\frac{dJ}{dW_r} = \frac{d(layer_r)}{dW_r} * \frac{d(transformation_r)}{d(layer_r)} *$$

$$\frac{d(layer_{r+1})}{d(transformation_r)} * \frac{dJ}{d(layer_{r+1})}$$

For biases:

$$\frac{dJ}{db_r} = \frac{d(layer_r)}{db_r} * \frac{d(transformation_r)}{d(layer_r)} *$$

$$\frac{d(layer_{r+1})}{d(transformation_r)} * \frac{dJ}{d(layer_{r+1})}$$

Once these gradients are computed, we can update the parameters for this layer:

$$W_r = W_r - \alpha * \frac{dJ}{dW_r}$$

$$b_r = b_r - \alpha * \frac{dJ}{db_r}$$

Finally, we must add our own "piece" to the glued domino, so the previous layer $r - 1$ can perform its own calculation in the same way. We compute the gradient with respect to our current layer:

$$\frac{dJ}{d(layer_r)} = \frac{d(transformation_r)}{d(layer_r)}$$

$$* \frac{d(layer_{r+1})}{d(transformation_r)} * \frac{dJ}{d(layer_{r+1})}$$

This procedure is repeated for every hidden layer in the network. Congratulations! Now that we know how to update parameters on a single layer, we effectively know how to train the whole network!

Now, let's zoom out from the math and consider how this translates to software design.

Imagine a general neural network. To manage complexity, we can think of a network as a collection of layers followed by transformations – many repeated building blocks of just two kinds:

1. Transformation – represented as a purple rectangle
2. Layer of neurons – represented as a stack of cyan circles

Let's visualize a general neural network and identify all the information we need to compute in order to update parameters on general layer r:

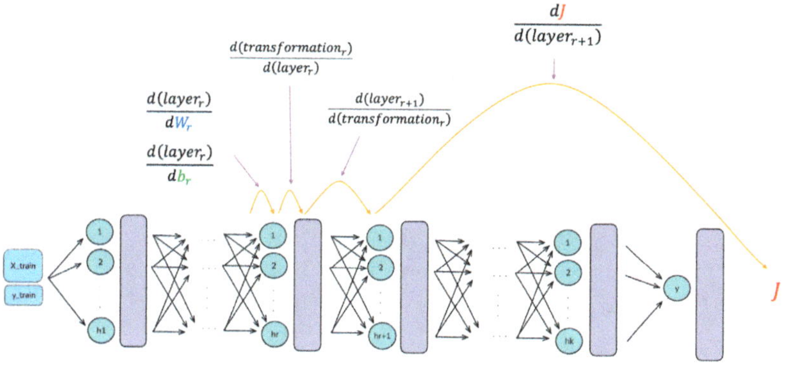

The effects are illustrated using orange arrows, where the tail of each arrow denotes the denominator (the cause) and the arrowhead denotes the numerator (the affected).

We want each building block to handle its own operations. To achieve this, we split gradient computation for an arbitrary layer r into two specific tasks.

1. The transformation block. This block handles the flow of the gradient backwards. It takes the "glued domino" from layer $r + 1$ and calculates gradient with respect to the current layer:

$$\frac{dJ}{d(layer_r)} = \frac{d(transformation_r)}{d(layer_r)} *$$

$$\frac{d(layer_{r+1})}{d(transformation_r)} * \frac{dJ}{d(layer_{r+1})}$$

We can represent three effects that are multiplied together as:

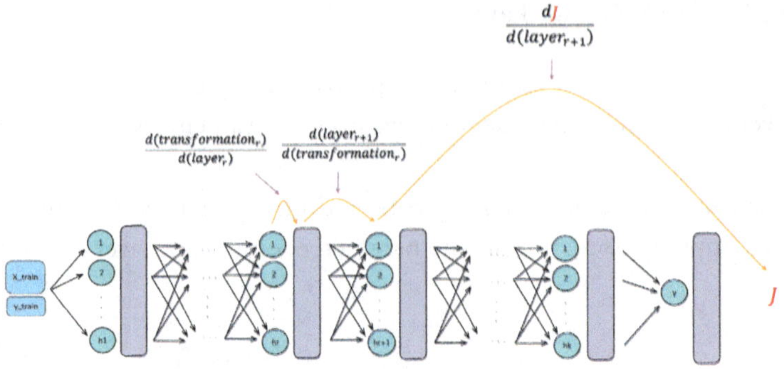

After the multiplication we get the indirect effect:

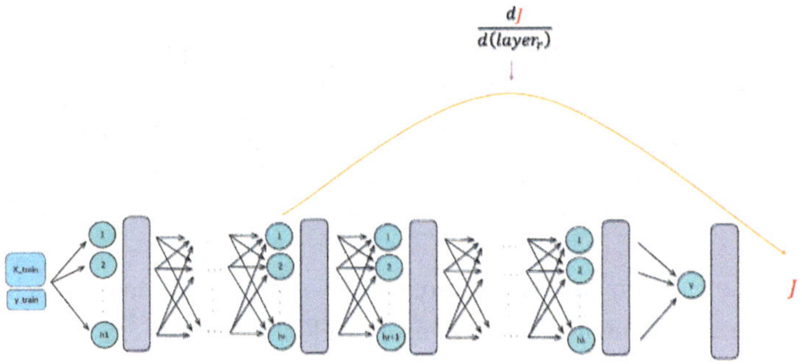

This information is then passed on to the part 2.

2. The layer block. This block handles the actual parameter updates. It takes the result from part 1 and applies the domino rule for the weights and biases:

$$\frac{dJ}{dW_r} = \frac{d(layer_r)}{dW_r} * \frac{dJ}{d(layer_r)}$$

$$\frac{dJ}{db_r} = \frac{d(layer_r)}{db_r} * \frac{dJ}{d(layer_r)}$$

We can represent two effects that are multiplied together as:

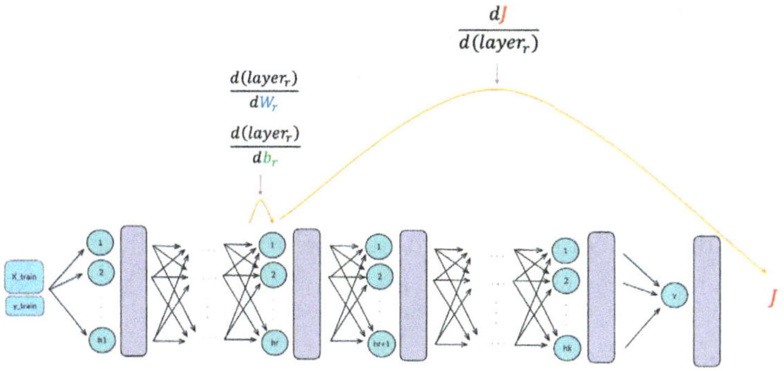

After the multiplication we get the final indirect effect of parameters on the cost:

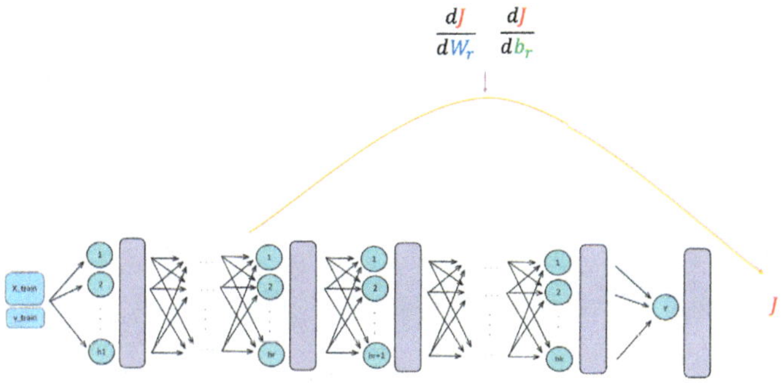

Great– now we can update parameters on the current layer r:

$$W_r = W_r - \alpha * \frac{dJ}{dW_r}$$

$$b_r = b_r - \alpha * \frac{dJ}{db_r}$$

Conclusion: We have simply broken down the complex computation of the gradient into two smaller parts. This complies with an important software design principle: each logical entity should handle its own computations.

Since we know that every layer of neurons is followed by a transformation, when we move backwards during training, we encounter the transformation first, and then the layer. You can think of it as the transformation block "gluing" its part to the domino chain and passing it safely to the layer block to finish the job – compute gradient with respect to parameters and update them.

Now that we have learned the mechanics of a single layer, let's zoom out and summarize the gradient computation from start to finish. It begins with the last layer and goes backwards – allowing us to "glue pieces" at the front.

1. The output layer $(k+1)$. First, we compute gradient with respect to parameters on the output layer. Since this is the end of the network, the "glued domino" was not yet constructed, and we directly compute gradient with respect to the final transformation, layer and parameters on it.

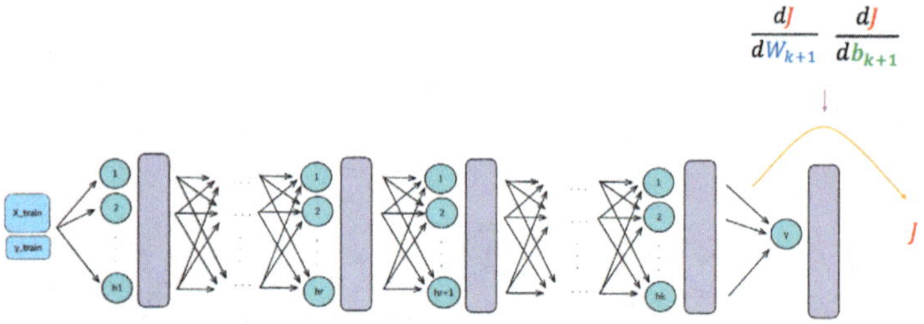

Next, we update parameters using the information we gained:

$$W_{k+1} = W_{k+1} - \alpha * \frac{dJ}{dW_{k+1}}$$

$$b_{k+1} = b_{k+1} - \alpha * \frac{dJ}{db_{k+1}}$$

2. The last hidden layer (k). Here, we leverage the information already computed in the previous step – effectively "gluing the domino pieces" together. All to compute gradient with respect to parameters on layer k.

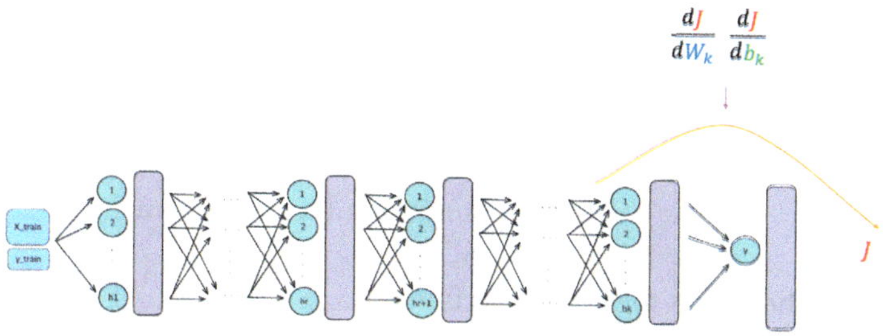

Next, we update these parameters:

$$W_k = W_k - \alpha * \frac{dJ}{dW_k}$$

$$b_k = b_k - \alpha * \frac{dJ}{db_k}$$

This process is repeated, going backwards layer by layer. At each step, we "glue" the piece we know (gradient with respect to the layer ahead) to the current calculation. The formula structure remains identical regardless of depth. Until finally we reach the first hidden layer.

3. The first hidden layer. Compute the gradient:

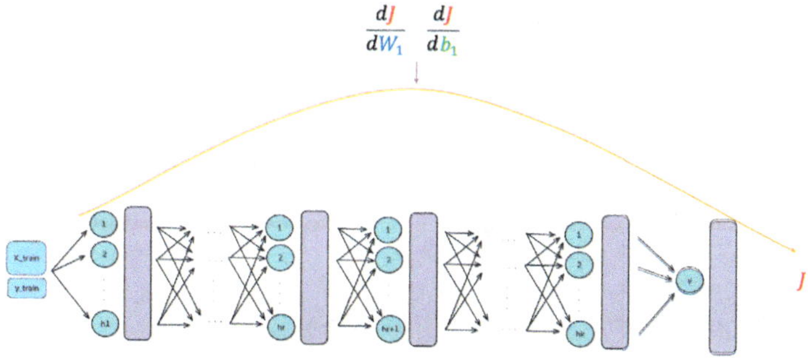

And update the final set of parameters:

$$W_1 = W_1 - \alpha * \frac{dJ}{dW_1}$$

$$b_1 = b_1 - \alpha * \frac{dJ}{db_1}$$

This concludes a single full training iteration of a neural network.

Let's put all the pieces together to define how to train a neural network from start to finish.

1. Start by initializing all parameters to random numbers

   Weights:

$$[W_1, W_2, \ldots, W_{k+1}]$$

   Biases:

$$[b_1, b_2, \ldots, b_{k+1}]$$

2. For a set number of iterations:

   - Pull the data forward through the network to compute y_{pred}:

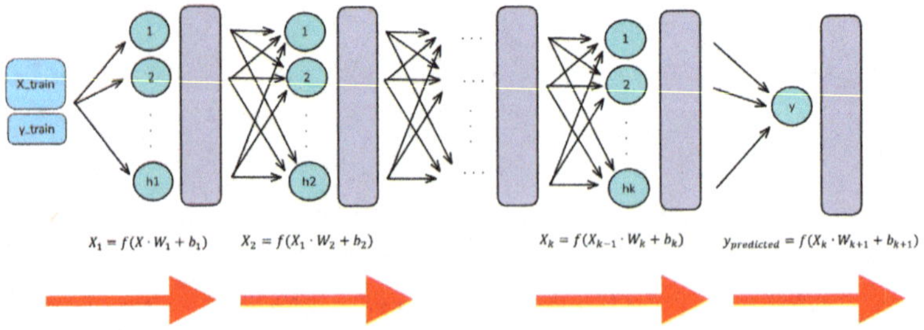

- Compute the objective J:

$$J = \frac{1}{n} * \sum_{i=1}^{n} l(y_{pred_i}, y_{actual_i})$$

For regression:

$$l = \left(y_{pred_i} - y_{actual_i}\right)^2$$

For binary classification:

$$l = -\left[y_{actual_i} * log\left(y_{pred_i}\right) + \left(1 - y_{actual_i}\right) * log\left(1 - y_{pred_i}\right)\right]$$

- Compute gradient of J with respect to parameters on each layer by going backward through the network:

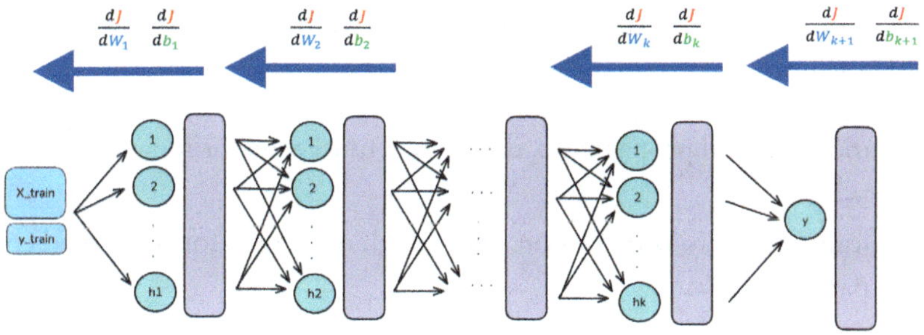

On each layer r we update parameters using the computed gradient:

$$W_k = W_k - \alpha * \frac{dJ}{dW_k}$$

$$b_k = b_k - \alpha * \frac{dJ}{db_k}$$

Once trained, making predictions is simple – pull the data forward through the network with optimal parameters:

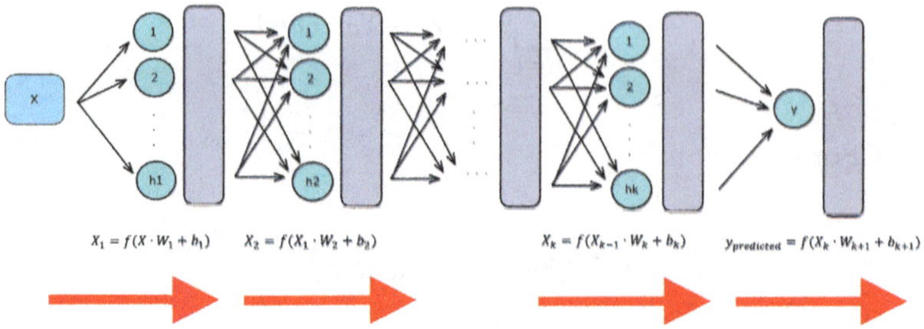

Generally, we can think of our neural network as a system with two modes:

- Forward propagation: The forward pass of the data through the network to make a prediction
- Backward propagation: The backward pass of gradients through the network to optimize the parameters

How do we code this efficiently? As before, we treat every layer and every transformation as separate building blocks.

- During forward propagation, each block must transform data to pass it forward
- During backward propagation, each block must transform the gradient to pass it backward

Therefore, every building block in our code must have both a "forward" and a "backward" method. This modular design allows us to create sequences of blocks of any kind, because each block handles its own preprocessing responsibilities internally.

Conclusion: A neural network is a stack of linear layers with non-linear transformations in between. The number of layers, and the number of neurons in each hidden layer, is completely up to us.

This makes neural networks extremely flexible. However, not everything is arbitrary. We still need to define two specific things that determine the problem type our model is solving:

- What kind of output do we want?
- How can we measure performance of the model?

Let's see how these two questions shape neural network for different problem types.

Regression:

- Predict a single continuous value. Therefore, we have 1 neuron on the output layer and no transformation (linear) after that layer.
- Measure how far the predicted value is from the actual target on average, while penalizing big errors more. Therefore, we use MSE (mean squared error) as our objective.

Binary classification:

- Predict a single probability between 0 and 1. Therefore, we have 1 neuron on the output layer, transformed by sigmoid function.
- Measure how far the predicted probability is to the actual target on average, while penalizing big errors more. Therefore, we use log-loss as our objective.

We can extend this to any problem type by answering these two questions! Let's tackle multiclass classification. Recall that for this problem, we want the model to predict the probability of an observation belonging to each class, then select the class with the highest probability.

Multiclass classification:

- Predict the probability for c different classes, ensuring they sum to 1 (100%). This requires c neurons on the output layer, transformed by a function that ensures they all sum up to 1.

A simple idea might be to divide output from each neuron by the total sum. That almost works, but layer outputs can be negative or very small, which causes problems when computing gradient. To fix this, we exponentiate each number before dividing by the sum. This ensures all probabilities are positive, the differences are amplified and the network can learn effectively.

Neural network used for multiclass classification outputs c probabilities corresponding to each class. Given output of neuron j is denoted as y_{raw_j}, probability of class j is:

$$y_{pred_j} = \frac{e^{y_{raw_j}}}{\sum_{j=1}^{c} e^{y_{raw_j}}}$$

We compute probability of each possible class and select one with the highest y_{pred_j} as our final prediction. This transformation is called Softmax.

- Measure how confident the model is about the correct target:

$$l = -log(y_{pred_{correct\ class}})$$

If the model assigns a low probability to the correct class, the loss shoots up. If it is sure about the correct class, the loss approaches zero. This loss function is called cross-entropy.

Neural network architecture for arbitrary multiclass classification problems looks as follows:

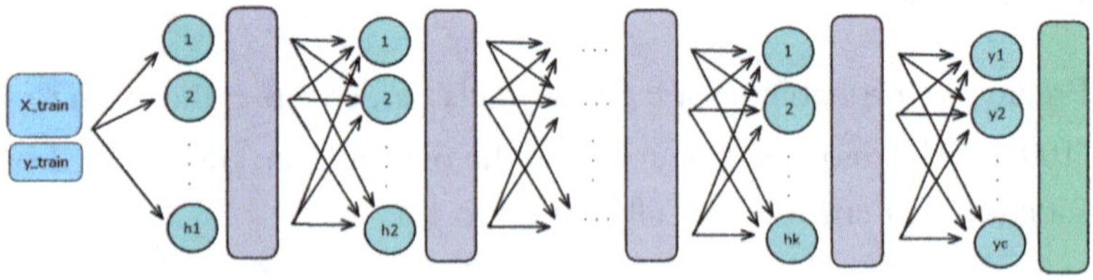

Where the mint rectangle represents Softmax transformation.

Conclusion: We can define a neural network with any number of layers and any number of neurons per layer, along with a wide choice of non-linear transformations (activation functions) to control how the model learns patterns.

What's determined by the problem type?

- The number of neurons on the output layer
- The transformation applied to the output layer
- The objective function

How does it learn?

Gradient descent computes how each parameter affects the objective, then adjusts every parameter based on that information until the model arrives at the optimal values for the parameters.

Implementation

Training a neural network is quite different from any other algorithm we have built so far. Unlike simpler algorithms, we cannot just run a single line of code. Instead, we must assemble building blocks (layers and transformations), define an objective function, and run gradient descent to find the optimal parameters. This is true for both our custom implementation and PyTorch.

Preface: All gradients in this implementation are computed using the definition introduced in the "Learning from Data (Optimization)" chapter. If you understand that, you don't need to derive every equation from scratch.

We always begin training a neural network with a conceptual blueprint. Before writing a single line of code, we draw the architecture to understand the data flow.

Let's begin with a simple neural network:

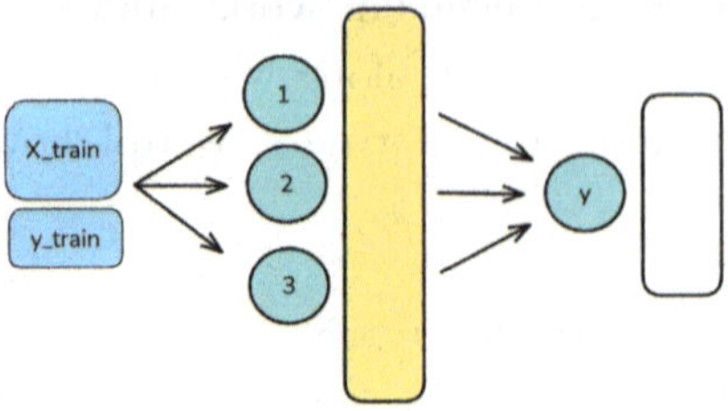

From this diagram, we can extract the essential requirements:

- Building blocks: A linear layer, followed by ReLU transformation and a final linear layer with no transformation.
- Dimensions: 3 neurons in the hidden layer, 1 neuron in the output layer
- Inputs: The first layer takes as many inputs as there are features. The output layer takes inputs from the 3 hidden neurons.
- The objective: Since the output layer has one neuron with no transformation – this a regression problem and thus we use MSE.

With this blueprint in mind, we can define the code interface we want to build. Using a library like PyTorch, the code would look nearly identical to this:

```
model = Sequential(
    Linear(num_features, 3),
    ReLU(),
    Linear(3, 1)
)

objective = MSELoss()
```

"Sequential" is what ties the entire architecture together, allowing us to think of it as a single coherent system – just as we use the term neural network rather than describing it as a mere sequence of neuron layers and transformations. The whole architecture is then defined as it is displayed in the diagram.

Note: We use MSE loss as our objective. Since cost is just the mean loss over samples, the loss function defines the cost, so we conventionally refer to the objective as "loss". Additionally, because each neuron can be represented by a linear equation, a collection of neurons is referred to as a linear layer.

Our goal now is to implement these classes ("Sequential", "Linear", "ReLU", "MSELoss") from scratch. How do we make these classes work? We know that training a neural network can be conceptualized as:

1. Initialize parameters
2. For a number of iterations:
    - Forward propagation
    - Backward propagation

All building blocks that form a neural network must move as a single whole, transferring all the information forwards to make a prediction and backwards to update the parameters.

To support this, every building block in our code must have both a "forward" and a "backward" method. This modular design allows us to stack blocks in any order, as each block handles its own computations internally.

Let's implement the components one by with NumPy.

```
import numpy as np
```

We begin with the linear layer, where we initialize parameters (weights and biases) based on the input size and number of neurons.

```
class Linear:

    def __init__(self, input_size, num_neurons):

        self.W = np.random.randn(input_size, num_neurons)
        self.b = np.random.randn(1, num_neurons)
```

Next, we define "forward" method that makes predictions – it's a simple linear equation.

```
    def forward(self, X):

        self.X = X

        return self.X @ self.W + self.b
```

Now we get to the "backward" method that receives the "glued domino", from the next building block, computes gradient with respect to its parameters and updates them. Finally, it updates and passes the "glued domino" backwards to the previous building block.

> Note: During back propagation we go backwards so every next layer passes the "glued domino" to the previous layer.

```
    def backward(self, glued_domino, learning_rate):

        dW = self.X.T @ glued_domino
        db = np.sum(glued_domino, axis=0, keepdims=True)

        glued_domino_new = glued_domino @ self.W.T

        self.W -= learning_rate * dW
        self.b -= learning_rate * db

        return glued_domino_new
```

Next, we implement ReLU transformation that introduces non-linearity in the model.

```
class ReLU:
    def forward(self, X):
        self.mask = (X > 0).astype(float)
        return X * self.mask

    def backward(self, glued_domino, learning_rate):
        return glued_domino * self.mask
```

In the forward pass MSE loss measures how far the prediction is from the target on average, while "backward" method measures how change in the prediction affects the cost. This value becomes the very first "glued domino" that gets passed back into the network to start the domino reaction of updates.

```
class MSELoss:
    def forward(self, y_pred, y):
        y = y.reshape(-1, 1)
        return np.mean((y_pred - y) ** 2)

    def backward(self, y_pred, y):
        y = y.reshape(-1, 1)
        return 2 * (y_pred - y) / y.shape[0]
```

Finally, "Sequential" unites the entire network. First, it stores all building blocks in an instance variable:

```
class Sequential:
    def __init__(self, *building_blocks):
        self.building_blocks = building_blocks
```

The forward pass iterates through each block, passing data forward through the network. Eventually, it returns the prediction.

```
    def forward(self, X):
        for block in self.building_blocks:
            X = block.forward(X)
        return X
```

The backward pass iterates through building blocks in reverse, propagating gradients ("glued domino") back through the network to update parameters on each layer.

```
    def backward(self, glued_domino, learning_rate):
        for block in reversed(self.building_blocks):
            glued_domino = block.backward(glued_domino,
learning_rate)
```

Now let's implement gradient descent algorithm to train the network.

On each iteration:

1. Make a prediction by passing data forward through the network
2. Compute the cost
3. Calculate gradient of the cost with respect to the prediction (the first "glued domino")
4. Pass computed gradient backward to update parameters layer by layer in the whole network

Lastly, print the cost on every 100 iterations to track the progress.

```
def train(model, objective, X_train, y_train, num_iterations=1000,
learning_rate=0.001):

    for i in range(num_iterations):

        y_pred = model.forward(X_train)
        cost = objective.forward(y_pred, y_train)

        gradient = objective.backward(y_pred, y_train)
        model.backward(gradient, learning_rate)

        if (i + 1) % 100 == 0:
            print(f"{cost:.3f}")
```

Great, now we are ready to train and test our model on the regression dataset.

```
from data_loader import Dataset, standardize

dataset_r = Dataset("regression")
X_train_r, X_test_r, y_train_r, y_test_r =
dataset_r.load_split_data()
X_train_r, X_test_r = standardize(X_train_r, X_test_r)
```

Begin by defining the model architecture using "Sequential" and all the building blocks we created, then we specify the objective and train the network.

```
num_features = X_train_r.shape[1]

custom_model_r = Sequential(
    Linear(num_features, 3),
    ReLU(),
    Linear(3, 1)
)

custom_objective_r = MSELoss()

train(custom_model_r, custom_objective_r, X_train_r, y_train_r,
num_iterations=1500, learning_rate=0.01)

0.740
0.589
…
0.453
0.452
0.451
```

As the training runs, you can see the cost steadily decreasing. This indicates that our model is successfully finding the "bottom of the hill" – the optimal parameters for our regression problem.

Great, we handled regression, but what about other problem types? The beauty of our modular design is that we only need to change the final transformation and the objective to solve entirely different tasks.

For binary classification tasks, we need to squash our output into a probability between 0 and 1. We achieve this by adding a sigmoid block as the final transformation and using log-loss (also called binary cross-entropy or BCE loss) as our objective.

Let's define sigmoid function – the "forward" method simply applies appropriate transformation and the "backward" method computes the gradient.

```
class Sigmoid:
    def forward(self, X):
        self.out = 1 / (1 + np.exp(-X))
        return self.out

    def backward(self, glued_domino, learning_rate):
        return glued_domino * (self.out * (1 - self.out))
```

The objective computes the average log-loss in the forward pass – penalizing confident wrong predictions heavily. The backward pass returns the gradient of the cost with respect to predictions (the first "glued domino" that gets passed on through the network).

```
class BCELoss:
    def forward(self, y_pred, y):
        y = y.reshape(-1, 1)
        return -np.mean(y * np.log(y_pred) + (1 - y) * np.log(1 -
y_pred))

    def backward(self,  y_pred, y):
        y = y.reshape(-1, 1)
        return (y_pred - y) / ( y_pred * (1 - y_pred) *
y.shape[0])
```

Now we can define a neural network to solve a binary classification problem.

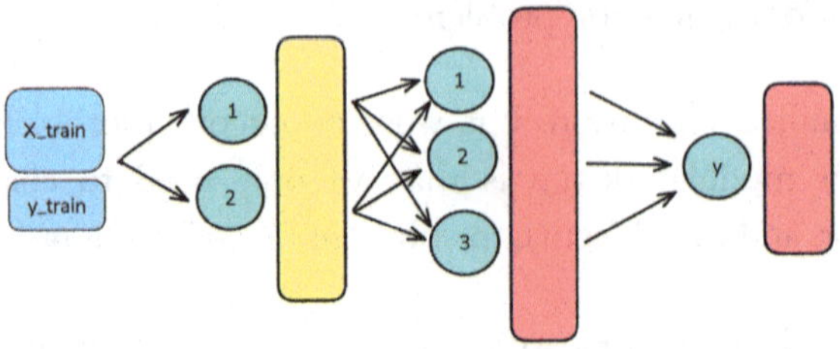

Let's train the network in the same way we did for regression – this time with different set of building blocks defined in the diagram above and the appropriate objective.

```
dataset_b = Dataset("binary classification")
X_train_b, X_test_b, y_train_b, y_test_b =
dataset_b.load_split_data()
X_train_b, X_test_b = standardize(X_train_b, X_test_b)

num_features = X_train_b.shape[1]

custom_model_b = Sequential(
    Linear(num_features, 2),
    ReLU(),
    Linear(2, 3),
    Sigmoid(),
    Linear(3, 1),
    Sigmoid()
)

custom_objective_b = BCELoss()

train(custom_model_b, custom_objective_b, X_train_b, y_train_b,
num_iterations=10000, learning_rate=0.01)

0.533
0.473
…
0.109
0.109
```

To save space – only the first and the last two cost function values are displayed. This is enough to realize our network is done training, achieving a relatively small cost.

Similarly, we can define and train a neural network for a multiclass classification problem by changing the number of neurons on the output layer to the number of classes, introducing Softmax transformation on the output layer and cross-entropy as our objective.

Both classes follow the same structure as we defined for other building blocks.

```
class Softmax:

    def forward(self, X):

        exps = np.exp(X)
        self.out = exps / np.sum(exps, axis=1, keepdims=True)

        return self.out

    def backward(self, glued_domino, learning_rate):

        dot = np.sum(glued_domino * self.out, axis=1,
keepdims=True)
        return self.out * (glued_domino - dot)

class CrossEntropyLoss:

    def forward(self, y_pred, y):

        y = y.reshape(-1, 1)
        losses = []

        for i in range(len(y)):
            losses.append(-np.log(y_pred[i, y[i]]))

        return np.mean(losses)

    def backward(self, y_pred, y):

        y = y.reshape(-1, 1)
        gradient = y_pred.copy()

        for i in range(len(y)):
            gradient[i, y[i]] -= 1

        return gradient / len(y)
```

Now, we can define and train a network to solve multiclass classification problem.

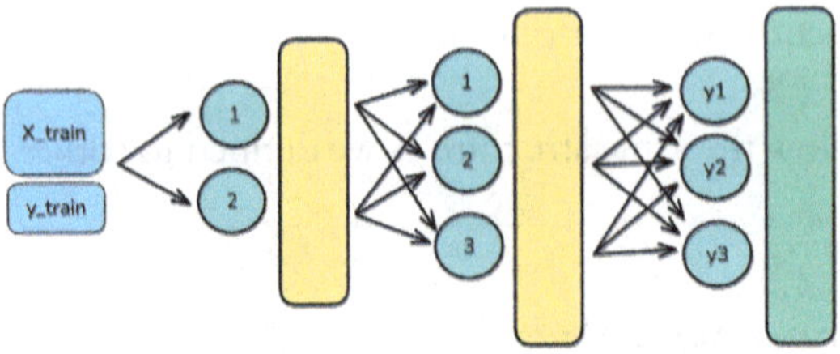


```
dataset_m = Dataset("multiclass classification")
X_train_m, X_test_m, y_train_m, y_test_m =
dataset_m.load_split_data()
X_train_m, X_test_m = standardize(X_train_m, X_test_m)

num_features = X_train_m.shape[1]
num_classes = len(set(y_train_m))

custom_model_m = Sequential(
    Linear(num_features, 2),
    ReLU(),
    Linear(2, 3),
    Sigmoid(),
    Linear(3, num_classes),
    Softmax()
)

custom_objective_m = CrossEntropyLoss()

train(custom_model_m, custom_objective_m, X_train_m, y_train_m,
num_iterations=20000, learning_rate=0.05)

1.101
1.082
…
0.087
0.086
```

You can define and train any architecture that aligns with the problem type at hand – play around with this to feel the flexibility of neural networks for yourself!

Test

Let's test our custom implementation.

```
from sklearn.metrics import mean_squared_error
from sklearn.metrics import accuracy_score

y_pred_custom_r = custom_model_r.forward(X_test_r)

print(f"Custom Regression MSE: {mean_squared_error(y_test_r,
y_pred_custom_r):.3f}")

y_pred_custom_prob = custom_model_b.forward(X_test_b)
y_pred_custom_b = (y_pred_custom_prob.flatten() > 0.5).astype(int)

print(f"Custom Binary Classification Accuracy:
{accuracy_score(y_test_b, y_pred_custom_b):.3f}")

y_pred_custom_prob = custom_model_m.forward(X_test_m)
y_pred_custom_m = np.argmax(y_pred_custom_prob, axis=1)

print(f"Custom Multiclass Classification Accuracy:
{accuracy_score(y_test_m, y_pred_custom_m):.3f}")

Custom Regression MSE: 0.472
Custom Binary Classification Accuracy: 0.993
Custom Multiclass Classification Accuracy: 0.967
```

This proves the models were able to learn the general pattern sufficiently well.

Next, let's implement and train the same networks using PyTorch.

First, we need to import the necessary library and convert NumPy arrays to PyTorch tensors. Tensors serve the same purpose as NumPy arrays, with most operations working identically. They're optimized for neural network operations, making them the standard data structure in deep learning frameworks.

```
import torch
import torch.nn as nn

X_train_r_tensor = torch.tensor(X_train_r, dtype=torch.float32)
y_train_r_tensor = torch.tensor(y_train_r,
dtype=torch.float32).view(-1, 1)
X_test_r_tensor = torch.tensor(X_test_r, dtype=torch.float32)
y_test_r_tensor = torch.tensor(y_test_r,
dtype=torch.float32).view(-1, 1)
```

Similarly, we transform the data for all problem types beforehand.

```
X_train_b_tensor = torch.tensor(X_train_b, dtype=torch.float32)
y_train_b_tensor = torch.tensor(y_train_b,
dtype=torch.float32).view(-1, 1)
X_test_b_tensor = torch.tensor(X_test_b, dtype=torch.float32)
y_test_b_tensor = torch.tensor(y_test_b,
dtype=torch.float32).view(-1, 1)

X_train_m_tensor = torch.tensor(X_train_m, dtype=torch.float32)
y_train_m_tensor = torch.tensor(y_train_m, dtype=torch.long)
X_test_m_tensor = torch.tensor(X_test_m, dtype=torch.float32)
y_test_m_tensor = torch.tensor(y_test_m, dtype=torch.long)
```

Begin by defining the same model architecture and objective we used to train the custom neural network.

```
num_features = X_train_r.shape[1]

pytorch_model_r = nn.Sequential(
    nn.Linear(num_features, 3),
    nn.ReLU(),
    nn.Linear(3, 1)
)

pytorch_objective_r = nn.MSELoss()
```

Then, we define a training function – unlike simpler algorithms, neural networks require more than a single line to train even with PyTorch.

```
def train_pytorch(model, objective, X_train, y_train,
num_iterations=1000, learning_rate=0.001):

    optimizer = torch.optim.SGD(model.parameters(),
lr=learning_rate)

    for i in range(num_iterations):

        y_pred = model(X_train)

        cost = objective(y_pred, y_train)

        optimizer.zero_grad()

        cost.backward()
        optimizer.step()

        if (i + 1) % 100 == 0:
            print(f"{cost.item():.3f}")

train_pytorch(pytorch_model_r, pytorch_objective_r,
X_train_r_tensor, y_train_r_tensor, num_iterations=1500,
learning_rate=0.01)

1.430
1.286
...
0.517
0.510
```

Let's explore how this is different from our implementation.

Here we explicitly specify gradient descent as our optimizer, while our custom version implicitly assumed its use. In our custom implementation, the "backward" method handled parameter updates directly. In PyTorch, these tasks are split: "cost.backward" calculates the gradients, and "optimizer.step" applies those gradients to update the parameters. Additionally, we call "zero_grad" because PyTorch accumulates gradients by default – this method clears them before each gradient descent iteration.

Next, we define the same architecture used to train our custom model for binary classification and train the PyTorch model.

```
num_features = X_train_b.shape[1]

pytorch_model_b = nn.Sequential(
    nn.Linear(num_features, 2),
    nn.ReLU(),
    nn.Linear(2, 3),
    nn.Sigmoid(),
    nn.Linear(3, 1),
    nn.Sigmoid()
)

pytorch_objective_b = nn.BCELoss()

train_pytorch(pytorch_model_b, pytorch_objective_b,
X_train_b_tensor, y_train_b_tensor, num_iterations=10000,
learning_rate=0.01)

0.685
0.664
...
0.111
0.110
```

Finally, we do the same for the multiclass classification problem.

```
num_features = X_train_m.shape[1]
num_classes = len(set(y_train_m))

pytorch_model_m = nn.Sequential(
    nn.Linear(num_features, 2),
    nn.ReLU(),
    nn.Linear(2, 3),
    nn.ReLU(),
    nn.Linear(3, num_classes)
)

pytorch_objective_m = nn.CrossEntropyLoss()

train_pytorch(pytorch_model_m, pytorch_objective_m,
X_train_m_tensor, y_train_m_tensor, num_iterations=20000,
learning_rate=0.05)

0.821
0.467
...
0.037
0.037
```

Note: Whenever the output layer has more than one neuron – PyTorch knows it's a multiclass classification problem. Therefore, it implicitly uses Softmax as the final transformation, which is why we didn't define it explicitly.

Now let's test all PyTorch models on the unseen data.

```
y_pred_tensor = pytorch_model_r(X_test_r_tensor)

y_pred_pytorch = y_pred_tensor.detach().numpy()

print(f"PyTorch Regression MSE:
{mean_squared_error(y_pred_pytorch, y_test_r):.3f}")

y_pred_pytorch =
pytorch_model_b.forward(X_test_b_tensor).detach().numpy()
y_pred_pytorch = (y_pred_pytorch.flatten() > 0.5).astype(int)

print(f"PyTorch Binary Classification Accuracy:
{accuracy_score(y_pred_pytorch, y_test_b):.3f}")

y_pred_pytorch_prob =
pytorch_model_m.forward(X_test_m_tensor).detach().numpy()

y_pred_pytorch = np.argmax(y_pred_pytorch_prob, axis=1)

print(f"PyTorch Multiclass Classification Accuracy:
{accuracy_score(y_pred_pytorch, y_test_m):.3f}")

PyTorch Regression MSE: 0.497
PyTorch Binary Classification Accuracy: 0.993
PyTorch Multiclass Classification Accuracy: 0.967
```

Both custom and PyTorch implementation demonstrate solid performance, verifying our approach!

Tips

Neural networks are super flexible and powerful. However, the term "neural network" isn't used to describe a single ML algorithm – it's a whole family of algorithms. What we've learned so far is called a multi-layer perceptron (MLP), which is the most fundamental member of this family.

An MLP is essentially a collection of linear layers followed by non-linear transformations, trained with gradient descent. When an MLP has multiple hidden layers (typically 3 or more), it's often called a deep neural network (DNN). The term "deep" simply refers to having many layers stacked together, allowing the model to learn increasingly abstract representations of the data at each level.

MLPs have practical limitations – for complex tabular data, classical methods like XGBoost are often preferred. With proper tuning, these tree-based methods learn complex patterns while being less prone to overfitting and more explainable.

Don't get discouraged just yet! Linear layers with non-linear activations form the backbone of all neural networks. Other architectures simply add specialized layers alongside these linear ones, allowing models to learn patterns better suited for specific problems. Ultimately, the core learning process remains the same across most deep learning algorithms: gradient descent with backpropagation, which we covered in detail for MLPs.

Just as there's flexibility in choosing layers and transformations, we can also customize the optimization process. We saw this in our PyTorch implementation, where we had to pick an optimizer because gradient descent comes in many different variations. While they all share the same core idea we explored, some have extra features like hyperparameters for momentum. Much like a person walking down a hill, momentum helps take larger steps when appropriate, allowing the model to avoid tiny local minima and speed up training.

Think of MLPs as a foundation of a house – essential and present in every structure, but different houses add specialized rooms for different purposes. In the MLP, every layer is just $X \cdot W + b$ followed by an activation function. In other neural network architectures, we introduce layers with different equations that involve parameters and data in ways that are optimal for specific data types.

For instance, convolutional neural networks (CNNs) add convolution layers optimized for images, while recurrent neural networks (RNNs) introduce recurrent layers for sequential data. The MLP concepts you've mastered form the backbone of today's most impactful AI: GPT language models, Face ID recognition on Apple devices, self-driving technology, medical diagnosis systems, and countless others. You now understand the fundamental mechanics behind the AI that has transformed the world.

You might have discovered that if you re-train an MLP without changing anything at all, it will come up with a different set of weights every time – hence, different performance. We haven't seen this before, algorithms like linear regression would always come up with almost identical parameters, no matter how many times we re-train them. Why is that?

Linear regression is quite simple in the way its parameters are arranged – this results in a smooth hill for our person. The landscape is like a simple bowl: no matter where you start, every path leads to the same global bottom. Therefore, the model always reaches the absolute minimum – parameters become optimal.

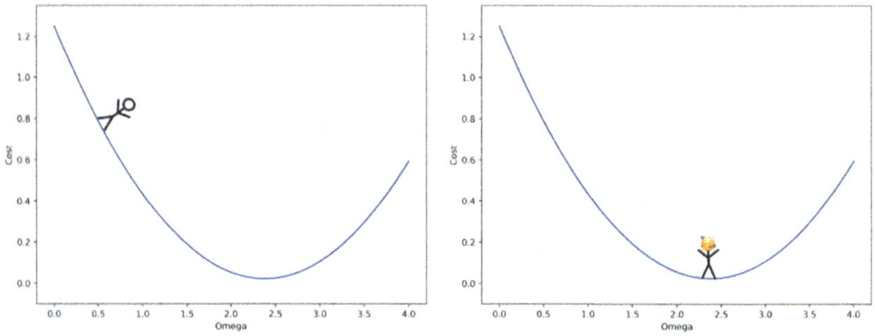

On the other hand, parameters in MLP are arranged in a much more complex way. Think about it: Each neuron on a layer takes all the outputs of the transformed previous layer. Therefore, every single parameter's value is affected by all the parameters on all previous layers. This very complex interdependence means that instead of one smooth valley at the bottom, there are many intermediate flat spots called local minima.

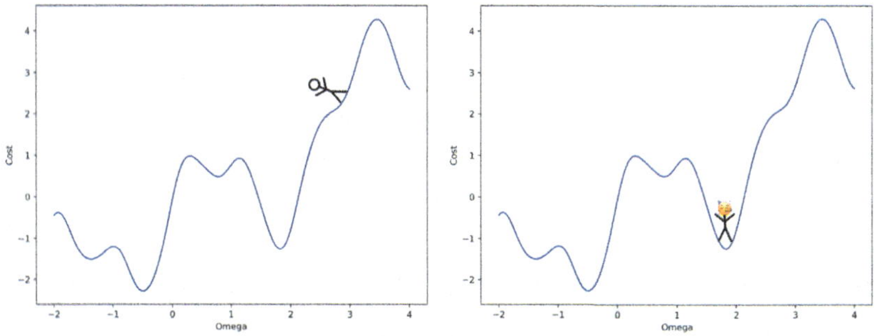

Recall that a parameter stops updating when it encounters a flat surface. In practice, neural network parameters typically reach local minima rather than the true global minimum. Therefore, depending on where the parameters started (their random initialization), they will likely reach different local minima, which may or may not impact the performance. This is why weights and performance vary across training runs.

We already know that the number of layers and neurons on each layer account for complexity or the number of "angles" our model can fit to the data. Learning rate and the number of iterations have the exact same role as in other iterative gradient-based methods. We aim for a combination of these parameters such that training error reduces progressively at a reasonable speed until the change becomes negligible, indicating we've reached a minimum.

Similarly to other methods that involve gradients, we can introduce regularization to prevent overfitting. There are two common approaches:

- L2 regularization. Just like with linear and logistic regression, this penalizes large weights by adding a term to the loss function. This distributes importance across neurons more evenly, preventing any single connection from dominating.
- Dropout regularization. This can be thought of as another layer applied after a layer of neurons that randomly "turns off" a fraction of neurons during training. Recall that the outputs of neurons are treated as features by the next layer. Hence, we can think of dropout as forcing the next layer to work with only a randomly selected fraction of features instead of all features. This introduces more randomness and reduces co-adaptation between neurons, which helps prevent overfitting. To use it, we simply add a dropout layer and specify the fraction of neurons to keep active (e.g. 0.8 means keep 80%, drop 20%).

This module acts as a fundamental building block to begin a deep learning journey for those interested in the topic. It provides the framework to think about neural networks, understanding how they are trained and used for inference to solve various types of problems.

Making the Best out of Models

Now that we know how core ML algorithms work, let's zoom out and explore how this knowledge fits in a real-world ML project – that is, how to approach a problem with ML.

ML project development can be viewed as an iterative process that revolves around three stages:

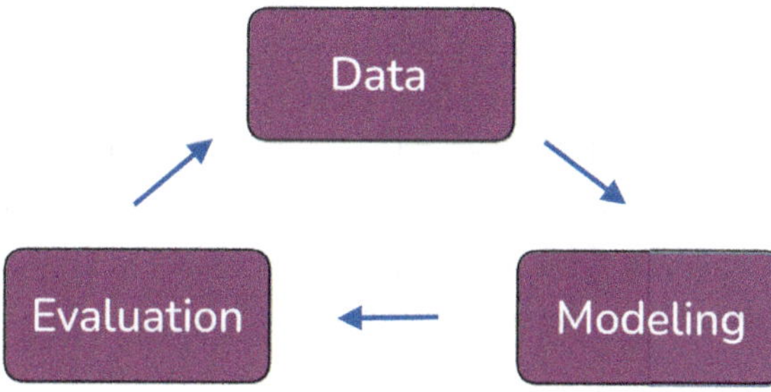

Let's jump into each stage in detail.

Data

The data stage is often overlooked, yet it's where professionals spend the most time and for good reason. At this stage, we need to clearly define our goal and understand what resources we have or may need to acquire. Specifically, we need to answer the following questions.

1. What do we want to predict (target y)?
2. What info do we have to make that prediction (features X)?
3. Is data valid (does it have duplicates, errors, biases, etc.)?
4. What features could potentially be useful/useless?
5. Is the relationship between variables linear or not?
6. What is the distribution of features and targets?
7. Can we potentially collect more data that would be useful for prediction?

We answer those questions by thoroughly exploring the data. A model can only be as good as the data. If there're errors (inconstancies in scales, annotation mistakes, biases, etc.) our best model will learn all of those, how useful would that model be? Not very much.

Recall that we can think of a model as a student and data as a textbook. As a good teacher, you should provide your student with a proper textbook that doesn't contain mistakes and makes learning easy. By understanding how core ML algorithms learn, we already have the best possible intuition for engineering useful features to make learning as easy as possible.

Once all cleaning and feature engineering decisions have been made, we split the data into training and test sets. The fraction depends on the case, but a general industry standard is 80% for training and 20% for testing. The whole point of the test set is to give us an idea of how the model would perform in the real world. Hence, we just need to ensure it is representative of the whole population.

At this point in the project, we have a solid understanding of the data. Answering the questions in from this section hints at what models could be suitable for the problem at hand.

Modeling

Throughout this book, we have learned what models tend to work well with linear versus non-linear relationships, many or few data points, many or few features, and which ones are suitable for different data types. We also learned that algorithms that leverage gradient descent or compute distances work better with features on the same scale. With all of this in mind, we select multiple ML algorithms that we think might be a good fit based on the information we inferred from the data.

We also know that most ML algorithms depend on hyperparameters that in turn heavily influence their performance. The truth is – for most ML algorithms, default hyperparameter selection determined by the library produces reasonable results. Usually, the optimal selection increases performance by less than 10%. This means that at the beginning, we should focus on what algorithms are most suitable for the problem at hand. Once the contenders are chosen, we train the models, assess and compare their performance with the goal of finding the best model(s) for our case.

Model Comparison

How do we decide which model is the best? Up to this point, we've been training models on the train dataset and testing them on the test dataset. However, if we use the test set to decide which model or hyperparameters are best, it is no longer truly unseen – we have effectively let it influence our decisions.

To preserve the test set as a genuine simulation of real-world unseen data, we need a third dataset: the validation set. We use the validation set to compare models and tune hyperparameters, and only once we have settled on the best model do we evaluate it on the test set – for the first and only time. Now we need to split the original data not into two but into three parts:

- A train set: to train the model
- A validation set: to select the best ML algorithm and hyperparameters
- A test set: to evaluate the final model

This way we both optimize the model and get a realistic assessment of its performance. As a rule of thumb, the respective proportions are 60-80% for training, 10-20% for validation, and 10-20% for testing, depending on the size of the dataset. The more data you have, the larger the training set should be, since smaller proportions for validation and test sets remain representative of the whole population. The key is that in the modeling stage we only work with training and evaluation datasets – we leave test data for the final stage, that is evaluation.

We will leverage our pre-defined code that randomly splits data into train (80%) and test (20%). As our example we will be using dataset for binary classification problem.

```
from data_loader import Dataset
from sklearn.model_selection import train_test_split

dataset = Dataset("binary classification")
X_train, X_test, y_train, y_test = dataset.load_split_data()
```

We want to create a validation set, such that the distribution of data between sets is 60-20-20. Therefore, we will randomly take 20% of the overall data from the train set and make it our validation set. Say our original dataset has 1000 points, at this moment 800 are in train and 200 are in test. We want to sample 20% of the original size, that is $0.2 * 1000 = 200$ from the train set. This translates into $\frac{200}{800} = 0.25$ fraction or 25% of the train set.

```
X_train, X_valid, y_train, y_valid = train_test_split(X_train,
y_train, test_size=0.25, random_state=1)
```

Now we have 60-20-20 distribution between train, validation and test datasets respectively. This means we are ready to train and compare performance of models we think might be a good as part of our first iteration.

For this problem we will compare multiple models that are known to be good at binary classification – logistic regression (with and without regularization), naïve bayes and XGBoost classifier. On the first iteration, we stick to default hyperparameters wherever possible, train and assess models on train and validation sets respectively. Then, we move forward with the most suitable models – ones that maximize performance on the validation set.

First, we construct a dictionary with all models of interest.

```
from sklearn.linear_model import LogisticRegression
from sklearn.naive_bayes import GaussianNB
from xgboost import XGBClassifier
from sklearn.metrics import accuracy_score

models = {
    "Logistic Regression (None)": LogisticRegression(penalty=None,
solver="lbfgs", max_iter=5000),
    "Logistic Regression (L2)": LogisticRegression(penalty="l2",
solver="liblinear", max_iter=5000),
    "Logistic Regression (L1)": LogisticRegression(penalty="l1",
solver="liblinear", max_iter=5000),
    "Logistic Regression (ElasticNet)":
LogisticRegression(penalty="elasticnet", solver="saga",
l1_ratio=0.5, max_iter=5000),
    "Naïve Bayes": GaussianNB(),
    "XGBoost": XGBClassifier()
}
```

Next, we train, evaluate and print the accuracy score for each model:

```
for name, model in models.items():

  model.fit(X_train, y_train)

  y_pred = model.predict(X_valid)

  accuracy = accuracy_score(y_valid, y_pred)

  print(f"{name} Accuracy: {accuracy:.3f}")

Logistic Regression (None) Accuracy: 0.964
Logistic Regression (L2) Accuracy: 0.971
Logistic Regression (L1) Accuracy: 0.971
Logistic Regression (ElasticNet) Accuracy: 0.971
Naïve Bayes Accuracy: 0.934
XGBoost Accuracy: 0.956
```

From the results above we conclude that all models were able to learn the patterns quite well. Considering size of the dataset – the difference between logistic models and XGBoost is negligible. While naïve bayes came close, there's no real point in considering it further because our dataset has 9 features (low-dimensional) and other more commonly used models showed slightly better results.

Since performance on validation set is great, we can now search for the optimal hyperparameters for both logistic and XGBoost to make the most out of their performance.

We were able to compare different models and select the best ones with the help of the validation set but we gave up 20% of our data for that opportunity. Another approach to model selection without losing the precious 20% of the data is called k-fold cross-validation. As before, we begin by splitting the data into train and test sets – the test set remains untouched until the final evaluation stage.

Instead of relying on a single random split to create a validation set, k-fold cross-validation divides the training dataset into k equal parts (called folds). The model is then trained and evaluated k times, each time using a different fold as the validation set and the remaining $k - 1$ folds as the training set.

For example, in 5-fold cross-validation, we split the data into 5 parts. We train on folds 1, 2, 3, 4 and evaluate it on fold 5, then train on folds 1, 2, 3, 5 and evaluate on fold 4, and so on. This gives us 5 different performance scores, then we average them to get a more robust estimate of the model's performance.

Let's make it visual. As the first step we separate train and test data, then divide the training data into 5 equally sized parts:

Next, we train and assess 5 identical models, each on a different combination of training and validation folds. The training and validation folds for each model are represented by green and red rectangles respectively:

Note: Each model is the same ML algorithm trained on a different subset of data. Since our goal is to find a model that solves our problem well in general – averaging out these scores provides a robust estimate of the algorithm's true performance.

The key advantage is that every data point gets to be in the validation set exactly once, giving us a more reliable picture of model performance that's less dependent on the luck of a single random split.

Recap: First, we divide training data into k equally sized parts. For each combination of hyperparameters we train k models, each model is trained on $k-1$ folds and validated on a single fold. This gives us k scores, one for each model – their average becomes our reliable estimate.

Let's see how k-fold cross-validation can be used in practice to do the same job as the validation set – just more efficiently.

```
from sklearn.model_selection import cross_val_score
import numpy as np

X_train, X_test, y_train, y_test = dataset.load_split_data()

for name, model in models.items():

    scores = cross_val_score(model, X_train, y_train, cv=5,
scoring="accuracy")

    print(f"{name} Mean Accuracy: {np.mean(scores):.3f}")

Logistic Regression (None) Mean Accuracy: 0.962
Logistic Regression (L2) Mean Accuracy: 0.960
Logistic Regression (L1) Mean Accuracy: 0.960
Logistic Regression (ElasticNet) Mean Accuracy: 0.960
Naïve Bayes Mean Accuracy: 0.952
XGBoost Mean Accuracy: 0.960
```

In the code above we use the same dictionary of models. On each iteration "cross_val_score" returns 5 (our k) accuracy scores controlled by "cv" and "scoring" arguments respectively. Finally, we average accuracy scores for each model before printing them.

The result provides a more reliable estimate of the performance, showing that variation in performance we observed with the validation set was likely due to randomness. Based on results from k-fold cross-validation we conclude the actual performance of all contender models is identical.

Now that have learned two ways to compare models and select the best ones – we can move on to selecting the optimal hyperparameters for the selected models to maximize their performance.

However, before that we need to touch upon a tiny but crucial detail that often gets overlooked. Recall, in the beginning of this book we defined that row-dependent operations must be performed after the data split to prevent leaking information from the unseen data. We must stay true to this rule regardless of whether we use the validation set or k-fold cross-validation. The main idea is that we compute the aggregated quantities on seen data and apply it to unseen data.

For our problem – we know that logistic regression benefits from standardization, which is a row-dependent operation on the data because it involves computing mean and standard deviation across rows. This means that to prevent leakage we need to compute mean and standard deviation for each column using seen data and then use those statistics with unseen data.

How can we integrate this into our model selection?

- For the validation approach: We compute all statistics using training data (seen), apply it to validation data (unseen). Once the model is selected and we move on to evaluation – we apply it to the test set the same way we did for the validation.
- For k-fold cross-validation: Each of k models of one ML algorithm, is trained and assessed on different subsets of data. Therefore, for each model we must compute a separate statistics using its seen data ($k - 1$ folds) and then apply it to its unseen data (1 fold). Once the model is selected and we move on to evaluation – we compute statistics and train the model of choice on full training dataset, then we apply those statistics to the test data.

Since we have already established that k-fold cross-validation is generally superior – we will use k-fold approach, this time combined with standardization and logistic regression. Fortunately, Scikit-learn makes this step very easy with "make_pipeline" function, which allows us to define a sequence of steps to put the data through. In this case we define logistic regression with elastic net and place it into the pipeline after the standardization step – then pass the pipeline into "cross_val_score" function.

```
from sklearn.pipeline import make_pipeline
from sklearn.preprocessing import StandardScaler

model_elastic = LogisticRegression(penalty="elasticnet",
solver="saga", l1_ratio=0.5, max_iter=5000)

pipeline_elastic = make_pipeline(StandardScaler(), model_elastic)

scores_elastic = cross_val_score(pipeline_elastic, X_train,
y_train, cv=5, scoring="accuracy")

print(f"Mean Accuracy: {np.mean(scores_elastic):.3f}")

Mean Accuracy: 0.960
```

In this example, the data was already approximately on the same scale, so standardization didn't improve performance – but as you have already seen, it's not always the case.

Generally, we can place other transformations into the pipeline, but for more advanced row-dependent operations, k-fold must be implemented from scratch. This involves writing a loop that manually splits the data into folds, computes statistics from the training folds only, applies them to the validation fold, then trains and evaluates the model – repeating this for each fold.

Finding the Optimal Hyperparameters

At this point, we can find the optimal set of hyperparameters for each of the selected ML algorithms. Fortunately, we know how algorithms work inside out, which means we know exactly how each hyperparameter affects them. While this knowledge on its own is not enough to guess the best set of hyperparameters from the first try, it is sufficient to approximate the range of values that covers an optimal value for a parameter (e.g., the number of weak learners in XGBoost can reasonably lie between 50 and 500).

Good news: Being able to define a reasonable range of values for each parameter is all we need! Given a range of possible values for every hyperparameter, how do we find the optimal combination? The core idea is simple: define a range of possible values for each hyperparameter, try different combinations, measure model performance for each one, and select combination that performs best.

There are a few approaches to checking these combinations:

- Grid Search: The simplest approach is to train the model with every possible combination and select the one that maximizes performance. It is guaranteed to find the best combination but often takes considerable time.
- Random Search: Chooses hyperparameter combinations randomly, checking only a fraction of combinations and selecting the best one among those tested. It is generally the fastest and least resource intensive.

- Bayesian Search: At its core, it uses Bayes' rule, the same principle behind naïve bayes, to update its beliefs about which hyperparameter combinations are likely to perform well based on what it has already tried. Rather than searching blindly, each evaluation informs the next, making it a smarter and more efficient search. It is often the go-to choice for professionals as it balances computational time and accuracy.

Finding the optimal hyperparameters for a model is like training a lot of models with a different set of hyperparameters and comparing their performance to find the best one. This sounds a lot like what we have done when selecting the best models among all contenders. In fact, it is – this time our contenders are the same algorithms with different sets of hyperparameters. Therefore, we can use the same approaches for contender assessment as we did before – validation or k-fold cross-validation. For illustration purposes we will stick with k-fold cross-validation because this way we get to train our final model on more data.

Let's explore practical implementation of hyperparameter tuning strategies with industry standard library Optuna. From the model comparison we determined that all models we explored perform very well. For the sake of illustration, we will consider that logistic regression and XGBoost are preferred for our problem at hand. Therefore, we will maximize their performance by selecting optimal hyperparameters for each model starting with logistic regression.

First, let's import the necessary libraries.

```
import optuna
```

Next, we define the hyperparameter search space that we want to explore.

```
param_grid = {
    "C": [0.01, 0.1, 0.5, 1, 5, 10, 15, 20],
    "penalty": ["l1", "l2"],
}
```

Here, *C* controls the regularization strength, and penalty specifies the regularization type. The goal of the algorithm will be to find the combination of those two hyperparameters that results in the average highest accuracy across all folds.

Now we define the objective function. This function tells Optuna how to evaluate a single trial, in other words, a combination of hyperparameters. The first step is to enter the hyperparameter space that we want to explore during a trial. The method "suggest_categorical" returns a suggested hyperparameter value selected from our search space.

```
def objective(trial):

    C = trial.suggest_categorical("C", param_grid["C"])
    penalty = trial.suggest_categorical("penalty",
param_grid["penalty"])
```

Next, we initialize our model given the suggested hyperparameters.

```
    model = LogisticRegression(C=C, penalty=penalty,
solver="liblinear", max_iter=5000)
```

In this example, "solver" is set to "liblinear" because it supports both L1 and L2 regularization. "max_iter" is set to 5000 to ensure that the solver has enough iterations to converge (reach the minimum). Those hyperparameters remain constant to ensure the model works as expected and doesn't take too long to train.

Finally, pass the model to k-fold cross-validation and return average score as our measure of performance that we need to maximize.

```
    scores = cross_val_score(model, X_train, y_train, cv=5,
scoring="accuracy")

    return np.mean(scores)
```

During each trial (evaluation of a combination of hyperparameters), this function measures the performance of the current combination. The optimization algorithm uses these measurements to identify the combination that maximizes the objective, which becomes our final set of hyperparameters.

At this point, we've defined a function that Optuna uses to sample hyperparameters, train the model, and assess its performance. Now we need to specify how Optuna samples from the search space – using grid, random or Bayesian search. Let's explore each approach, starting with grid search.

First, we initialize a sampler with our hyperparameter search space. Then we create a study, specifying the sampling method and our goal to maximize the objective function. Finally, we run the optimization to find the optimal hyperparameter combination.

```
sampler_grid = optuna.samplers.GridSampler(param_grid)

study_logistic = optuna.create_study(direction="maximize",
sampler=sampler_grid)

study_logistic.optimize(objective)
```

The algorithm outputs report about each trial, which includes a hyperparameter combination used, its respective accuracy and the best trial so far. Ultimately, we want to know accuracy score and hyperparameter values for the best trial.

```
print(f"Grid Search best hyperparameters:
{study_logistic.best_params}")
print(f"Grid Search best performance:
{study_logistic.best_value:.3f}")

Grid Search best hyperparameters: {'C': 5, 'penalty': 'l1'}
Grid Search best performance: 0.962
```

At this point we know the optimal combination of hyperparameters for the logistic regression and corresponding average accuracy across all folds.

For illustration purposes, we will explore other sampling algorithms. Fortunately, our objective and hyperparameter search space can stay the same, we just need to specify a different sampler. Unlike grid search, random and Bayesian search explore only a set number of trials, which we need to specify with "n_trials".

Random search:

```
sampler_random = optuna.samplers.RandomSampler()
study_logistic = optuna.create_study(direction="maximize",
sampler=sampler_random)
study_logistic.optimize(objective, n_trials=10)
```

```
print(f"Random Search best hyperparameters:
{study_logistic.best_params}")
print(f"Random Search best performance:
{study_logistic.best_value:.3f}")

Random Search best hyperparameters: {'C': 5, 'penalty': 'l1'}
Random Search best performance: 0.962
```

Optuna uses Bayesian search by default; therefore, there's no need to specify the sampler. Bayesian search:

```
study_logistic = optuna.create_study(direction="maximize")
study_logistic.optimize(objective, n_trials=10)

print(f"Bayesian Search best hyperparameters:
{study_logistic.best_params}")
print(f"Bayesian Search best performance:
{study_logistic.best_value:.3f}")

Bayesian Search best hyperparameters: {'C': 10, 'penalty': 'l1'}
Bayesian Search best performance: 0.962
```

In this case, all searching algorithms came down to the same accuracy with a different choice of hyperparameters. For the sake of illustration, we let random and Bayesian search explore 10 trials, while grid search explored all possible 15 trials. In this example, the dataset and hyperparameter search space were very small, which makes time and performance difference between these methods negligible. In the real-world the choice of the searching method can have significant impact on the performance as well as the time it takes to run the algorithm.

Next, we will follow a similar procedure to find approximately the optimal set of hyperparameters for XGBoost via k-fold cross-validation.

```
param_grid = {
    "n_estimators": [50, 350],

    "subsample": [0.8, 1.0],
    "colsample_bytree": [0.8, 1],

    "learning_rate": [0.01, 0.3],
    "reg_lambda": [0.01, 5],
    "gamma": [0.01, 5],

    "max_depth": [3, 7],
    "min_child_weight": [0.5, 10]
}
```

Here, instead of manually defining the search space, we use range for every hyperparameter. The range between two numbers is a continuous space, which means it has infinitely many numbers in between (e.g. 9.99991 is different from 9.99992). Grid search cannot work with continuous ranges because it is impossible to check every single combination. Thus, for this example we could only decide between the other two search algorithms. Since the dataset is small and we will not run into computational limitations, we will choose Bayesian search. Let's define the objective.

```
def objective(trial):

    n_estimators = trial.suggest_int("n_estimators",
param_grid["n_estimators"][0], param_grid["n_estimators"][1])

    subsample = trial.suggest_float("subsample",
param_grid["subsample"][0], param_grid["subsample"][1])
    colsample_bytree = trial.suggest_float("colsample_bytree",
param_grid["colsample_bytree"][0],
param_grid["colsample_bytree"][1])

    learning_rate = trial.suggest_float("learning_rate",
param_grid["learning_rate"][0], param_grid["learning_rate"][1])
    reg_lambda = trial.suggest_float("reg_lambda",
param_grid["reg_lambda"][0], param_grid["reg_lambda"][1])
    gamma = trial.suggest_float("gamma", param_grid["gamma"][0],
param_grid["gamma"][1])

    max_depth = trial.suggest_int("max_depth",
param_grid["max_depth"][0], param_grid["max_depth"][1])
    min_child_weight = trial.suggest_float("min_child_weight",
param_grid["min_child_weight"][0],
param_grid["min_child_weight"][1])

    model = XGBClassifier(
        n_estimators=n_estimators,
        max_depth=max_depth,
        learning_rate=learning_rate,
        subsample=subsample,
        colsample_bytree=colsample_bytree,
        reg_lambda=reg_lambda,
        gamma=gamma,
        min_child_weight=min_child_weight,
    )

    scores = cross_val_score(model, X_train, y_train, cv=5,
scoring="accuracy")

    return np.mean(scores)
```

As before the objective function uses suggested combination of hyperparameters to train the model, make prediction and assess its average performance across folds.

> Note: Some hyperparameters must be integers (e.g. the number of estimators and maximum depth), so we use "suggest_int" to define their ranges. Other hyperparameters can have floating-point values, requiring "suggest_float". For categorical hyperparameters, such as those we saw with logistic regression, we use "suggest_categorical".

Once the search space and objective are defined, we run the study use Bayesian search (default).

```
study_xgb = optuna.create_study(direction="maximize")
study_xgb.optimize(objective, n_trials=50)

print(f"Bayesian Search best hyperparameters:
{study_xgb.best_params}")
print(f"Bayesian Search best performance:
{study_xgb.best_value:.3f}")

Bayesian Search best hyperparameters: {'n_estimators': 292,
'subsample': 0.8418008970155431, 'colsample_bytree':
0.8888586644577937, 'learning_rate': 0.02633287862561345,
'reg_lambda': 3.807450852170324, 'gamma': 1.5863712694546885,
'max_depth': 6, 'min_child_weight': 5.98554065960626}
Bayesian Search best performance: 0.969
```

Now we know the near-optimal set of hyperparameters for our XGBoost model along with corresponding average accuracy across folds.

At this point we finished tuning hyperparameters for our best models, reaching 96% and 97% average accuracy across folds for logistic regression and XGBoost respectively. The performance is nearly identical, and we can't really go wrong at this point.

We could even combine them into a simple ensemble, averaging their predicted probabilities – but given the near-identical performance, that's likely overkill unless the models are making systematically different mistakes.

Since XGBoost slightly outperforms logistic regression, we will take it as our winner and move on to the final step.

Evaluation

Throughout this book, depending on the problem type, we have used two primary metrics to measure performance: MSE for regression and accuracy for classification. We did this to ensure our custom implementations aligned with well-established libraries. In the real world, however, the choice of evaluation metric is more important than many realize. While it is largely dependent on your data and the project goals, the main question remains the same: What do we want our model to be good at?

It sounds straightforward, but to answer this, you must always keep your data's context in mind. For instance, if we evaluate a house value prediction model using MSE and get a value of 4, is that good or bad?

It depends entirely on the scale of your targets. If targets are expressed in thousands of dollars, a loss for a single observation might look like$(3000 - 3002)^2 = 4$. MSE of 4 is excellent at this scale, as 3000 and 3002 are very close. However, if targets are expressed in hundreds of thousands (where 5 represents 500,000), a loss of $(5 - 3)^2 = 4$ is huge. While the MSE value is the same, the actual prediction is off by $2,000 and $200,000 respectively. Therefore, MSE must be interpreted in context.

In this section we will dive deeper into evaluation metrics for different problem types, starting with regression.

Regression

Another famous regression metric is MAE (mean absolute error). Previously, we used the square of the difference to prevent positive and negative errors from canceling each other out. We can achieve a similar result by taking the absolute difference:

$$J(y_{pred}, y_{actual}) = \frac{1}{n} * \sum_{i=1}^{n} |y_{pred_i} - y_{actual_i}|$$

How does this affect our interpretation compared to MSE? Let's look at two cases – one with small scale (e.g. prediction is 0.3 while the actual target is 0.5) and a large scale (e.g. prediction is 1,000 while the actual target is 800).

MSE:

$$(0.3 - 0.5)^2 = 0.04$$

$$(1000 - 800)^2 = 40000$$

MAE:

$$|0.3 - 0.5| = 0.2$$

$$|1000 - 800| = 200$$

MSE makes small errors (less than 1) even smaller and large errors significantly larger. In contrast, MAE distributes the penalty evenly. Which is better? It depends on your priorities. If you cannot afford large outliers and want more consistent, small errors, use MSE. If you don't want to over-penalize outliers, use MAE.

For example, weather forecasters might prefer MSE. Being off by 10 inches on a single rainfall prediction could mean missing a flood warning, while being off by 1 inch on ten predictions is just minor inaccuracy. While MAE treats both scenarios equally (total error of 10), MSE heavily penalizes the large error (100 vs. 10).

These metrics depend on the scale of the targets, but not all metrics do. We can create a scale-independent metric by measuring prediction error as a percentage of the true value:

$$J(y_{pred}, y_{actual}) = \frac{1}{n} * \sum_{i=1}^{n} \left| \frac{y_{actual_i} - y_{pred_i}}{y_{actual_i}} \right| * 100$$

Conceptually, we measure how large the error is relative to the target on average – this metric is called MAPE (mean absolute percentage error). For instance, MAPE of 20% indicates that on average the model is off by 20% relative to the true target.

MAPE seems like a universal choice for measuring model performance since it's easily interpretable, but there's one caveat. When the target is 0, we encounter division by zero, and when it's very close to 0, we see inflated errors.

For example, suppose one target in the dataset is 0.1 and our prediction is 1.5. The percentage error for this single prediction would be $|\frac{0.1-1.5}{0.1}| * 100 = 1400\%$. Even if the model made 100 other excellent predictions contributing around 2% error each, the overall MAPE would be $\frac{100*2+14000}{101} \approx 16\%$ dominated by a single problematic prediction.

As you can see, MAPE is highly sensitive to outliers and near-zero targets. Whenever you use MAPE, it's essential to examine the distribution of individual errors for a more complete understanding of model performance.

Now that we covered some of the core regression metrics, let's dive into binary classification.

Binary Classification

So far, we have relied on accuracy – the fraction of correct predictions. This is intuitive but can be misleading with imbalanced datasets. Consider a bank's loan approval model where 97% of applicants are historically approved. A "dummy" model that always predicts "Approve" would achieve 97% accuracy, yet it is completely useless at identifying risky loans.

To solve this, we look at all possible mistakes a binary classification model can make:

- Predict class 1 when actual class is 0 – Type I error
- Predict class 0 when actual class is 1 – Type II error

By simply measuring those two errors we can understand how good the model is at predicting each class. In our loan example (100 points, 97 approved, 3 rejected), the model that always predicts "1" would have:

$$Type\ I = \frac{3}{3} = 100\%$$

$$Type\ II = \frac{0}{97} = 0\%$$

These errors tell us that the model completely fails to identify class 0 but always correctly identifies class 1. Type I and Type II error rates can also be thought of as $error = 1 - accuracy$ for each class independently.

Recall that while our final model has a binary output, under the hood a classifier doesn't just predict a hard label of 0 or 1. Instead, it produces a probability for each class, which we then convert into a label using a threshold (commonly 0.5). A robust classifier assigns high probability to the correct class. For example, if the true class is 1, we'd prefer the classifier to predict 90% rather than just 51%. The higher the confidence in the correct decision, the more reliable and useful the classifier becomes.

To quantify prediction reliability, we use the ROC curve (Receiver Operating Characteristic curve). Fun fact: It was first introduced during WWII, to measure reliability of the radar systems in detecting enemy communications.

Despite the difficult name, the concept is straightforward – it measures the model's performance across all possible thresholds, not just the default 0.5. For instance, if a classifier predicted all class 1 observations correctly with 0.51 confidence each, it would have 0% Type I and Type II errors at the 0.5 threshold. However, this same classifier would have 100% Type II error at 0.52 or any threshold above that. The ROC curve captures this subtlety, while every other metric we've discussed would simply ignore it.

You might wonder why we would care about thresholds other than 0.5. In practice, using 0.5 blindly can be risky. Consider a model predicting whether a patient has a certain condition – how reliable is a diagnosis when the model predicts only 51% probability? Models that assign high probabilities to the correct classes are generally much more stable and trustworthy. Therefore, it makes sense to evaluate model reliability across all decision thresholds.

To construct the ROC curve, we make predictions on the entire dataset for every threshold value from 1 to 0. We then compute and plot the Type I error rate on the x-axis and $1 - \textit{Type II}$ error rate on the y-axis. In other words, the x-axis measures how often the model misclassifies class 0, while y-axis measures how accurately it identifies class 1. This gives us an informative visualization of the model's confidence in the correct predictions.

Let's see how it can be useful by looking at an example:

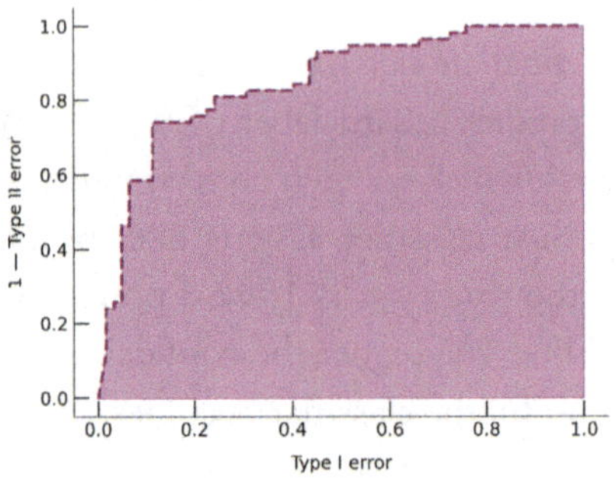

Each point along this curve represents a different threshold, which alters the model's performance as shown by the x and y coordinates.

Let's pick a random threshold and assess it, say 0.56:

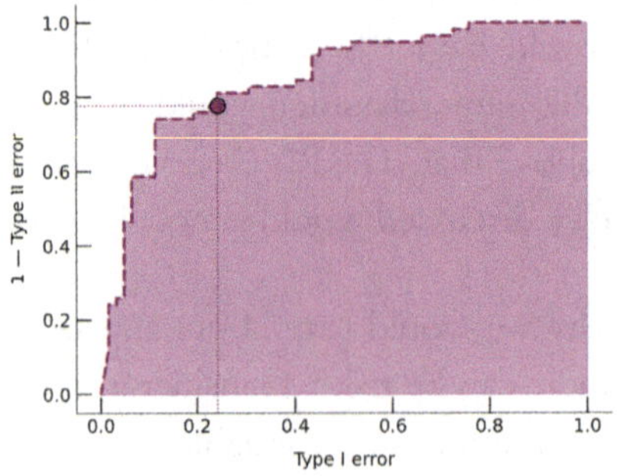

This means that after the classifier predicts the probability of an observation belonging to class 1, we classify probabilities of 56% or higher as class 1 and the rest as class 0.

The threshold value is not displayed on the graph, just its corresponding performance metrics. Specifically, at this threshold value, Type I error is around 0.24 (24%) and 1 minus Type II error is around 0.78 (78%), which means Type II error is 0.22 (22%). This threshold balances both types of errors, meaning the predictions are roughly equally reliable for each class.

Let's consider a perfect binary classification model – how would it appear on this graph? Ideally, it should assign 100% probability to all class 1 observations and 0% probability to all class 0 observations. This would mean that at any threshold, the model would be perfectly correct, resulting in a curve that covers the entire upper-left area of the graph:

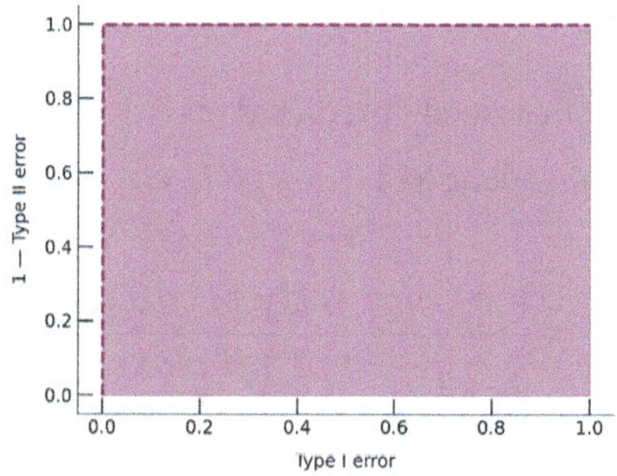

Thus, we can infer that the more reliable the model is, the larger the area the ROC curve covers, with a maximum area of 1 $(1 * 1 = 1)$. In fact, professionals often simply look at the area under the curve (AUC) to assess a model's reliability. However, the plot can also be used to select an optimal threshold that balances errors in the way most suitable for your specific situation.

Let's take a look at two realistic ROC curves and their corresponding AUC scores:

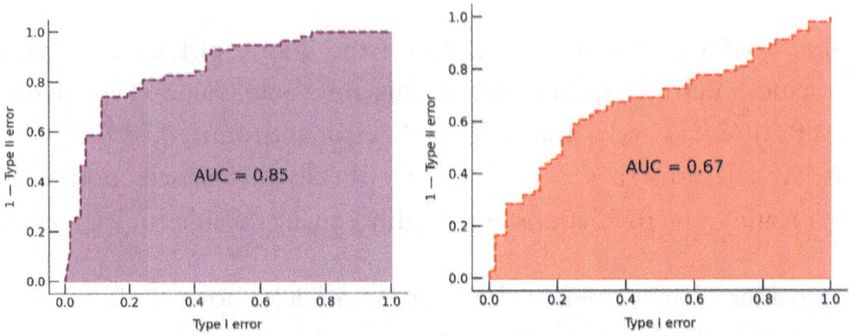

By measuring accuracy, Type I and Type II errors, and ROC/AUC, you develop a comprehensive understanding of model performance. However, practitioners commonly use three additional metrics – recall, precision, and F1 score.

- Recall is fraction of correctly predicted class 1 observations over all class 1 observations (equivalent to $1 - Type\ II$ error).

$$Recall = \frac{\#\ of\ correctly\ predicted\ class\ 1}{\#\ of\ all\ class\ 1}$$

- Precision is fraction of correctly predicted class 1 observations over all predicted class 1 observations.

$$Precision = \frac{\#\ of\ correctly\ predicted\ class\ 1}{\#\ of\ all\ predicted\ class\ 1}$$

- F1 score is a harmonic mean of recall and precision. Harmonic mean is a type of average that penalizes strong difference in recall and precision, prioritizing balance between them.

$$F1 = 2 * \frac{Recall * Precision}{Recall + Precision}$$

All three metrics take values between 0 and 1, with higher values indicating better performance. They focus on class 1, which in many real-world problems represents the class of primary interest. Now, let's move on to multiclass classification.

Multiclass Classification

The core idea is similar – we care about how accurate our model is for every class in the dataset. Overall accuracy works the same way as for binary classification and, as before, can be misleading, especially with imbalanced datasets.

The key difference with multiclass problems is that we need to understand how well the model performs for each individual class. Just as with binary classification, we can calculate recall, precision, and F1 score, but now we calculate them separately for each class.

For binary classification, it was sufficient to get a single score for precision and recall for class 1, because it implicitly informed us about performance for class 0. However, with multiclass problems we need to compute a score for each class separately. This gives us a detailed view of how the model performs on each class individually. Some classes might be easier to predict than others, and these per-class metrics reveal those patterns.

To get a single metric that summarizes performance across all classes, we take the average. There are two common methods to average across classes:

- Macro average: Simply average the metric across all classes, treating each class equally
- Weighted average: Average the metric across all classes but weight each class by the proportion of instances it has in the dataset

The same averaging approach applies to ROC curves and AUC. Just as we calculate recall, precision and F1 for each class separately, we can calculate an AUC score for each class by measuring how well the model distinguishes that class from all the others. We then take the macro or weighted average of these per-class AUC scores to get an overall measure of model reliability.

By examining overall accuracy, per-class recall, precision, F1 scores, and the average AUC, you get a comprehensive picture of your multiclass model's performance. As always, which metrics matter most depends on your answer to the main question: What do we want our model to be good at?

This concludes our exploration of different metrics that enable us to gain a full understanding of model performance for the most common problem types.

Let's illustrate how we would evaluate XGBoost model that we chose as our winner in the previous section. We start by importing all necessary metrics and defining the model with the best hyperparameters found via Bayesian search.

```
from sklearn.metrics import (
    accuracy_score,
    precision_score,
    recall_score,
    f1_score,
    roc_auc_score
)

model = XGBClassifier(**study_xgb.best_params)
```

Finally, we train the model and evaluate it using all binary classification metrics we explored in this section.

```
model = XGBClassifier(**params)
model.fit(X_train, y_train)

y_pred_raw = model.predict_proba(X_test)[:, 1]
y_pred = model.predict(X_test)

type_1 = np.sum((y_pred == 1) & (y_test == 0)) / np.sum(y_test ==
0)
type_2 = np.sum((y_pred == 0) & (y_test == 1)) / np.sum(y_test ==
1)

print(f"Accuracy: {accuracy_score(y_test, y_pred):.3f}")

print(f"Type I: {type_1:.3f}")
print(f"Type II: {type_2:.3f}")

print(f"Recall: {recall_score(y_test, y_pred):.3f}")
print(f"Precision: {precision_score(y_test, y_pred):.3f}")
print(f"F1: {f1_score(y_test, y_pred):.3f}")

print(f"AUC: {roc_auc_score(y_test, y_pred_raw):.3f}")

Accuracy: 0.993
Type I: 0.000
Type II: 0.021
Recall: 0.979
Precision: 1.000
F1: 0.989
AUC: 1.000
```

With 99% accuracy, perfect precision, and an AUC of 1, our XGBoost model is about as close to perfect as it gets. Congratulations! You have now seen how everything in this book comes together in practice!

Conclusion

Throughout this book you've built something much more valuable than just technical knowledge – you've developed an ML practitioner's mindset. You are now equipped to solve real-world problems with machine learning, not by memorizing formulas or treating models as black boxes but by understanding the fundamental principles that make ML work.

In this journey you gained practical skills that support this mindset:

- Ability to build core ML algorithms from scratch and apply them in a practical setting using industry standard libraries like Scikit-learn and PyTorch
- A structured approach to ML projects, following best practices throughout data preparation, modeling, and evaluation stages

You now understand when, how, and why core ML techniques work, enabling you to adapt to new problems and use this strong foundation to expand your knowledge in the field. The path forward is wide open – whether that's diving into deep learning, MLOps, or domain-specific applications, the thinking skills you have built here will carry you there.

The best next step you can take is to build and share. Take the from-scratch implementations in this book and extend them – add the remaining enhancements to XGBoost, experiment with different activation and loss functions in the MLP or try new splitting criteria in the decision tree. Another path is to apply the end-to-end project workflow from the last chapter to a problem you care about. Then put it on GitHub, write about it, share it with the community. Building develops your skills, while sharing develops your reputation. The practitioners who grow fastest are the ones who build in public – it's how you get noticed, connect with the community and open doors.

It would mean a lot to hear about your experience with this book via a review on Amazon or Goodreads.

Thank you!

Made in United States
North Haven, CT
10 November 2026

22095613R00173